IDEAL OF THE COURTLY GENTLEMAN IN SPANISH LITERATURE:

ITS ASCENT AND DECLINE

FRANCESCO RAIMONDO, PH.D.

Order this book online at www.trafford.com
or email orders@trafford.com

Most Trafford titles are also available at major online book retailers.

Printed in the United States of America.

ISBN: 978-1-4669-8109-6 (sc)
ISBN: 978-1-4669-8108-9 (hc)
ISBN: 978-1-4669-8110-2 (e)

Library of Congress Control Number: 2013903111

Trafford rev. 01/28/2014

www.trafford.com

North America & international
toll-free: 1 888 232 4444 (USA & Canada)
fax: 812 355 4082

CONTENTS

PROLOGUE

Although it is difficult to set a concrete point of departure or trace historical connections between social situations and man's preoccupation for an ideal of conduct, it seems that the art of sociability was first and most eminently cultivated among Greek philosophers. It is said, for example, that Alcibiades, "Socrates' enormously seductive disciple," was most polished and accomplished in this art. Later Roman writers like Seneca, Quintilian, and Cicero also placed great emphasis on the qualities of sociability and worldliness in man. During the age of Augustus, writes Guez de Balzac, it was Maecenas who excelled as a model of aristocratic taste and worldly perfection. But the real process of establishing a code of manners which would identify and reflect the self-consciousness of a whole class of people, and later provide the basis for modern standards of civilized behavior, has its starting point in the Middle Ages' institution of chivalry.

The knight, whose chivalrous ideals and duties were at first defined in the prayers of the knighting ceremony, was mainly a bearer of arms. His conduct was governed by a few crude and ordinary precepts dealing with his behavior in battle and his obligations to church and society. Near the end of the twelfth century, by a mere succession of social and political developments, the knight began to acquire a new self-awareness. His primitive, rudimentary class ideology and manners were softened by his constant association with court nobility, better living standards, stable political conditions, great emphasis on ceremony, and most of all, by the influence of women. He had gradually become a gentle knight whose highly prized virtues were not just prowess, loyalty, and obedience to his king and society, but also noble birth, love, and courtesy. The attainment of these new worldly qualities made the knight fashionable and entertaining company in mixed society and symbolized the knight's transition from chivalrous to courtly gentleman.

At the beginning of the fifteenth century, following the path of Tristan, Lancelot, Percival, and other legendary heroes, Amadís of Gaul emerges in Spain, and later in the courts of Europe, as a true ideal of knightly virtues and the expression of the new spirit of social refinement. One influence, however, that is generally negligible in the ideal of chivalry and the education of the knight is that of classical humanism, with its concomitant emphasis on the aesthetic elements of social and cultural life. It was Baldassare Castiglione who, taking inspiration from the Roman concept of "humanitas," fashioned in his *Courtier* the new Renaissance ideal of the perfect gentleman living at the court of princes. The "Courtier" is both a humanist and an extended version of the ideal knight: he is a soldier and a scholar, whose primary pursuits are the possession of all the finer graces and the search for an aesthetic ideal of self-perfection in all aspects of human endeavor.

Il Cortegiano, without a doubt one of the most significant books in the history of courtly literature, exercised a strong influence on the literary life of the time, but by the end of the sixteenth century had already become outmoded by changing social and political conditions. By this time the concept of courtliness had already been redefined, modified, and transformed. The "courtier," fueled by his own ambiguous morality, had become a favorite target of satire and was soon replaced by the more functional and practical-minded literary prototypes of the seventeenth century.

CHAPTER I

Amadís De Gaula As A Courtesy Book

The Background and the Ideal

The quest to formulate and define modes of behavior for the ideal man of society has been a constant intellectual pursuit in all literary traditions. The study of classical literature and folklore indicates that questions of refinement and etiquette occupied the Greco-Roman mind as well as that of related preceding civilizations.

It was during the Middle Ages, however, that for the first time an unprecedented, group-oriented, and exclusionary code of behavior, intended to mirror the lifestyle and the self-image of an elect few, began to emerge in the code of chivalry. Reflecting the highest aspirations of the military aristocracy and landed nobility, chivalry, an outgrowth of the knightly system of ideals, with its exclusive set of values and an array of elaborate rituals, social prescriptions, and legendary heroes, became the new distinctive discipline of the upper-class society. Chivalric ceremonies and symbolism served to promote group identity, fixed patterns of life for the wealthy, and at the same time served to hinder penetration of the aristocratic class by the less privileged. Rituals and symbols, in fact, were the force of social cohesion vital to the unity and continued existence of the elite in the face of political instability and social changes.

The royal courts of the thirteenth and fourteenth century provided the proper atmosphere for the development and maintenance of these autocratic values, interests, and activities. Aiming at setting the standards of the courtly aristocracy, apart from many chivalric manuals and courtesy books, were various novels of chivalry with scores of fictional heroes who were to serve as real-life models for those who sought the ultimate in social perfection.[1]

The fifteenth century saw a gradual decline and waning public interest in this form of literature whose hallmarks were the mysterious and the miraculous. At the time when the influence of the genre had begun to fade and "it appeared that the romance of chivalry would vanish, just as the knight that it glorified was disappearing from the courts and battlefields of Europe,"[2] Spain produced the greatest *libro de caballarías*, the *Amadís de Gaula* by Garci Rodríguez de Montalvo.[3]

---

[1]   For a study of "courtesy books" in the Middle Ages, see A. T. Byles, "Medieval Courtesy Books and the Prose Romances of Chivalry" in *Chivalry*, ed. Edgar Prestage (New York: Alfred A. Knoff. 1928), pp. 183-206.

[2]   Anthony Mottola, "*The Amadís de Gaula* in Spain and in France" (unpublished PhD dissertation, Fordham University, 1962, p. iv.)

[3]   Edwin B. Place, ed. *Amadís de Gaula* (4 vols.; Madrid: Consejo Superior de Investigaciones Cienteíficas, 1962-1971). All quotations and references to *Amadís de Gaula* will be made from Edwin Place's edition, considered among critics as the best annotated and most up-to-date reproduction of Montalvo's text. Vol. I fully discusses the early editions, adaptations, and translations of *Amadís*. Vol. II has a bibliography and linguistic notes on I and II. Vol. III discusses the novel's early form as well as its characters and geography. Vol. IV contains notes on Montalvo's life and reviews his adaption of *Amadís* "primitivo." Edwin Place's edition replaces as the standard text El *Amadís de*

Amadís de Gaula, an adaptation of an early edition appeared in 1508. Together with the revival of chivalric romanticism, represented a new outburst of enthusiasm for the heroic life and a new literary vogue for chivalric novels. Amadís himself and the other principal characters of the novel were the new stereotyped symbols that were to reflect the ideals and conceptions of virtue in which the sixteenth-century court aristocracy disguised their ideology. Montalvo's text not only became *el código caballeresco de la vida española*,[1] but also the court bible and the symbol of refining influence all over Europe.

That *Amadís de Gaula* should have emerged as a literary fantasy with a definite didactic purpose is clearly stated in the prologue to the text. The author intended, as a means of imparting instruction, to utilize the original version of Amadís' knightly adventures, which he calls "hystorias fengidas en que se hallan las cosas admirables fuera de la orden de natura, qué mas por nombre de patrañas que de crónicas con mucha razón deuen ser tenidas y llamadas."[2] And by intercalating rhetorical questions, courtly sermons, moralizing reflections, and instructions in the proper conduct and obligations of knighthood, Montalvo elevated it to the dignity of a book of "buenos enxemplos y doctrinas" according to the beliefs and teaching of "todo lo que la Sancta Yglesia tiene y manda."[3]

The homelistic intention of Montalvo in his reconstruction of *Amadís'* early text becomes manifest,

Gaula, ed. Pascual de Gayangos ("Biblioteca de Autores Españos," Vol. XI; Madrid: Rivadeneyra, 1880).

[1] Angel Rosenblat, *Amadís de Gaula* (Buenos Aires: Losada, 1940), p. 9.

[2] Place, ed., *Amadís de Gaula*, I, 9.

[3] *Ibid.*, 10.

even more significantly, if one compares corresponding parts of the Montalvo's version with the manuscript fragments of the *Amadís* "primitivo" found by Antonio Moreno Martín in 1954, and dated ca. 1420, according to a paleographic study done by Augustín Millares Carlo.[1] A comparative analysis of the two texts reveals that Montalvo altered some material; added some details; and dropped, at times, entire paragraphs to suit his didactic and artistic purpose.[2] By both omission and addition, Montalvo presented the story of Amadís in terms quite different from the older text, which reflected the state of chivalric ideals at the time of its composition. His adaptation of the primitive text emerges as a practical sophisticated code of behavior aimed at meeting the needs and satisfying the aspirations of the more socially emancipated and intellectual constituency of the early Renaissance. Edwin Place decries the interpretation and deletions of the original version as damaging to its artistic quality and unity: "Si Montalvo se hubiese limitado a refundir los tres *Libros* primitivos sin rechazar el trágico desenlace del III, ni añadir enredo de su propia cosecha, lo obra hubiere resultado dos veces más distinguida de lo que es hoy día."[3] Although it is debatable whether Montalvo really diminished the literary merit of the *Amadís* "primitivo" by projecting his own personality and attitudes in the original work, there is no doubt as to the influence of his version on the courtly conduct and manners of the sixteenth century.

---

[1]   Mottola, 79.

[2]   The *Amadís'* fragment is reproduced in A. Rodríguez-Moñino's edition, *El primer manuscrito del "Amidís de Gaula"* (Madrid: Imprenta de Silverio Aguirre Torre, 1957), p. 15.

[3]   *Ibid.* III, 935.

The question of whether *Amadís de Gaula* can be properly classified as a courtesy book has been sparingly debated, and only a few critics have addressed themselves to this topic. Prof. Place says, "A nadie, con la posible excepción de Reyner, quien le dedica un párrafo, se le haya ocurrido clasificarla en la misma categoría que comprende el *Cortegiano* de Castiglione y el *Galateo* de Giovanni della Casa, es decir, la de manual de urbanidad cortesana."[1]

The term "courtesy book," according to the definition given by Virgil Heltzel in his introduction to the *Check List of Courtesy Books*, applies to

> any work, or significant part of work which sets forth for the gentleman (or gentlewoman) first, the qualities or criteria inherent or acquired which he must possess; second, his formation (including his various interests, exercises, recreation and amusements and his education); and, third, his conduct.[2]

Under the first head, Hetzel includes "works which deal with such matters as birth, wealth, honor, arms, learning and good breeding"; under the second, "works concerned with sports (hunting, riding, etc.), or with recreations such as . . . games, art and poetry or with the aim and method of education or with advice about studies to be pursued";; and under the third, "works treating moral

---

[1]   Edwin B. Place, "El *Amadís* de Montalvo como manual de cortesanía en Francia," *Revista de Filología Española*, XXXVIII (1954), 151.

[2]   Virgil Heltzel, *Check List of Courtesy Books* (Chicago: Newberry Library, 1942), p. vii.

and social conduct and obligations in human intercourse or works on the pursuit of occupation or profession."[1]

In view of the expert and comprehensive definition supplied by Prof. Heltzel and despite the fact that *Amadís de Gaula* is not mentioned in his long checklist of courtesy books, the purpose of this chapter is to study whether Montalvo's text contains the essential criteria that would warrant its classification among the great courtesy books of all times.

An appraisal of *Amadís de Gaula* as a courtesy book is made by Menéndez y Pelayo in *Orígenes de la Novela*. He calls *Amadís de Gaula* "el doctrinal del cumplido caballero, la epopeya de la fidelidad amorosa, el código del honor, . . . el manual del buen tono, el oráculo de la elegante conversación, el repertorio de las buenas maneras y de los discursos galantes."[2] A similar evaluation of *Amadís* is given by Edwin Place. After comparing a few passages from Montalvo's text, with its French adaptation and translation by Herberay des Essart, and after rejecting the contention of some critics as to the superior artistic quality of the latter, Prof. Place concludes:

> El *Thrésor d'Amadís* no sólo entra plenamente en la categoría de manual de urbanidad cortesana, sino que, como tal, ejerció mas influencia en la tosca clase superior francesa del Renacimiento que ningún otro "courtesy book". . . .[3]

---

[1]   *Ibid.*, p. viii.

[2]   Marcelino Menéndez y Pelayo, *Orígenes de la Novela* (Santander: Aldus, S. A. de Artes Científicas, 1943), lp. 375.

[3]   Place, "El Amadís de Montalvo como manual de cortesanía en Francia," p. 168. For other studies on the influence of *Amadís de Gaula* in France, see Eugene Baret, *"De l'Amadís de Gaule" et de son influence sur les moeurs et al litterature au XVI^eet au XVII^esiecle* (Paris, 1973); Edward Bourciez, *Les*

El *Thrésor d'Amadís* ensesña al caballero y a la dama por inducción—es decir—por medio de [arengas] ejemplares sacados del *Amadís*.[1]

The case for *Amadís* as a courtesy book is also made by Jacques Gahorry. He believes that the author, following the conventional literary technique of enunciating and demonstrating through the lesson of the story certain virtues and principles of conduct, presents in *Amadís* a definite ethical and social message made plain by example rather than by direct instruction. The narration of heroic adventures, love intrigues, and pleasing tales is for the author, in Gahorry's view, a way of combining the pleasant with the useful and making the moral teachings of the romance more palatable to the readers. Gahorry also suggests that, as in the case of Apuleius' *Golden Ass* and Boccaccio's *De Genologia Deorum*, many episodes in *Amadís* are to be interpreted allegorically, if one wishes to derive proper perspective and meaning.[2]

The principal criticism of *Amadís* as a guide to proper conduct and manners came from many Spanish humanists, namely Juan Luís Vives, Antonio de Guevara, Pedro Mejía, Diego Gracián, Melchor Cano, and others who were quick in pointing out the contradictions and inconsistencies between the didactic intent of the book and its content as well as exposing, what they considered in

---

Moeurs Polies et la litterature de cour sous Henri II (Paris, 1886), pp. 60-100; Gustave Reynier, *Le Roman sentimental avant l'Astrée* (Paris, 1968), pp. 200-204; also Hugues Vaganay, "Les Trésors d'Amadís," *Revue Hispanique*, LVII (1978), pp. 115-126.

[1]   *Ibid.*, p. viii.

[2]   Jacques Gahorry, *X^e^livre d'Amadís de Gaule* (Paris: Lucas Breyer, 1571), quoted by John O'Connor in *Amadís de Gaule and its influence on Elizabethan Literature* (New Brunswick: Rutgers University Press, 1970), pp. 62-3.

their views, the pernicious influence of *Amadís* on youth and society in general.[1] A similar judgment is expressed by A. Cioranescu, a modern critic: "*Amadis*," he says,

> fut considéré pendant tout le XVI siécle, comme, le contraire de ce qu'll était en réalité, comme une école de guerre, de morale et de vertu. Il fut l'un des livres que l'on mit le plus souvent entre les mains de garcons et de jeunes personnes, afin qu'll leur ouvrît le yeux sur lés conditions de la vie.[2]

Apart from the different evaluations and conclusions reached by the critics on the influence of *Amadís* on the customs and morality of the period, a study of Montalvo's test shows that instances of ethical and social instruction are spread throughout the book. The didactic tone in the text, however, does not become pressing until *book 4*, where a complete code of knightly discipline is outlined and becomes an integral part of the narration. Francisco Delicado, in the epigraph to the edition of *Amadís* published in Venice in 1533, says:

> En el cual libro cuarto os serán contadas cosas muy sabrosas de leer y entender. . . . Enseña Asimismo a los caballeros el verdadero arte de caballería, a los mancebos a seguirla, a los

---

[1]   A list of works in which many Spanish writers criticized Amadís' morality is given in Arturo Souto's edition of Rodríquez de Montalvo, *Amadís de Gaula* (México City: Porrua, 1975), p. xxii.

[2]   Al. Cioranescu, *L'Arioste en France des Origines a la fin du XVIIIᵉSiécle* (Paris: Les éditions de Presses Modernes, 1939), pp. 27-8. On the question of *Amadís'* influence over Spanish moral and ethical ideals of the time, see Henry Thomas, *Spanish and Portuguese Romances of Chivalry* (Cambridge University Press, 1920), pp. 160-79.

ancianos a defenderla. Oltrosí aquí está encerrado el arte del derecho amor, la lealtad, la cortesía con que las damas se ha de usar, las defensas y derechos que a las dueñas los caballeros les deben de razón, las fatigas y trabajos que por las doncellas se han de paras; así que, cuanto los caballeros y hombres buenos, condes, duques y marqueses, reyes, soldanes y emperadores deben ser obligados a las mujeres. . . . Conviene a saber: tomar por enjemplo el modo, la virtud y bondad que de Amadís se cuenta, y de los otros muy valientes caballeros, para por aquel camino seguir . . . porque digo yo, a mi paracer, que la historia de Amadís puede ser apropiada a todo buen caballero.[1]

Sharing similar views is Menéndez y Pelayo: "Este libro cuarto . . . constituye un doctrinal de caballeros, el más perfecto y cumplido que pueda imaginarse."[2]

Indeed, the text of *Amadís* could not have been considered during the sixteenth century the "arbiter elegantiarum" and the most influential handbook of knightly conduct unless it surpassed all other romances of chivalry in practical examples of knightly virtues and social graces deemed necessary to the formation of the courtly gentleman. In respect to other novels of chivalry, *Amadís* had a twofold advantage. First, it shared with other chivalric romances such as *Lancelot* and *Tristan* a common literary origin since these novels, like *Amadís*, have their roots in the Arthurian theme of the Round Table or "the *Vulgata*, as is more commonly known among

---

[1] Souto's edition, p. 274.

[2] Menéndez y Pelayo, p. 364.

scholars."[1] Second, and of more importance, Montalvo's text, while vividly restating the principles of chivalric tradition, also reaffirmed, in the light of the new social and political realities of the sixteenth century, a code of conduct which reflected the modus vivendi and the interests of the courtly class whose exclusiveness was being threatened by the emergence of a new, wealthier, and more militant Renaissance Bourgeoisie.[2] Responding as well to the ethical and religious preoccupation of the Castillian society, Montalvo also raised the moral tone of the *Amadís* story by minimizing "el amor cortés adúltero,"[3] quite common in the Arthurian romances, and by stressing instead the love devotion of Amadís and Oriana. By a mere process of emphasis and modification, Montalvo, a true interpreter of the Castillian mind, sought, by the edification of Amadís' noble and virtuous examples, to bridge the gap between chivalric precepts and Christian doctrines and to reconcile secular interests with spiritual concerns. As a result, he presents in *Amadís* a more contemporary scheme of ideals and manners, of good and bad, which reflects the tastes and prejudices of the Spanish court under the *Reyes Católicos* understandably

---

[1]   Place, ed., *Amadís de Gaula* by Rodríguez de Montalvo, I, xiv. The literary connection between the early *Amadís* and Arthurian sources has been convincingly treated by Grace Williams in "The Amadís Question," *Revue Hispanique* XXI (1909), 1-167. See also W. J. Entwistle, *A lenda arturiana nas literaturas da peninsula ibérica* (Lisboa, 1942), pp. 197-200.

[2]   For some interesting insights on the dynamics of Spanish classes during the Renaissance, see J. H. Elliot, *Imperial Spain: 1469-1716* (New York: The New American Library, 1966), pp. 193-5.

[3]   Place's edition, *Amadís de Gaula*, III, p. 928.

preoccupied with questions of ethics and morality, at least on the surface.[1]

There were undoubtedly many Spanish literary precedents to mold Montalvo's vision of the ideal knight and gentleman. Besides the various epic poems, "cancioneros" and "crónicas," there were the *Siete Partidas*, a compendium of laws and customs; *El Victorial*, an idealized biography of the knight Don Pedro Niño; *Libro del Paso Honroso*, an Arthurian flavored historical account of a tourney held at Orbigo in 1434; and in particular, *El Cabballero Cifar*, which has been said to contain "the germ of the Renaissance novel of chivalry"[2] and held until recently as "one of *Amadís'* innumerable progeny"[3] These literary specimen must have provided ample examples for Montalvo's forging his "libro de caballerías" and tailoring it to the standards of conduct and manners of the courtly aristocracy, whose traditional guide to noble behavior had been the code of chivalry.

It has been repeatedly stated that *Amadís de Gaula* was "el código caballeresco" of the sixteenth century. But what is the nature of the ideal it embodies, to what extent and in what sense is Montalvo's text truly a courtesy book are questions that need to be explored. I believe that the best avenue of approach to these questions is to study *Amadís* in the content of its relation to the concept and ideal of chivalry, a term that by the end of the fifteenth century became descriptive and synonymous with the English

---

[1]   A perceptive account of the moral and social milieu in the era of the Catholic kings can be found in Jean Hippolyte Mariejol, *The Spain of Ferdinand and Isabella*, trans. Benjamin Keen (New Brunswick: Rutgers University Press, 1961), pp. 39-58, pp. 176-91.

[2]   Richard Chandler and Kessel Schwartz, *A New History of Spanish Literature* (Baton Rouge: Louisiana State University, 1961), p. 162.

[3]   Henry Thomas, p. 11.

word "courtliness" and the French word *courtoisie*. Both of these terms have been used since the twelfth century to describe, in the words of Jean Frappier, *un code de politesse et de galanterie* as well as *un mode de vie, un attitude sociable.*[1] It is useful to point out that the Spanish equivalent *cortesanía* does not appear in Spain with the same connotation, as the English and French terms, until the translation of *Il Cortegiano* of Castiglione by Juan Boscán in 1534.[2] Prior to this date, the terms *arte fina e palenciana* or *gentileza* were used.[3]

The connection between "courtliness" and "chivalry" is clearly explained by A. J. Denony. He defines "courtliness" "as the ideal of the social and moral decorum of the courts and nobility." "By the fourteenth century," he adds, "there is clear evidence that *courtoisie* is synonymous with *curialitas*, the *nobilitas morum*, the cardinal worldly virtue, so to speak, of the chevaler, the embodiment of the social and ethical ideal of chivalry."[4] The same thought is shared by Prof. Hearnshaw: "First, 'chivalry' was used to connote simply a body of knights and horsemen equipped for battle . . . It was later in the Middle Ages that chivalry was used in a broader sense

---

[1] Jean Frappier, *Amour courtois et Table Ronde* (Genéve: Librairie Droz, 1973), p. 20.

[2] Margherita Morreale, Castiglione y Boscsán: *El lideal cortesano en el Renacimiento español* (Añejos de Boletín de la Real Academia Española, Añejo I; Madrid: 1959), p. 116.

[3] Bernardo Blanco-González, *Del Cortesano al Discreto: Examen de una "decadencia"* (Madrid: Editorial Gredos, 1962), p. 188.

[4] Alexander J. Denomy, "Courtly Love and Courtliness," *Speculum*, 28 (1953), pp. 47-8.

to include the whole knightly system with its peculiar religious, moral, and social customs."[1]

Although our knowledge of the essence of medieval courtliness and its descriptive features is not exact, a survey of the fifteenth century literature and earlier seems to indicate that there are three widely accepted basic qualities that eminently describe and define the Spanish *caballero*, the English knight, and the French *chevalier*. These are noble birth, skillfulness in arms, and gallantry in love. It was commonly thought among medieval and Renaissance theoreticians of knightly virtues, ranging from Lull to Caxton, from Castiglione to Della Casa, that from the possession and interplay of these three essential and correlated qualities within the individual were derived all the other worldly attributes.

A textual analysis of *Amadís* will show that these fundamental characteristics distinctive of the ideal knight, combined with other expressly Spanish idiosyncrasies of the Amadís' character, are at the basis of Montalvo's literary creation. Let us first examine how the question of nobility is treated in *Amadís*.

Knightly Qualities

Nobility

The most important attribute of the knight is that of noble birth. Within the code of chivalry, remarks Prof.

---

[1] F. J. Hearnshaw, "Chivalry and its Place in History," in *Chivalry*, ed. E. Prestage (New York, 1928), pp. 1-2.

Kilgour, "every noble was not a knight, but every knight was of necessity a noble."[1] Ancestry, says A. W. Reed, is the true mark of the gentleman: "all other derivations seem whimsical. He is a man of birth, a man of extraction."[2] Ramón Lull, the Catalonian scholar, mystic, and missionary, in his *Order of Chivalry* (ca. 1280), unequivocally states that *Parage and chyualrye accorden to guder.*[3] In the *Siete Partidas* we find: "Solo puede ser armado caballero el escudero de noble linaje."[4]

The theme of ancestry in *Amadís* is treated extensively. References to Amadís' nobility are a constant reminder throughout the text. The terms *linaje, nobleza, estan noble condición, persona de alto logar* are repeated almost at regular intervals. There seems to be a deliberate effort to stress the concept of hereditary nobility and associate noble birth with good deeds and good manners.

Amadís' royal extraction is emphasized from the very beginning. Before Amadís was placed in a chest and abandoned in the river, Elisena's maid took special care in writing and placing on the neck of the newly-born child a sealed letter attached to a string with the inscription:

[1] Raymond Lincoln Kilgour, *The Decline of Chivalry as Shown in the Decline of French Literature of the Late Middle Ages* (Cambridge: Harvard University Press, 1937), p. xix.

[2] A. W. Reed, "Chivalry and the Idea of a Gentleman" in *Chivalry*, ed. E. Prestage, p. 207.

[3] William Caxton, The Book of the *Ordre of Chyvalry*, ed. A. T. P. Byles (London: E.E.T.S., 1926), p. 58

[4] Blanco-Gonzalez, p. 49.

Este es Amadís Sin Tiempo, hijo de rey.[1]

Later in the text, the same reiteration is made when Oriana discovers and reads the letter and realizes that Amadís is of noble blood:

> Estuuo pensando vn poco, y, entendío que el Donzel del
> Mar hauía nombre Amadís y vio que era hijo de rey;[2]

When Gandalac releases young Galaor to the Hermit so that he may rear him and educate him in knightly virtues, he tells the Hermit:

> Este niño vos doy que lo criéis y enseñéys de todo lo que
> conuine a cauallero, y dígoos que es fijo de rey y reyna.[3]

An offspring, however, cannot be truly noble unless both parents are of noble descent. Urganda *la Desconocida*, prophetizing Amadís' heroic deeds, says to Gandales:

> Sabe que viene de reyes de ambas partes.[4]

When Cendil, Lisuarte's messenger, delivers to Amadís and his allies King Lisuarte's challenge and warnings, Don Quadragante retorts:

---

[1]   Place, ed. *Amadís de Gaula*, I, i, 23.

[2]   I, viii, 67.

[3]   I, iii, 37.

[4]   I, 11, 30.

Pero dezidle vos por mí que . . . de fidfalguía no
le deuo nada
que no es é de más derechos reyes de ambas
partes que yo.[1]

The same point is made in a letter sent by Celinda,
King Hegido's daughter, to Lisuarte, her former lover.
Celinda asks the king to confer knighthood upon their son,
whom he does not yet know or recognize:

Honrralde y amalde, mi buen señor, haziéndole
cauallero,
que de todas partes de reyes viene.[2]

Urganda also assures Lisuarte of the same:

Pero yo vos juro por la fe que a Dios deuo que
de ambas partes viene de reyes lindos.[3]

One of the principles inherent in the concept of
hereditary nobility is that it establishes and perpetuates
a closed caste system in which only the well-born are
permitted to move freely. This caste system must be
defended against outside penetration even under threat or
personal danger. The principle is well illustrated in a letter
Celinda writes to King Lisuarte:

Bién se vos acordará . . . donde me vos hallastes
cercada, en el mi castillo que del Gran Rosal se
nombra, de Antifón el Bravo, que por ser de mi

---

[1]   III, lxiii, 663.

[2]   III, lxvi, 695.

[3]   III, lxvi, 693.

desechado en casamiento por no ser en linaje mi
ygual, toda mi tierra tormarme quería.[1]

Only proof of noble ancestry gains Galaor admission to
the palace of Aldeya, daughter of the King of Serolis:

> Señor cauallero, antes que entréys conuine que
> me digáys cúyo hijo sois. –Dexad vos desso-
> dixo él-, que yo tengo tal padre y madre que
> hasta que mas valga no osaría dezir que su
> hijo soy. –Todavía-dixo ella- conuiene que me
> digáys, que no será de vuestro daño. –Sabed que
> soy fijo del rey Perión y de la reyna Helisena . . .
> –Entrad- dixo ella.[2]

The point that only those of noble birth have the
privilege of mingling with the noble is made by a knight
to Don Florestán, whose noble ancestry he ignores,

> no conuine a cauallero de tal linaje como vos
> tener en su guarda muger de alta guisa como la
> donzella es.[3]

Amadís is almost at odds with himself when, for
a moment, ponders how he, not yet certain about his
ancestry, has dared to aspire to Oriana's love:

> -Ay, catiuo Donzel del Mar, sin linaje y sin bien,
> ¿ cómo fueste tan osado de meter tu coracón y tu

---

[1]   III, lxvi, 695.
[2]   I, xii, 104-5.
[3]   I, xliii, 348.

amor en poder de aquella que vale más que las
otras todás de bondad y fermosura y de linaje?[1]

In *Amadís*, nobility, military prowess, and good
manners are often linked together. Nasciano calls Amadís

flor y espejo de todos los caualleros del mundo
assí en linaje como en esfuerço y en todas las
otras buenas maneras que cauallero deue tener;[2]

Nobility, however, is more closely linked to fine
conduct than military prowess. Commenting on the fine
manners and polite answers given by Amadís, disguised
as the Knight of the Green Sword, to the emperor and
empress of Constantinople, the author remarks:

Gran plazer houo destas razones que passaron el
emperador y la emperatriz . . . y muy bién les
pareció las graciosas respuestas que el cauallero
de la Verde Spada daua a toto lo que le dezían;
assí que esto les fazía creer, ahún mas que el su
gran esfuerço, ser él hombre de alto lugar, porque
el esfuerço y valenteía muchas vezes acierta en
las personas de baxa suerte y gruesso juyzio, y
pocas la honesta mesura y polida criança, porque
esto es deuido aquellos que de limpia y generosa
sangre vienen.[3]

Noble ancestry is also associated with moral and
spiritual strength in the face of adversity. The hermit

---

[1]   I, viii, 67.

[2]   IV, cxiii, 1, 125.

[3]   III, lxxiv, 823.

of Peña Pobre tells Amadís, who is shedding tears of desperation and is threatening to do away with his life for the supposed loss of Oriana's love:

> Según vuestro entendimiento y el linaje tan alto donde venís, no os dueríades matar ni perder por ninguna cosa que vos aueniese.[1]

On the same note, Mabilia, commissioned by Oriana to relieve Queen Sardamira's affliction for the loss of her husband, says:

> Noble reyna y senõra, no conuiene a persona de tan also lugar como os assí se vencer y sojuzgar de la fortuna;[2]

and adds that show of courage in the face of hardship is an obligation that those of noble birth have toward their ancestors:

> Mucho bien paresçe en los antiguos enxemplos de aquellos que con sus fuertes animos quisieron pagar la deuda a sus antecessores mostrando en las cosas adversas la nobleza del linaje y sangre donde vienen.[3]

Nobility in *Amadís* is also seen as a stimulus to virtue. Oriana, who has just found evidence of Amadís' noble ancestsry in the inscription of a letter, sends *la doncella de*

---

[1]   II, xlviii, 393.

[2]   IV, lxxxii, 961.

[3]   Ibid.

Denamarca to inform Amadís, who is fighting in the war of Gaula, that he is

> hijo de rey y que pues él era tan bueno quando
> no lo sauía, agora pure de ser mejor.[1]

Galaor, after expressing his desire to be knighted and after being told by the hermit, "Soys hijo de rey y de reyna," responds:

> El pensamiento que yo fasta aquí tenía por grande en querer ser cauallero tengo agora por pequeño, según lo que me hauéys dicho.[2]

Later in the text Galaor asks Urganda:

> -¿Es verdad . . . que el rey Perión es mi padre y la reyna mi madre, y que soy hermano de aquel tan buen cauallero? –Sin falta- dixo ella- es – A Dios merced –dixo- él- agora os digo que soy puesto en mucho mayor cuydado que ante y la vida en mayor peligro, pues me conuine ser tal que esto que vos, donzella, dezís.[3]

Those of noble lineage have a greater obligation to give good example. When Oriana reveals to Nasciano her illicit love relation with Amadís:

---

[1]   I, viii, 67.

[2]   I, v, 55.

[3]   I, xi, 96.

> El hombre bueno fue muy maravillado de tal
> amor en persona de tan alto lugar, que muy mas
> que otra obligado era a dar buen exemplo de sí.[1]

Noble birth is also associated with intelligence and ability to learn. It is said of Amadís:

> Su ingenio era tal, y condición tan noble, que
> muy mejor que otro ninguno y más presto todas
> las cosas aprendía.[2]

Noble breeding is clearly recognizable by the garments one wears, body marks, and outward appearance. Gandales, after narrating to King Lisuarte the circumstances of Amadís' discovery in the water, and after describing the ring and the sword that were found with him, and also giving the details of the rich clothes in which he was wrapped, exclaims:

> Que assí Dios me salue, según el aparato que él
> tráya yo creo que es de muy gran linage.[3]

Similarly Nasciano, after describing to Lisuarte how he had found Esplandián *en ricos paños,* remarks,

> - Cierto, señor, yo creo que al niño es de alto
> logar . . . y cuando le baptizé, falléle en la diestra
> parte del pecho vnas lettras blancas en escuro
> latín . . . y en la parte siniestra en derecho de

---

[1]   III, lxxi, 780.

[2]   I, iii, 34.

[3]   I, iii, 34.

coracón tiene siete letras más ardientes y coloradas como vn fino rubí.[1]

A person of noble lineage feels and acts nobly. His intuition and impulses are such that he instinctively seeks the pursuit of virtue and great deeds. In King Lisuarte's mind, being of good extraction is an indispensable quality and requirement to entering the order of knighthood. When Amadís expresses to the king his wish to become a knight, Lisuarte answers him:

-Vos queréys ser cauallero, y no sabes si de derecho os conuiene, y quiero que sabéys vuestra hazienda como yo lo sé.[2]

He then informs Amadís of how he was found by Gandales in an arch in the open sea and that his ancestry was unknown. Amadís, in his answer to the king, seems to suggest that those of noble blood have a superior order of sensitivity and propensity to bravery:

Mas a mí no pesa de quanto me dezís, sino por no conocer mi lenaje, ni ellos a mí. Pero yo me tengo por hidalgo, que mi coraçón a ello me esfuerça. Y ahora, señor, me conuiene más que ante cauallería, y ser tal que gane honra y prez.[3]

From the various allusions and remarks spread throughout the text, it is evident that there is a marked tendency in *Amadís* to associate noble birth with virtue

[1]   III, lxxi, 775.
[2]   I, iv, 42.
[3]   I, iv, 42.

in general. *Virtud* and *nobleza* are repeatedly paired. The idea that "those who sprung from better ancestry are likely to be better men, for nobility is excellence of race" can be traced as far back as Aristotle.[1] The same thought is also expressed in the drama of Euripides: "Unto the noble, everything is good."[2] In Roman antiquity parallel views are found in the works of Sallust, who sees noble birth "as a lamp to posterity,"[3] and in Plutarch who associates keen mind, good appearance, behavior, strength, and larger body size with noble ancestry.[4] These thoughts during the Middle Ages were readily embraces by the landed aristocracy, which saw in the appropriation of noble ancestry and claim to excellence a means of preserving their exclusiveness and wealth.

The case against the Aristotelian view of hereditary nobility is well outlined in Seneca's remarks: "It is within the realm of every man to live nobly."[5] "All men descend from the same original stock; no one is better born than another except insofar as his disposition is nobler or better suited for the performance of good actions."[6] Similar views on nobility are also expressed by Juvenal: "Sanctus

---

[1] Politics iii. 13.1283a, trans. Benjamin Jowett, *The Basic Works of Aristotle*, ed. Richard McKeon (New York: Random House, 1941), p. 1194.

[2] Euripides, *Danoe*: Fragment, quoted in the *Home Book of Quotations*, ed. Burton Stevenson (New York: Dodd, Mead and Co., 1967), p. 1407.

[3] *Dictionary of Quotable Definitions*, ed. Eugene E. Brussel (Englewood Cliffs: Prentice Hall, Inc., 1970), p. 18.

[4] Charles E. Little, *Historical Lights* (New York: Funk and Wagnalls Co., 1886), p. 450.

[5] Seneca, *Epistulae ad Lucilium*, Epis. xxii, 17, in Eugene E. Brussell, *Dictionary of Quotable Definitions*, p. 1408.

[6] Seneca, De Beneficiis, iii. 28 in *Moral Essays*, trans. John W. Basore (Loeb Classical Library; Cambridge, Mass.: Harvard University Press, 1928-1935), III, 177.

haberi, justitiaeque tenax, factis, dictisque mereris? Agnosco procerem."[1]

The concept of nobility based on individual merit was shared by many medieval writers. Jean Clopinel in his *Roman de la Rose* writes, "Noblece vient de bon courage/Car gentillece de lingnage."[2] Andreas Capellanus in his *De Amore* states that it is excellence of character that blesses man with nobility rather than high birth. He argues that since all human beings derive from the same stock, it is logical that "rank" was originally derived from self-worth. Comparable beliefs are also held in Dante's *Convivio*, Macchiavelli's *Discorsi*, Francisco de Osuma's *Abecedario Espiritual,* Chauser's *Gentilesse,* and in many other Renaissance texts.[3] On the other hand, Montalvo, bound by the very nature of the romance of chivalry and committed, perhaps, by his own convictions, adhered to the principle of hereditary nobility.

The doctrine of true nobility based on birth rather than virtue was a creed fiercely defended by the court elite of the fifteenth century.[4] The acceptance of this doctrine left no possibility of social advancement or mobility and was used by the courtly aristocracy as the main argument to ascertain their class supremacy and guard against any attempt by the lesser nobility to infiltrate their ranks. The tenets on noble birth exposed in *Amadís* not only

[1] Juvenal, Satires viii, 1. 24, in Eugene E. Brussell, *Dictionary of Quotable Definitions*, p. 1407.

[2] *Roman de la Rose*, ed. Ernest Langlois (5 vols.; Paris; Societé de Anciens Texts Français, 1914-1924), Vol. IV, vv. 18619-186622.

[3] Leonard Mades, *The Armor and the Brocade: A Study of "Don Quijote" and "The Courtier"* (New York: Las Americas Publishing Co., 1968), pp. 35-36.

[4] Elliot, pp. 218-19. On the power of the nobility in Spain during this time, see the chapter on "Nobility" *in The Spain of Ferdinand and Isabella* by Jean Hippolyte Mariejol.

reiterated in an aura of romantic nostalgia old principles and convictions on the subject, but also reinforced among the court aristocracy the belief that high birth was one of the outstanding qualities that defined the ideal of courtliness. To the nobly-born, Amadís was a convenient symbol of identification and social aspiration. To the less privileged classes, together with the psychological effect of limited expectability, he was the mirror of a world beyond their reach. Commenting on the modes of thought of the early Renaissance, Alfred Von Martin points out that the "bourgeoisie" was easily impressed by the "gentleman of noble birth" and that "it bestowed its admiration where it could not really follow."[1] In the social milieu of the sixteenth century, so sensitive to class differences and so impressed by wealth and status, it is not surprising that *Amadís de Gaula*, a romance dealing with personal relationship of knights, princes, and kings, should have been seized by the courtly nobility as a vehicle for self-image and projection.

Arms

Like nobility, skillfulness and proper conduct in the profession of arms are central to the concept of chivalry and courtliness. In a society where "noble life is seen as an exhilarating game of courage and honor,"[2] the nobleman must demonstrate his virtue in feats of strength and valor.

---

[1] Alfred Von Martin, "Sociology of Renaissance" in *Renaissance Medieval or Modern*, ed. Karl H. Dannenfeldt (Boston: D. C. Heath and Co., 1957), pp. 46-47.

[2] J. Huizinga, *Homo Ludens: A Study of the Play-Element in Culture* (Boston: The Beacon Press, 1964), p. 101.

Although, as has been pointed out, noble birth in *Amadís* is not necessarily associated with military prowess; the performance of great deeds in the pursuit of honor and the lady's love is the text's main theme. The fighting spirit in *Amadís* certainly found a real-life manifestation in the gallantry and bravery of many Spanish noblemen who served heroically in the long-fought struggle against the Moors. Montalvo himself, in the prologue to book 1 of *Amadís*, alludes to "al esfuerço de los caualleros, en las rebueltas, escaramuças y peligrosos combates."[1] Resonances of the Spanish heroic spirit are also found in the chronicles and epics of the *Reconquista* of which *El Cid* is the outstanding example. Spanish military valor and spirit, in Montalvo's time, were not less alive in the exploits of adventure and conquest of the New World. Although confined within the boundaries of myth and legend, the knightly examples of Amadís' courage, conduct, and martial skills must have provided for the sixteenth-century aristocracy a "fair seeing" of what was expected in the training of the noble Spanish gentleman educated at the court of kings.

The knight's main purpose was to fight for his lord, and as part of an essentially military society, his education had to be geared to warfare. His training at first consisted in mastering the skills of horsemanship and building courage, as well as learning to endure pain and uncertainty. In Montalvo's text we find Amadís, from a very early age, being educated in the court of King Lisuarte in the basic skills of knightly sportsmanship:

---

[1] Place, ed. *Amadís de Gaula*, I, p. 7.

> El amaua tanto caça y monte que si lo dexassen
> nunca dello se apartara tirando con su arco y
> ceuando los canes. . . .

> No ouo cauallero que más apuesto en la silla
> pareciesse.[1]

Esplandián, in his early training, also received instruction in the skills of horsemanship, hunting, and archery. In his first youthful appearance, we find him sharing with King Lisuarte the take of his hunting:

> -Señor, tomad vos el cieruo para os y para
> vuestsros compañeros. [2]

Similarly, Galaor, under the tutelage of the giant, learned

> a caualgar y a esgremir y todas loas otras cosas
> que a cauallero conuenían.[3]

And under the care of the hermit:

> Seyendo ya en edad de diez y ocho años, hízose
> valiente de cuerpo y membrudo; y siempre leýa
> en vnos libros que el buen hombre le daua de
> los fechos antiguos que los caualleros en armas
> passaron: de manera que quasi con aquello como

---

[1]   I, iii, 34.

[2]   III, lxxi, 779.

[3]   I, xi, 89.

con lo natural con que nasciera fue movido a
gran deseo de ser cauallero.[1]

Chivalry finds its best model in Amadís; Oriana
calls him

> flor y espejo de toda cauallería, . . . gran caudillo
> y capitán, assí en las armas como en todas
> las otras virtudes, donde los que en él biuen
> enxemplo podían tomar.[2]

In the duel against King Abies, a chorus of voices
chants:

> En este es caualleri á bien empleada pues que
> sobre todos la mantiene en la su gran alteza![3]

Agrajes, Amadis' cousin, after witnessing one of his
great duels, exclaims:

> - Caualleros, mirad al mejor cauallero y más
> esforçado que nunca nasció.[4]

And Urganda la Desconocida, in her prophesy, has
these words to say about Amadís:

> - Será flor de los caualleros de su tiempo; éste
> fará estremecer los fuertes; éste començará todas
> las cosas y acabará a su honra en que los otros

---

[1]   I, v, 54.
[2]   I, xx, 183.
[3]   I, ix, 76.
[4]   I, viii, 73.

fallescerion; éste fará tales cosas que ninguno cuydaría que pudiessen ser començadas ni acabadas por cuerpo de hombre.[1]

The life of the knight is a life of action in battle; therefore, one of the knight's first virtues is bravery. It is said of King Perión:

> Su fuerte coraçón no era contento sino quando el cuerpo ponía en los grandes peligros.[2]

And of his siblings:

> Eran aquellos que siempre sus fuertes coraçones no eran satisfechos sino quando las cosas en que los otros fallecían que ellos las prouauan, desseándolas acabar sin ningún peligro temer.[3]

The many encounters of Amadís with knights, giants, lions, magicians, and other nonhuman opponents are symbolic of his unmatched courage. In one of his many descriptions of knightly combats, the author writes:

> Allí veriades al Donzel del Mar haziendo cosas estrañas, derribando y matando quantos ante sí hallaua, . . . y metíase en los enemigos haziendo dellos corro, que parescía vn león bravo.[4]

---

[1] I, ii, 25.

[2] I, ii, 25.

[3] II, xliv, 363.

[4] I, vii, 73.

But courage alone is not enough. It has to be combined with physical strength. Amadís was of such body strength:

> que muy mayor que ninguno pudiera pensar la
> tenía, ahunque de gran cuerpo no era.[1]

Apolidón was the greatest knight of his time because

> así de fortaleza del cuerpo como esfuerço de
> coracón en su tiempo ninguno ygual le fue.[2]

On the other hand, Agrajes could not match Amadís' valor because his courage was not complemented by his physical vitality:

> Éste fue vno de los caualleros del mundo más
> biuo de coraçon y más acometedor en todas las
> afrentas, y si assí la fuerça como el esfuerço le
> ayudara, no ouiera otro ninguno que de bondad
> de armas le passara[3]

Only through courage and feat of arms can the knight pursue honor and establish his good reputation. Since honor is more important than life itself, the knight often has no choice but to fight against overwhelming odds. Don Florestán, Amadís' brother, who is trying to establish his reputation in combat, refuses, even at the risk of dying, to submit to Galaor's request that he reveal his identity:

---

[1]   I, xxvii, 234.

[2]   II, p. 355.

[3]   I, viii, 72.

Antes querría morir en la batalla que lo dezir;[1]

When Galaor is told by a damsel that he was fighting his own brother, he offers Florestán *le espada y la honra de la batalla.* To this gesture Florestán replies:

> -Señor, perd ónadme, que si vos erré en me combatir con vos no lo sabiendo, no fue por ál sino porque sin vergüeça me pudiese llamar vuestro hermano, como lo soy, paresciendo en algo al vuestro gran valor y gran prez de armas.[2]

The major threat to the knight's honor is cowardice. King Lisuarte points out to Amadís, who has just expressed his desire to become a knight:

> -Quien este nombre de caualleria ganar quisiere y mantenerlo en su honrra, tantas y tan graves son las cosas que ha de fazer, que muchas vezes se le enoja el coraçón, y si tal cauallero es que por miedo o codicia dexa de hazer lo que conuiene, mas le valdría la muerte que en vergüença buiir.[3]

On a similar note, King Perión says to a group of knights he is about to lead into battle:

> -Nobles príncipes y caualleros, . . . todos somos muy obligados en defendimiento de nuestra

---

[1]   I, xli, 327.

[2]   I, xli, 328.

[3]   I, lv, 40.

honrras y estados a poner las personas en todo
peligro por las defender.[1]

Not to appear cowardly in front of King Lisuarte,
Amadís, who was just about to defeat Dardán in a
horse-mounted combat, reluctantly consents to his
opponent's wishes to continue the fight on foot, although
in Amadís' view it is not proper that *"cauallero deue dexar
su caballo en quanto pudiere estar en él."*[2] When later in
the fight Amadís, at the sight of Oriana, lost concentration
in the battle and began to lose momentarily,

> -Ouo tan gran vergüença que quisiera ser muerto
> con temor que creería su señora que hauía en el
> couardía.[3]

At this thought, he regained his composure and
defeated Dardán.

Nothing can stand in the way of the knight's pursuit of
honor, and in the case of Galaor, not even his own family.
Galaor feels obligated to honor his pledge of loyalty to
King Lisuarte, although it meant that he would have to
fight against King Perión, his father, and against Amadís,
his brother.

The possession of honor reflects itself not just on the
individual but also on his family and his siblings. Florestán
says to Galaor:

---

[1]   IV, cxiii, 1, 134.

[2]   I, xiii, 119.

[3]   I, xiii, 120.

Si alguna cosa yo valiere, tanto es la honra
vuestra como mía.[1]

Mabilia, Amadís' cousin and Oriana's confidant,
expressing her feelings of pride in Amadís' reputation and
honor, exclaims:

Señor, . . . bendito seas porque tan bueno
cauallero heziste en nuestro linaje.[2]

Later in the text, Agrajes, commenting on Mabilia's
feelings of pride, remarks:

Con gran razón mi hermana de tal cosa se deuía
sentir y no solamente ella, más todos los que de
su linaje somos.[3]

To be faithful to one's word is one of the essential
principles of the knight's code of honor. Amadís is tricked
into making a promise to a mourning lady, only to discover
later that she was the wife of his worst enemy, Arcaláus:

-Sabed, mi señor Amadís, que soy mujer de
Arcaláus el Encantador, el que vos tenéys preso.
Demándoosle, que me lo deys . . . que vos soys
el mayor enemigo que él tiene.[4]

Amadís, in order that

---

[1]   I, xliii, 346.

[2]   I, viii, 126.

[3]   I, xxiii, 209.

[4]   IV, cxxx, 1, 305.

su palabra y verdad por ninguna guisa por dudosa
se juzgasse, acordó de fazer lo que pedía.[1]

In similar fashion, King Lisuarte is tricked into
accepting from a stranger a beautiful mantle and a crown
on the condition that he return them on a specified day or
grant a boon. The king gave his word:

> Cierto, cauallero, essa promessa terné yo quanto
> la vida tuuiere.[2]

As anyone would expect, the crown and the mantle
disappeared, and the king, who had given his word of
honor, had no choice but handing over his daughter
Oriana, whom the stranger asked in exchange:

> - Ay, cauallero!- dixo el rey, -mucho me auedes
> pedido . . . pero el rey que era el más leal del
> mundo, dixo: - No vos pese, que más conuiene la
> pérdida de mi fija que falta de mi palabra.[3]

Loyalty ranks very high among the knightly virtues.
King Arban calls loyalty:

> una de las más preciadas cosas del mundo.[4]

Amadís is often called *"el más leal cauallero."* His
pledge of loyalty is a lifelong commitment, as expressed
to King Perión:

---

[1] IV, cxxx, 1, 306.
[2] I, xxix, 242.
[3] I, xxiii, 273.
[4] I, xxxvii, 294.

-Señor, . . . en la vuestra ayuda me hauréys vos quanto mi persona durare.[1]

But above all, the knight must be loyal in honoring his lady. When Amadís was asked by Angriote to admit that the beauty of his lady was superior to that of Oriana, he answers,

> Tan gran mentira nunca otorgaré si por fuerça no me lo hazen dezir o la vida no me quitan.[2]

Moments later we find that

> Amadís se combatía por razón de la hermosura de su señora, donde ouiera él por mejor ser muerto que fallescer vn punto de lo que deuía.[3]

One of the knight's duties is the protection and defense of the needy, especially women, in the face of violence and villainy of unscrupulous knights. Urganda proclaims Amadís *"amparo y reparo de muchos,"* and Nasciano calls him *"reparador de muchos cuytados."*[4] In one of his many rescues of distressed damsels, Amadís tells two knights:

> No vos dexaré si no juráys que nunca tomaréys dueña ni donzella contra su voluntad.[5]

Later he remarks that it is cowardice,

---

[1]   I, xviii, 71.

[2]   I, xvii, 60.

[3]   I, xviii, 163.

[4]   IV, cxiii, 1, 125.

[5]   I, xiii, 113.

forçando las mujeres, que muy guardadas deuen
ser de los caualleros.[1]

In redressing wrongs against women, the knight can
acquire great honor. After being freed from the Roman
ships, Oriana says to Amadís:

-Agora paresce la vuestra gran bondad en auer
hecho este socorro a mí y a estas infantas, que
en tanta amargura y tribulación, puestas éramos.
Por todas las tierras del mundo será sabido y
ensalçado vuestro loor.[2]

While fighting, the knight is bound by a prescribed
code of conduct. In *Amadís*, wars, small group combat,
and duels are fought in accordance with certain rules of
etiquette. Almost invariably, all encounters start with a
challenge consisting of a declaration or a complaint. This
may be followed by an insult or a demand for a concession
requiring an immediate satisfaction by way of surrender
or combat. For reason of personal honor, the challenge
always results in armed conflict. To the victor goes *el prez,
el provecho,* or *la honra* of the battle. Armed combat is a
serious matter that compromises not just the life and honor
of the knight but also the physical and moral wellbeing of
those he is there to defend. For example, it is not part of
the chivalric code that the knight risks any advantage that
he might gain in the course of the battle. When Galpano,
already tired, suggests to Amadís that they stop the fight
and rest before continuing, Amadís responds:

[1]   I, xix, 179.
[2]   III, lxxxi, 914.

> Esso no ha menester . . . que yo no me combato contigo por cortesía, más por dar emienda aquella donzella que deshonoraste.[1]

Although there are instances when the rules of chivalry do not apply, especially when fighting against unprincipled opponents—and there are in *Amadís* many fights that occur outside the boundaries of chivalry—even then, the knight must still struggle to keep within the limits of chivalric courtesy. When Amadís, for instance, arrives at the castle of Galpano to avenge the honor of a lady who had just been raped—a crime that in Amadís' words calls for immediate justice—he still allows Galpano to take arms:

> Armad vos luego, si no, matar vos he assí desarmado; que con los malos como vos no se deuía tener templança.[2]

Finally, when participating in larger wars and the outcome is allowed to rest on the fight between two champions, the knight, if necessary, must have the courage to offer himself in one-to-one combat as a means of avoiding needless bloodshed. The old Merovingian concept of "better for one to fall than the whole army" is well demonstrated in Amadis' challenge to King Abies, who has come with a larger army to fight the small contingent of Perión:

---

[1]   I, vi, 60.

[2]   I, vi, 59.

No hay razón porque ninguno otro padezca, y
sea la batalla entre mi y vos.[1]

This custom during the Middle Ages resulted in many
prearranged single battles among commanders of armies.[2]
Many times the challenge to single combat was offered
by one king or another. However, no one really expected
them to fight, but it was a grand chivalric gesture.[3]
Francis I twice was challenged by Charles V. Elaborate
preparations were made, but "the battle royal never came
off. . . . [It was] a piece of empty ceremonial between two
royal houses."[4]

Addressing himself to the question of proper conduct
in battle, as it appears in medieval romances of chivalry
and its influence on the military code of behavior and the
tenets of warfare of the Late Middle Ages, Huizinga points
out that in the name of chivalric courtesy:

> Kings exposed themselves to the danger of the
> most violent battles. The best commanders were
> risked in prearranged single combats; a battle
> would be accepted for the sake of chivalric
> honor; a straight path through enemy territory
> would be chosen because a roundabout way was
> unchivalric.[5]

---

[1] I, viii, 75.
[2] Huizinga, *Homo Ludens*, pp. 92-3.
[3] Kilgour, p. 10.
[4] Huizinga, p. 92.
[5] Johan Huizinga, "Historical Ideals of Life" in *Men and Ideas* (New York:
Meridian Books, Inc., 1966), p. 88.

Numerous examples of how the fictional accounts in the romances of chivalry became a living reality in the lives of many Spanish *caballeros* of the fourteenth and fifteenth centuries are contained in a well-documented study of Martín de Riquer, *Cavalleria fra realtá e letteratura nel Quattrocento.*[1] In this work, Riquer recounts many episodes in which many Spaniards in "carne e ossa imitando ció che avevano letto in alcuni libri vissero sorprendenti avventure testimoniate storicamente con rigore."[2]

Fernando de Pulgar, in his collection of biographical sketches of many fifteenth-century personalities, also refers to the current vogue of imitating the chivalric feats of arms of fictional heroes:

> Yo por cierto no ví en mis tiempos, ni leí que en los pasados viniesen tantos cavalleros de otros reinos e tierras estrañas a estos vuestros reinos de Castilla y de León por fazer en armas a todo trance, como ví que fueron cavalleros de Castilla a las buscar por otras partes de la Cristianidad. Conocí al conde don Gonçalo de Guzmán, e a Juan de Merlo; conocí a Juan de Torres, e a Juan de Polanco, . . . e oí dezir de otros castellanos que con ánimo de cavalleros fueron por los reinos estraños a fazer en armas con qualquier cavallero que quisiese fazerlas con ellos, e por ellas ganaron honra para sí, e fama de valientes

---

1 Martín de Riquer, *Cavalleria fra realtá e letteratura nel Quattrecento* (Bari: Adriatica Editrice, 1970).

2 *Ibid.,* p. 5.

y esforçados cavalleros para los fijosdalgo de Castilla.[1]

At a time when many noble and valiant Spaniards ventured in search of chivalric pursuits, Amadís must have been a well-suited symbol of courage in action, and the text of *Amadís de Gaula* a complete book of military and chivalrous conduct.

Even more significantly, *Amadís* offered not just a romanticized image of the stubborn warrior qualities of the knight-errant who sets out into the world with no other possession except his horse, armor, and weapons, but also a real-life example of the knight's military code of behavior as outlined in chivalric and courtesy manuals. These texts, like Lull's *Ordre of Chyualry*, the brought-up-to-date version of Vegetius' *De Re Militari*, and Egidio Colonna's *De Regimine Principum*, all widely circulated in Spain, contained the instructional ideas and elements necessary to raise a superior military class. The principles of warfare, chivalric conduct, and military training of the knight as expressed in *Amadís* were not in essence different from the pragmatic formalized instruction found in the manuals of chivalry or the "ius military" of the sixteenth-century aristocracy, whose hereditary occupation was fighting. The obvious difference was in that while military manuals provided a comprehensive account of the duties of the knight in the form of precepts, *Amadís* instructed by way of example. There is no doubt that in the *Amadís'* ideal of noble strife and knightly conduct, the young Spanish

[1] Fernando del Pulgar, *Claros varones de Castilla*, ed. J. Domínguez Bordona (Madrid, 1923), p. 115.

On the influence of chivalric romances on the youth in Montalvo's time, see Carmelo Viñas y Mey, "Espíritu castellano de aventura y empresa y la España de los Reyes Católicos," *Archivo de Derecho público*, V (1951), pp. 13-83.

aristocrat of the sixteenth century could have found the professional code of the soldier, the rules of social aesthetics, and the examples of deeds of strength that he was called to live up to and perform as part of his heritage and noble upbringing, both in war and in peacetime tournaments, jousting, and other chivalric games played in mock-seriousness. As Huizinga points out, the noble young men had to be fully prepared to imitate the feats of courage and strength of the heroic life:

> The game of living in imitation of antiquity was pursued in holy earnest. Devotion to the ideals of the past in the matter of plastic creation and intellectual discovery was of a violence, depth and purity surpassing anything we can imagine. . . . The splendours of the Renaissance are nothing but a gorgeous and solemn masquerade of the accoutrements of an idealized past.[1]

Love

It seems evident from the study of *Amadís* that the episodic plot of the romance is held together by the prowess of its heroes, but it is also evident that the presence of adventure and feats of arms, however abundant, are subordinate to the theme of love. War and love are closely related and mutually indispensable in *Amadís*: the greatest warrior is also the best and most loyal lover. Amadís travels extensively and accomplishes much but his faithful love for Oriana is responsible for his going, for his return, and his deeds of courage. The

---

[1] Huizinga, "Historical Ideals . . ." in *Men and Ideas,* p. 180.

pursuit of glory, the call for adventure, and the desire to fulfill his missionary obligations cannot overpower his unending affection for his lady. John J. O'Connor points out that in *Amadís* "love and his lady occupy almost as much of the hero's attention as fighting and there is little doubt that in the sixteenth century *Amadís de Gaula* was read principally as a book of love." In fact, he says, "ladies provide the incentive for many a battle and are often the cause of war."[1] Frank Pierce in his study of *Amadís* says that "the characters, many of whom are little more than types and remain rather shadowy, reveal themselves in more depth in an area of great significance in our romance, namely love."[2] And according to Menéndez y Palayo, *Amadís* belongs to that genre of novel in which "el amor, que en las canciones heroicas no tenía importancia alguna, se convirtió en el principal motivo de las acciones de los héroes."[3]

Before the appearance of the Arthurian romances of Chrétien de Troyes, the praise of the prowess of the hero and the glorification of the homeland had been at the center of the epic literature of Europe. When occasionally women appeared in these epics, their role was always one of minor importance, and when the theme of love was introduced, it was treated in "a highly moral and socially acceptable way."[4]

It was during the twelfth century that new attitudes toward women and a new concept of love blossomed, first in France, in the court of Marie of Champagne and Henry the Liberal. These new sentiments and ideas soon became

---

[1]   O'Connor, p. 43.

[2]   Frank Pierce, *Amadís de Gaula* (Boston: Twayne Publishers, 1976), p. 95.

[3]   Menéndez y Pelayo, p. 353.

[4]   Mottola, p. 61.

the dominant forces in the development of literature throughout Europe. The literary flowering of France in the twelfth century was the result of the "fruitful meeting" and collaboration of different intellectual traditions assimilated and enriched by a court audience with sophisticated and eclectic tastes. It was, in fact, the court of Champagne, famous for the education of its literary patrons and for the prominence of many writers and scholars, that served as the center for the "dissemination of the doctrine of *l'amour courtois.*"[1] Although the term was unknown in medieval times, it was coined by Gaston Paris in 1883 to define the concept that most clearly reflected the poetry of the troubadours and in particular the lyrics of Bernant de Ventardon, who wrote during the last half of the twelfth century. One cannot emphasize enough the importance of the concept of "courtly love" in the development of chivalric literature. Charles Moorman states:

> I am inclined to believe that it is courtly love which supplies the knight not only with a character, a set of values and a potential conflict capable of literary treatment—knight-errantry—out of which plot and action may be constructed. It seems well-nigh certain to me that the real knight, at any period preceding off a-questing. He had at first his castle to defend and later his religion, and for both these causes he fought in group. It is only the courtly lover in time of peace who had time to go out alone wandering about the countryside, and it is courtly love which alone gives him a motive for

---

[1]   John Benton, "the Court of Champagne as a Literary Center," *Speculum*, XXXVI (October, 1961), 551.

> wandering—the fulfillment of the vows made
> to his lady. . . . And this is a completely new
> concept of the mission of the knight, the knight
> errant could not have existed before courtly love
> supplied the motivation for his quest. . . . It is
> the courtly lover who becomes the knight of
> literature.[1]

"Courtly Love" is defined by Prof. Denomy as

> a species of that movement inherent in the soul
> of man towards a desired object. It is object,
> the final object, which specifies love and
> differentiates its manifestations one from the
> other. When the object of love is the pleasure of
> sense, then love is sensual and carnal; directed
> towards a person of the opposite sex, sexual;
> towards God, divine. Courtly Love is a type of
> sensual love and what distinguishes it from other
> forms of sexual love, from mere passion, from
> so called platonic love, from married love is its
> purpose or motive, its formal object, namely, the
> lover's progress and growth in natural goodness,
> merit and worth.[2]

Although it is almost impossible, because of its long
period of development, to frame exactly the nature of the
essence of "courtly love" in a simple defining statement,
there seem to be three basic elements that distinguish
"courtly love" from all other conceptions of love.
Briefly summarized these are: (1) the concept of "love"

[1]   Charles Moorman, "The First Knights," *Southern Quarterly*, I (1962), 21-2.
[2]   Denomy, p. 44.

is an ennobling force that heightens man in the scale of goodness and virtue; (2) the belief that "love" elevates the beloved to a place of superiority above the lover; and (3) the conception of love as an ever-unsatiated, unappeasing desire. We will see that these thoughts are well reflected in the story of *Amadís*.

The question of the origin and of the appearance of "courtly love" in the romances of chivalry has been a topic of extended debate among critics.[1] The consensus is that the system of "courtly love" is for the most part an amalgamation of ideas from troubadours' songs, Ovidian erotic works, Celtic poems, Christian doctrine, medical treatises, and discussions fashionable in European courtly circles. But in the light of recent studies, the roots of "courtly love"—in its sensual and mystical manifestations—have been traced to Spanish-Arabian poetry. One of the most enthusiastic advocates of the Hispano-Moorish origin of *amour courtois* is Robert S. Briffault. After contrasting specific excerpts from Moorish works and the poems of Guilhelm de Poitiers, which according to Jeanroy contain the "germ" of "courtly love," Briffault concludes that "all the examples which Jeanroy cites . . . are found in similar form and even more distinctly in the Hispano-Moorish poetry, in the treatise of

---

[1]   The subject of "courtly love" has been treated extensively and its bibliography is voluminous. Among the best studies are: L. F. Mott, *The System of Courtly Love as an Introduction to the Vita Nuova of Dante* (Boston, 1896); C. S. Lewis, *The Allegory of Love* (London: Oxford University Press, 1936). On the origin of "courtly love" two good studies are those of W. A. Neilson, *The Origins and Source of the Courts of Love* (Harvard, 1899) and T. P. Cross and W. A. Nitze, *Lancelot, Guenevere: A Study of the Origin of Courtly Love* (Chicago, 1930).

Iban Hazn and in the songs of Ibn Quzman."[1] On a similar note A. Denomy says:

> I am sure that the troubadours derived their teaching of "fin' amors" from Arabian mysticism and specifically from some such tract as the *Treatise on Love* by Avicenna . . . that the troubadours took their morality of love from the Arabs and were able to maintain it alongside the norms of Christian morality.[2]

"Courtly love," however, is not just a set of theories, it is also a well-defined system of etiquette that characterizes almost all aristocratic treatment of love in medieval literature. In its social aspect, "amour courtois" is fundamentally a question of manners idealized into a cult by polite society and taught by examples in chivalric romances and by direct instruction in manuals for lovers.

The codification of the rules, social conventions, and psychology of "courtly love" was undertaken by Andreas Capellanus in his *De Amore*, ca. 1186; this book soon became the best known reader and abecedarium for lovers among the courts of Europe. According to Capellanus, "love is a certain inborn suffering derived from the sight and excessive meditation upon the beauty of the opposite sex which causes each one to wish above all things the embraces of the other and by common desire

---

[1] Robert S. Briffault, *The Troubadours* (Bloomington: Indiana University Press, 1965), pp. 24-9. See also Jeanroy, "La poésie provençale au moyen âge," *Revue des Deux Monde* (1903), p. 668. On "courtly love" and its religious origins, see the classical study of Denis Rougemont, *Love in the Western World* (New York: Pantheon, 1916), pp. 58-122.

[2] Denomy, p. 45.

to carry out all of love's precepts in the other's embrace."[1] After exploring who are the suitable objects for the passion, Andreas lists a series of precepts that sets the conditions for reciprocal affection and union. Reflecting the tenets of Ovid's *Ars Amatoria* and the sentiments of the troubadours, Capellanus rather subtly condones adultery and sets aside marriage as "no real excuse for not loving."[2] As a complement to this axiom, he emphasizes the necessity for secrecy and the duty of loyalty on the part of the lover. Jealousy is another important component in the value system of "courtly love." "Love cannot exist without jealousy."[3] It is jealousy between lovers that "increases the feeling of love and is commended by every man experienced in love."[4] Turning pale in the presence of the beloved, shyness, loss of appetite, sleeplessness, and palpitations of the heart are other manifestations of being in love. Service and obedience even to the caprice of love distinguish the true lover who wishes to achieve "the ecstatic possession of the beloved." The lover must also be courteous, courageous, and willing to perform feats of arms for his lady's sake. C. S. Lewis summarizes the long list of rules and ideals of Andreas Capellanus' doctrine in four basic principles: humility, courtesy, adultery, and the religion of love.[5]

At the same time that Andreas was writing his treatise, Chrétien de Troyes was incorporating the same precepts of social behavior, the sentimental theories, and the ethnical

---

[1] Andreas Capellanus, *The Art of Courtly Love*, trans. J. J. Parry (New York, 1941), p. 28.

[2] *Ibid.*, pp. 184, 159.

[3] *Ibid.*, p. 102.

[4] *Ibid.*, pp. 74-75.

[5] C. S. Lewis, *The Allegory of Love* (London: Oxford University Press, 1936), p. 2.

values assembled in *De Amore* in the romances of *Tristan* and *Lancelot*. In similar fashion court poets tried in their songs to verbalize the system of ideas that Capellanus had exposed and codified almost scientifically in his text.

Although, in the words of Alfonso Reyes, "la aparición del Ciclo Bretón en España es relativamente tardía"[1] and the first known translation of an Arthurian text does not become available in Spain until the beginning of the fourteenth century, there is sufficient evidence to indicate that the theme of "courtly love," as it appears in the French lyrics and Arthurian romances, passed into the Iberian Peninsula at an early date.[2] Guiralt de Cabrera, a Catalan troubadour writing ca. 1170, already makes mention and shows to be familiar with the theme of "courtly love" and the Knights of the Round Table.[3] In her study, *Arthurian Literature in Spain and Portugal*, Lida de Malkiel also points to the early availability and popularity of the Arthurian romances in their original untranslated form among the aristocratic Spanish class and the courtly troubadours.[4] Otis Green explains that the doctrine of *fin' amors* appeared in Spain at first in the *Cancioneros* and that it was for the most part not very different from the basic concepts existing in the troubadouresque tradition of other European courts.[5] The views of the troubadours,

[1] Alfonso Reyes, "Influencia del ciclo artúrico en la literatura castellana" in *Capítulos de Literatura Española* (México, 1945), p. 131.

[2] Helaine Newstead, "the Origin and Growth of the Tristan Legend," in *Arthurian Literature in the Middle Ages* (Oxford: Clarendon Press, 1959), p. 137.

[3] *Ibid.*

[4] María Rosa Lida de Malkiel, *Arthurian Literature in the Middle Ages* (Oxford: Clarendon Press, 1959), p. 137.

[5] Otis H. Green, "Courtly Love in Spanish Cancioneros" in the *Literary Mind of Medieval and Renaissance Spain* (Lexington: The University Press of Kentucky, 1970), p. 40.

says Green, combined with Arthurian elements already present in the Peninsula and with preexisting Ovidian erotic precepts, as well as other medieval ideas on love, were gradually, over a period of centuries, modified and adopted to Spanish ideals and conditions of life.[1] By the sixteenth century, this gradual process of transformation and adaptation is clearly reflected in Montalvo's treatment of the love theme.

The presentation of the love topic in *Amadís* is, in general, similar in psychology, rhetorical devices, plot situations, and literary sources to the exposition given the same matter in the Arthurian romances of Chrétien de Troyes but it differs in moral tone, ethical evaluation, and intent. This divergence is consistent, less a few exceptions, e.g. *Libro de Buen Amor*, with Spanish precedents that steadily tend to underplay the graphic presentation of the sensual element or the introduction of relationships that would undermine the social order. El Cid, who during the thirteenth and fourteenth century still remains the greatest Castillian hero, is far distant, except for his courage, in moral character and perception from the heroes of Arthurian romances. Nor does Doña Ximena "bear the slightest resemblance to the haughty Guinevere or the passionate Isolt."[2] It was later that El Cid, in the hands of Guillén de Castro, "devint un galant beau diseur, et Chiméne un dame romanesque et sentimentale."[3]

It is a matter of literary and historic record that until the dawning of the fifteenth century the concept of love in

---

[1]   *Ibid.*

[2]   Mottola, p. 84.

[3]   Duchesne Julien, *Histoire de poémes épiques français du XVIIesiécle* (Paris: Hachette, 1870), p. 136.

Spanish and French epics and chivalric romances generally followed different directions. Prof. Mottola states:

> The all powerful and all demanding love of the North which made the knight its slave and sometimes its victim, leading at times to spiritual and moral tragedy had no counterpart in Castillian literature of chivalry. In the latter literature, the hero maintained his supremacy, love was more controlled and more rational and womanhood tended for the most part to be the model of fidelity and virtue. It is to the credit of *Amadís de Gaula* . . . to bring about a confrontation of these contradictory ideas.[1]

It is evident, in view of the favorable reception accorded to *Amadís de Gaula* in religious and public circles, that Montalvo, by skillfully blending outside literary currents with patterns of traditional Spanish thought on courtship and marriage, was able to present and modify the theme of "courtly love" in a manner that met the approval of the church and the Spanish reader. While Amadís and Oriana, in their love passion, faithfully reflect the essence of "courtly love" with its irresistible force over the mind and the body, the subjugation of the will, its rounds of jealousy and bouts of despair, the refinement of manners, and bestowal of rewards for faithful service, they also represent in the denouement of their mutual affection the spiritual exaltation of the Christian idea of love in the institution of marriage. These concepts of Christian love and wedded union are unprecedented in novels of chivalry and are in opposition to the adulterous conduct of

---

[1]   Mottola, p. 85.

many of Chrétien's heroes and heroines and Capellanus' code of *fin' amors* that excludes the possibility of love in marriage.

The different aspects and dimensions of the concept of love in *Amadís* have been to various extents studied by several critics, especially in relation to the artistic and literary precepts borrowed from Arthurian romances. The best informed studies are those of Marcelino Menéndez y Pelayo, Justina Ruiz de Conde, Grace Williams, Rodríguez Lapa, Anthony Coppola, and Frank Pierce. For the purpose and scope of this study, it is best to limit our analysis to those aspects of Amadís' love passion that best define the social ideal of courtliness and make *Amadís* a book of love in fashionable society.

The didactic note struck by Montalvo in his *Prólogo* should safely stir us as to the purpose and social significance of the sentimental theme in *Amadís*. True to his assumed pedagogical role, the author makes a deliberate effort to portray in the characters of Amadís and Oriana the career of two model lovers who are to reflect the general standards of conduct and the real love experiences of noble knights and gracious ladies, exponents of a self-conscious and discriminating culture. By a series of literary techniques, namely the use of the object lesson of the story, the careful delineation of the characters, and at times by direct comment, Montalvo seeks to reject those principles of "courtly love" that defy or ignore the church moral code or don't hold up to the sympathy and emulation of the reading public. By the same process, he also strives to underscore those aspects of *fin' amors* consistent with Spanish social and ethical ideals of the time that ought to be the prized possession of a refined and noble heart.

As in the doctrine of *amour courtois,* love is presented in many chapters of *Amadís* as an elemental and compelling force beyond willful restraint and also as an instinctive desire whose fulfillment implies the acceptance of certain social responsibilities upon which the survival of society and the protection of individual honor and reputation are based. The irresistible compulsion of love and the idea of concomitant obligation when yielding to its passion are two maxims that Montalvo stresses at the very inception of *Amadís'* story in the description of the love affair between Elisena and King Parión. Without much psychological elaboration of the characters, the author, relying strictly on the exuberant power inherent in youth, the physical attractiveness, the social charm, and the atmosphere of leisure at the court of King Garinter, presents Elisena's and King Perión's mutual love fascination as an inescapable magnetic force:

> Pues estando en aquel solaz, como aquella infanta tan hermosa fuese y el rey Perión por el semejante, y la fama de sus grandes cosas en armas por todas las partes del mundo divulgados, en tal punto y ora se miraron, que la gran honestad y santa vida della no pudo tanto que de incurable y muy gran amor presa no fuesse, y el rey assimismo della, que fasta entonces su coraçón sin sojuzgado a otra ninguna libre tenía, de guisa que assí el vno como el otro estuuieron todo el comer quasi fuera de sentido.[1]

---

[1] Place, ed. *Amadís de Gaula*, I, p. 13.

Later, Darioleta, Elisena's maid and go-between, advises her lady to freely surrender to the king for the power of love is inexorable:

> - Quedad, señora, con essse cauallero, que ahunque vos como donzella hasta aquí de muchos vos defendistes, y él assí mesmo de muchas otras se defendió, no bastaron vuestras fuerças para vos defender el vno del otro.[1]

Darioleta, however, promises to escort beautiful Elisena to King Perión's quarters only after receiving from the king the commitment to marry Elisena at the proper time:

> - Mi señor, si me vos prometéys como rey en todo guardar la verdad a que más que ningún otro que lo no sea obligado soys, y como cauallero, que según vuestra fama por la sostener tantos afanes y peligros aurá passado, de la tomar por muger, quando tiempo fuere, yo la porné en parte donde no solamente vuestro coraçón, satisfecho sea, mas el suyo, que tanto o por ventura más que él es en cuyta y en dolor dessa mesma llaga herido, y si esto no se haze, ni vos la cobraréys, ni yo creeré ser vuestras palabras de leal y honesto amor salidas.[2]

King Perión without hesitation gives Darioleta his noble word and answers:

---

[1]   I, i, 19.

[2]   I, 15.

> - Yo juro en esta cruz y espada con que la orden
> de cauallería recibí hazer esso que vos donzella
> me pedís, cada que por vuestra señora Helisena
> demandado me fuere.[1]

Obviously Elisena and King Perión's love relationship and arrangement for marriage meet with society's demands of individual honor and the moral obligation of the lovers to each other, but Montalvo does not completely sanction their conduct. In the midst of the narration, the author seizes the opportunity to interject his comments and sounds his warning to other wealthy and noble damsels not to follow the example of Elisena:

> que en cabo de tanto tiempo que guardarse quiso,
> en solo un momento veyendo la grand fermosura
> de aquel rey Perión, fue su propósito mudado
> de tal forma que si no fuera por la discreción
> de aquella donzella suya, que su honra con el
> matrimonio quiso, en verdad ella de todo punto
> era determinada de caer en la peor y más baxa
> parte de su deshonra, assí como otras muchas
> que en este mundo contar se podían, por se no
> guardar de lo ya d icho lo fizieron y adelante
> farán no lo mirando.[2]

Although the awakening and development of Amadís' passion for Oriana and her surrender to love have been described by the author in more lengthy detail throughout the text's numerous chapters—almost in a perfect application of the hereditary principle *de tal palo tal*

---

[1]   I, 15.

[2]   I, i, 20.

hastilla, Amadís' virtuous comportment and sense of moral responsibility parallel the noble example given by King Perión, his father. From an early stage, Amadís' spiritual and emotional commitment to Oriana remains constant throughout the novel:

> Este amor turó quanto ellos turaron, que assí como la él amaua ass*i* amaua ella a él. En tal guisa que vuna hora nunca de amar se dexaron.[1]

His promise of absolute faithfulness to Oriana is rigidly observed. Amadís is *el leal enamorado.* He enters *el arco de los leales amadores*:

> sin temor ninguno, como aquel que sentía no hauer errado a su señora, no solamente por obra, mas por el pensamiento.[2]

Since an early age he aspired to be Oriana's faithful servant:

> ¡Ay, Dios, señor, y quando veré yo el tiempo en que seruir pueda aquella señora![3]

His service in love is one of total surrender:

> Me tengo y me terné por vuestro para seruir, sin que otra ni yo mismo sobre mi señorio tenga en quanto biua.[4]

---

[1]   I, iv, 40.

[2]   II, xliv, 365.

[3]   I, ix, 81.

[4]   I, iv, 43-4.

The pursuit of love presents many challenges. The knight is often called to perform feats of arms to defend and protect his lady from other worthy competitors. Amadís is often challenged into combat, as in the following example, to justify his claim to Oriana's love:

> Vos, cauallero que estáys folgando conuiene
> que os levantéys y que veamos como sabéys
> mantener amoar de que en vos tanto loáys.[1]

Similarly by force of arms, Amadís is called to rescue Oriana from Arcaláus, and later in the text, from the ship of the Roman emperor.

Love is an inspiring force, a source of strength, and an incentive to valor:

> ¡O, mi señor Oriana, de os me viene a mi todo el
> esfuerço y ardimiento. . . .

> Este vencido coraçón sin el fauor de cuyo es no
> podrá ser sostenido en inguna afrenta.[2]

Without love man's spiritual and physical prowess is weakened:

> -Sábate—says Amadís—que no tengo seso, ni
> coraçón, ni esfuerço, que todo es perdido quando
> perdí la merced de mi señora, que della y no
> de mí me venía todo, y assí ella lo ha leuado, y
> sabes que tanto valgo para mi combatir quanto

---

[1]   II, xlvi, 382-3.
[2]   II, xliv, 367.

vn cauallero muerto, . . . que no ay catiuo, ni tan
flaco cauallero que ligeramente no me matase,
si con el me combatiesse, que te diré que soy el
más vencido y desesperado que todos los que en
el mundo son.[1]

But with the return of love, Amadís,

fue tan mejorado, que ya su coraçón le mandaua
que a las armas tornasse.[2]

Love is an ennobling force from which all virtue and
worth come:

-Amor, Amor—says a knight under the spell of
love—mucho tengo que vos agradecer por el bien
que de vos me viene y por la grande alteza en que
me auéys puesto sobre todos los otros caualleros,
leuándome siempre de bien en mejor.[3]

Love, however, does not always deliver its expected
rewards. After undeservingly losing Oriana's affection,
Amadís decries love's erratic ways and false promises:

-Que yo soy de aquellos desamparados dél, y soy
sólo el que jamas en él fiara, porque con grandes
seruichios que le fize me dió mal galardón no lo
meresciendo.[4]

---

[1]   II, xlvi, 382.

[2]   II, lii, 426.

[3]   II, xlvi, 381.

[4]   II, xlvi, 383.

Indeed the path of love is irregular and unsettling. The emotional upheaval, the inner conflicts that from love emanate, affect the body, the mind, and the will:

a] Quando Amadís se vio ante su señora, el coraçón le saltaua de vna y otra parte. . . . [1]
Quando, 'el oyó mentar a su señor estremeciósele el coraçón tan fuertemente que por poco cayera del cauallo.[2]

b] Mi juyzio no puede resistir aquellos mortales desseos de quien cruelmente es atormentado.[3]

c] El coraçón muy turbado y de sobrado amor preso, no dexa la lengua en su libre poder; y porque assí como con vuestra sabrosa menbrança todas las cosas sojuzgar pienso, assí con vuestra vista soy sojuzgado sin quedar en mi sentido alguno para que en mi libre poder sea.[4]

Love is a refiner of manners. Its refining influence, however, is only limited to the gentle heart. In the religion of "courtly love," "only the courteous can love," says C. S. Lewis, "but it is love which makes them courteous. . . . It is the noblest hearts which love designs to enslave."[5] The uncouth and the villain are excluded from its bondage. In

---

[1]   I, xxx, 246.
[2]   I, v, 54.
[3]   I, xiv, 129.
[4]   I, xiv, 128.
[5]   Lewis, *The Allegory of Love*, p. 2.

like manner, love in *Amadís* is an affliction of the refined and gentle heart whose depth and sensitivity only the sophisticated at love can appreciate. In a very touching scene of reunion and love between Amadís and Oriana the author exclaims:

> ¿Quién sería aquel que baste recontar los amorosos abraços, los besos dulces, las lagrimas que boca con boca allí en vno fueron mezclados? Por cierto no otro sino aquel que seyendo sojuzgado de aquella misma passión y en semejantes llamas encendido, el coraçón atormentado de aquellas amorasas llagas pudiese dél sacar.[1]

One of the legacies of love is gallantry. Love demands that men graciously yield to women's requests and charm. King Lisuarte, after Amadís' duel with Dardán, begs him not to leave the court. Despite the king's promises and inducements, Amadís still refuses and prepares to depart. Lisuarte then commissions the queen, who in turn seeks the help of Oriana in an effort to convince him to stay:

> -Cauallero—says the Queen—el rey mi señor quisiera mucho que quedáredes con él y no lo ha podido alcançar; agora quiero ver qué tanta más parte tienen las mugeres en los caualleros que los hombres, y ruégovos yo que seáys mi cauallero y de mi hija y de todas estas que aquí veys; . . . y llegaron todos a ge lo rogar, y Oriana le fizo seña con el rostro qu lo otorgasse; la reyna le dix: - Pues cauallero, ¿ qué faréys en esto de nuestro

---

[1] II, lxvi, 467.

ruego? – Señora- dijo él -, ¿ quién faria ál sino vuestro mandado, que soys la mejor reyna del mundo demás destas señoras todas? yo señora, quedo por vuestro ruego y de vuestra hija, y después de todas las otras.[1]

Even in the face of treason and life threat, Amadís and Galaor manage to be courteous and gracious:

-Dueña—says Galaor—no consentiremos que nuestras manos ate sino vos, que soys dueña y muy hermosa, y somos vuestros presos, y conuiene de vos catar obediencia.[2]

If love demands gallantry in men, it insists upon modesty in women. A lady's heart must be reluctant to be won; easy conquests and the offer of love unsought compromise women's discretion and honor. On their way to a crossroad, the knight Balay's remarks to a damsel whom he had just freed from a group of molesters:

A los caualleros conuine seruir y codiciar a las donzellas y querellas por señoras y amigas, y a ellas guardarse de errar como lo vos queréys hazer; porque como quiera que al comienço en mucho tenemos auer alcançado lo que dellas desseamos, mucho más son de nosotros preciadas y estimadas quando con discreción y bondad se defienden, resistiendo nuestros malos apetitos,

---

[1] I, xv, 135.
[2] I, xxxiii, 267.

guardando aquello que perdiéndolo ninguna cosa
les quedaría que de loar fuesse.[1]

The damsel responds:

En tanto más se deue tener este socorro de la
honra que el de la vida.[2]

The text of *Amadís* is replete with similar reference
to women's decorum, reputation, and defense of honor.
Although the author is sensitive to female erotic needs
and passions, he is never sympathetic to women's lack of
restraint in matters of love. When illicit love relationships
do occur in the course of the novel, he never fails to give
due recognition to the moral responsibility and social
obligation of the individuals. Throughout the text of
Amadís, there seems to be an uncompromising effort to
present love in relation to society. It also seems evident
that Montalvo tries to raise the concept of human and
physical attraction above the plane of sensuality by
purifying it through religious and ethical considerations
that satisfied the standards of morality of the court of *los
reyes Católicos* and catered to the prevailing tastes of the
time. The high degree of idealism on the question of love
clearly transpires through the characterization and the
praise afforded to the various heroes and heroines in the
story who at times become personifications of virtues,
vices, and prejudices—illustrating social and religious
principles, as well as class consciousness and sentiment.
Our author, however, is not just a moralist, he is also an
artist. As a moralist he had to adhere to the purposes and

---

[1]   I, xxviii, 238.

[2]   *Ibid.*

goals of his homily; as an artist he had to be faithful to the spirit of the characters and techniques of narration of the novels of chivalry. Without compromising his credibility of serious pedagogue, Montalvo resolves an obvious artistic dilemma and an obvious moral conflict implicit in the illicit love relationship of Amadís and Oriana before marriage by resorting to an equally obvious expedient, namely *el matrimonio secreto.*

In reference to Amadís' and Oriana's love affair and Montalvo's gimmick, Menéndez y Palayo states:

> La pasión constante y noble de estos amantes no es de absoluta pureza moral, ni tal cosa puede esperarse de ningún libro de caballerías, conociendo la sociedad que los engendró . . . No se ha de perder de vista sin embargo, que el *Amadís* se escribió dos siglos antes de que el Concilio de Trento declarase nulos los matrimonios clandestinos. De este género es el de Amadís y Oriana en que faltan los testigos pero no la "forma esencial" del sacramento, que es el mutuo consenso por palabras de presente. El autor prefirió sin duda el matrimonio secreto por ser más novelesco, pero procede con toda la corrección canónica que su tiempo permitía, haciendo que el santo ermitaño Nasciano imponga a Oriana una penitencia por el pecado de "clandestinidad," aunque reconociendo la validez del matrimonio. . . . Si esta doctrina no hubiese sido enteramente ortodoxa, la Iquisición no la hubiese dejado pasar, tratándose de materia tan delicada.[1]

---

[1]   Menéndez y Pelayo, *Orígenes de la Novela*, p. 353.

Anthony Mottola adds:

> It is clear that it would have been impossible for Montalvo to produce a romance in the tradition of the great stories of chivalry, given the romantic character of Amadís and the passionate warmth of Oriana, and keep them united throughout the story by a purely idealistic love that is not consummated until their formal marriage in chapter forty-three of the fourth book.[1]

It is important to notice that Montalvo does not openly endorse his novelistic solution to the love of Amadís and Oriana, nor does he suggest by the attitudes of the two lovers that principles of morality have been violated. What is clear, however, is that only after their legal marriage Amadís and Oriana are blessed with the benefits of social advancement together with a rise in fortune and possession of great wealth in the *Insula Firme*. In this context, only faithful love that culminates in marriage is a true source of worldly gain.

There is in Amadís' passion that ignores morality and disregards social conventions. For example, no ideal of moral conduct is evident in Galaor's several amorous affairs, but Montalvo dismisses Galaor's ordinary humanity and illicit escapades with one of his frequent comments:

> En los autos semejantes, que a buena conciencia ni a virtud no son conformes, con razón deue hombre

---

[1]   Mottola, p. 96.

por ellos ligeramente passar, teniéndolos en aquel
pequeño grado que merescen ser tenidos.[1]

Although Galaor and other minor characters in *Amadís*
are of great importance in the development, purpose, and
lesson of the story, most of the attention of the author
centers on the characterization and prominence of the hero
whose main function is to arouse the spirit of admiration
and emulation of those who seek to identify with his virtues
and ideals. As a lover, Amadís combines the finest in human
and moral qualities. He is a man of noble deeds and fine
feelings; he is gentle and valiant, strong and sentimental.
He inherits all the afflictions of *fin' amors*—trembling,
sighing, loss of appetite, sleeplessness, changing of color,
crying—but his lachrymose sentimentality and his apparent
heroic effeminacy are tempered by his courage, sense
of honor, and skill at arms. Amadís mirrors the ideal of
physical beauty, a quality associated throughout the text
with noble birth, gentle heart, and noble deeds. He also
embodies the maximum in personal refinement, politeness
of manners, elegance of speech, and all the other courtly
virtues prized by social and sentimental culture. But above
all, Amadís is the symbol of deep religious faith and trust
in God, whom he constantly implores for help in his
mission as a knight-errant, as well as the picture of the true
Christian in his observance of religious obligations, church
rituals, and Christian charity. In short, Amadís "mirrored
with sufficient fidelity the Spanish gentleman's dream of
himself . . . It would have been a rare young man in the XVI
century Spain who had not heard of Amadís and did not
want to be like him."[2] In *Amadís*, says Menéndez y Pelayo:

---

[1]   I, xii, 105.

[2]   O'Connor, p. 8.

el ideal de la Tabla Redonda aparece refinado, purificado y ennoblecido. Sin el vértigo amoroso de Tristán, sin la adultera pasión de Lanzarote, sin el equívoco misticismo de los héroes del Santo Grial, Amadís es el tipo del perfecto caballero, el espejo del valor y de la cortesía, el dechado de vasallos leales y de finos y constantes amadores, el escudo y amparo de los débiles y menesterosos, el brazo armado puesto al servicio del orden moral y de la justicia.[1]

Befitting the ideal knight and lover is the ideal lady. Montalvo certainly spares no effort to make Oriana the most gracious, noble, loyal, and inspiring symbol of love's beauty. Oriana is described as

la más hermosa criatura que se nunca vio. . . . [2]

Aquella que vale más que las otras todas de bondad, fermosura y de linaje.[3]

She is warm and passionate. She tells Amadís:

Si yo del mundo he sabor, por vos que en él biuís lo he.[4]

Amadís is

---

[1] Menéndez y Pelayo, p. 351.
[2] I, iv, 39.
[3] I, viii, 67.
[4] I, xxx, 247.

Aquel que más que a sí amaua.[1]

She suffers the anguish of love:

Yo soy la donzella herida de punta de espada por
el coraçón, y vos soys el que me feristes.[2]

Unlike other heroines of chivalric romances such as
Guinevere or Isolt, who conform to the more mundane
and shallow conventions of "courtly love," Oriana firmly
asserts her individuality and independence of sentiment.
Falling in love against her parents' wishes, she is
caught between her heart's desires and her sense of duty
toward her family, and in particular toward her father,
King Lisuarte, who wants to give her in marriage to the
emperor of Rome. Undoubtedly, this kind of matrimonial
arrangement is reflective of the pressures placed on
many ladies and damsels of court society, whose nuptials
were usually decided by parental consent rather than by
personal choice. Oriana rose to the emergency by choosing
in favor of Amadís. The unbreakable strength and sincerity
of Oriana's love vows make her a true symbol of feminine
fidelity, moral fortitude, and freedom of choice in love. In
the face of obstacles, hardships, and parental pressures:

> como determinado estuviesse el rey Lisuarte
> en entregar a su fija Oriana a los romanos . . .
> llegado el plazo por el prometido, fablo con ella
> tentando muchas maneras para atraer que por su
> voluntad tomasse aquel camino que a él tanto

---

[1]   I, iv, 43.
[2]   II, xliv, 371.

le agradaua, mas por ninguna guisa pudo sus
llantos y dolores amanzar.[1]

Although idealized in her heroine's role, Oriana, of
course, is not an angel and even less a saint. Her social
graces, feminine charm, moral and spiritual strength are
tempered by her bouts of jealousy, anger, and despair. It is
perhaps this combination of virtue and human frailties that
make Oriana the embodiment of what Menéndez y Pelayo
calls "*lo eterno feminino.*"[2]

By and large, in the total context of the novel Oriana is
as important as Amadís.[3] She is, in fact, the unifying agent
of the story, the cause of Amadís' life-errant, the principal
excuse for his fighting, the stimulus to his courtesy, and
the main determinant of his moods, thoughts, and feelings.
Together, Amadís and Oriana represent the highest form
of individual and human perfection achievable in marriage
and the true symbol of "l'union spiritualle d'une dame et
d'un chevaliere."[4] From this perfect union in love is born
a new model of chivalrous perfection—Esplandián—
Montalvo's Renaissance ideal of the Christian prince and
gentleman:

> El es de alto linaje, . . . será tan fuerte, tan brauo
> de coraçón que a todos los valientes de su tiempo
> porná en sus fechos de armas gran escuridad. Será
> manso, mesurado, humildoso, y de muy buen
> talante, y sofrido más que otro hombre que en
> el mundo aya. . . . Será en gran manera sesudo y

---

[1]   III, lxxxi, 910.

[2]   Menéndez y Pelayo, p. 353.

[3]   *Ibid.*

[4]   Baret, p. 131.

de gran entendimiento, muy católico y de buenas palabras. Y en todas las sus cosas será pujado y estremado entre todos, y amado y querido de los buenos tanto que ningún caballero será su ygual. Y los sus grandes fechos en armas serán empleados en el seruicio del muy alto Dios, despreciando él aquello que los caualleros deste tiempo mas por honra de vana gloria del mundo que de buena conciencia siguien y siempre traerá a sí en la su diestra parte, y a su señora en la siniestra.[1]

The Influence of "Amadís"

Closely related to the theme of love in *Amadís* is the social background in which the main characters act and live. The author takes special care, through the description of small details, in showing how the chosen class lived and moved under the influence of current and traditional ideals and customs. The elaborate meals at the table of kings and the ensuing social relaxation, the tournaments and the pageantry that accompanied the *cortes* of King Lisuarte, the festivities and courtly receptions afforded to Amadís and other heroes in their return from battle, the lavish ceremony of Angriote's wedding—all suggest and outline activities that are the exclusive domain of the wealthy and aristocrats. Although these functions were staged primarily to enhance and exhibit the qualities of the hero and therefore contribute to the glorification of his virtues, they also provided, together with glimpses of medieval society, a picture of contemporary court life and customs.

---

[1]   III, lxxi, 776-7.

The center of social life in *Amadís* is the court of Lisuarte, described as the king "más rico y más poderoso de tierra y gente."[1] His court was the place where, in the words of Amadís,

> es mantenida caualleria en la mayor alteza que en ninguna casa de rey ni emprerador que en el mundo haya.[2]

And in the words of Don Galvanes,

> tantos caualleros buenos biuían porque allí mas que en otra parte honra y fama podrían ganar.[3]

Together with great feasting and dancing, one of the most important events of King Lisuarte's court was fashionable society's favorite pastime: the tournament or *cortes*. Although the *corte[s]* seem to be of little significance in the development of *Amadís'* plot, they certainly afforded the author the opportunity to present the details of sportsmanship and pageantry of court life. Following is a description that marks the beginning of one of Lisuarte's *cortes*:

> Partió el rey Lisuarte de Vindilisora con toda la caualleria, y la reyna con sus dueñas y donzellas a las cortes que en la cibdad de Londres se auían de juntar; la gente paresció en tanto número, que por marauilla se deuría contar. Auía entre ellos muchos caualleros mancebos ricamente

---

[1]   I, xxxii, 258.

[2]   I, x, 86.

[3]   I, xvi, 143.

armados y ataviados, y muchas infantas hijas de
reyes y otras donzellas de gran guisa, que dellos
muy amadas eran por las quales grandes justas
y fiestas por el camino fizieron. . . . El rey y la
reyna con toda su compaña fueron a descalualgar
en sus palacios, y allí e vna parte dellos mandó
posar a Amadís y a Galaoar y Agrajes y don
Galvanes, otros algunos de los más preciados
caualleros. . . . Assí holgaron aquella noche y
otros dos dias con muchas danças y juegos, que
en el palacio y fuera en la cibdad se hizieron,
en los quales Amadís y Galaor eran de todos
tan mirados, y tanta era la gente que por los ver
acudían donde ellos andauan. . . .[1]

Another function suitable for great display of pageantry
was the celebration of weddings. Here is a part of the
description of the elaborate formalities of Amadís' and
Oriana's wedding:

Venido el día señalado, todos los nouios se
juntaron en la posada de Amadís, y se vestieron
de tan ricos y preciados paños como su gran
estado en tal auto demandaua. Y así mesmo
lo hizieron las nouias, y los reyes y grandes
señores los tomaron consigo y caualgando en sus
palafrenes muy ricamente guarnidos, se fueron
a la huerta, donde fallaron las reynas y nouias
assí mesmo en sus palafrenes. Pues assí salieron
todos juntos a la yglesia donde por el Santo
hombre Nasciano la missa aparejada estaua.[2]

---

[1] I, xxxi, 251.

[2] IV, cxxv, 1, 227.

Undoubtedly these detailed accounts of functions, customs, and ceremonies in *Amadís* serve to give the fictional world of the romance an aura of reality. At almost every opportunity, the author also seems to make an effort to give the characters in the story the appearance of lifelike naturalness even in their most extraordinary experiences. The scenes of battles, love episodes, and courtly formalities are narrated in realistic terms that suggest the report of an eyewitness and are remindful of narrative techniques employed in the *Novela Costumbrista* of the nineteenth century. The artistic talent of Montalvo in manipulating details and creating the impression of real-life scenes in a world of fairy tales is evidenced in this vignette of prosaic exactness in which Oriana commissions Gandalin to deliver a message to Amadís:

> - Amigo, ve a tu señor y díle que venga esta noche muy escondido y entre en la huerta, y aquí debaxo es la cámara donde yo y Mabilia dormimos, que tiene cerca de tierra vna finiestra pequeña con vna redezilla de fieroo, y por allí le fableremos.[1]

It is this ability of the author to skillfully pair the idyllic with the real that makes the exceptional look plausible and makes *Amadís* a truly valuable book of chivalrous examples fit for the imitation of the noble and the affluent. Montalvo seems to have found in the relation of fiction with society a way to make his text a guide to courtly life and behavior. The world of *Amadís* is not entirely "chimerical," says O'Connor:

---

[1]   I, xiv, 125.

> The book was not read simply as entertainment or escape from bleak reality. Rather it gave its readers a reflection of the world they recognized—heightened, to be sure, but seldom wholly distorted. Many of the characters became household names, and the romance was highly regarded, both by its champions and its critics, as a practical guide to manners. In Spain where the long struggle against the Moors had culminated in the fall of Granada in 1492, *Amadís* reflected a background that seemed familiar . . . and a parallel—not very exact, of course—with Spanish victory was easily made. To the nobility faced with the absolutism of Ferdinand and Isabella the troubled relationship between Amadís and his lord King Lisuarte, must have seemed relevant. . . . Hence the sixteenth-century redaction of Montalvo combined nostalgia for a vanished age with pride in a victorious present. The emphasis in *Amadís* upon ceremony and refined manners was bound to seem appropriate in view of the new emphasis at court upon the social graces.[1]

Roy C. Strong points out that Spanish royalty readily found counterparts in *Amadís* and cites a passage of Don Guerau Despes, the Spanish ambassador to England in 1569, which declares that the prominent members of the Spanish Court were accustomed to address their queen as Oriana.[2] Moreover, a comparison of eyewitness accounts

---

[1] O'Connor, p. 8.

[2] Roy C. Strong, "Queen Elizabeth and Oriana," *Studies in Renaissance*, VI (1959), p. 254.

in various chronicles of the sixteenth century indicate that much of the pageantry displayed in ceremonial entrances, coronations of kings, entertainment, tournaments, jousting, and duels at the court of Charles V are reminiscent of episodes in *Amadís*. In *Crónica de don Francesillo de Zúñiga* we find the following passage with regard to the tournaments that were to take place in 1527 on the day of the birth of Infante Felipe:

> El Emperador tenía concertados torneos y aventuras de la manera que *Amadís* lo cuenta, y muy gracioso, y todo lo que en aquel libro se dice, se había de hacer acá de veras.[1]

Maxime Chevalier in *Lectura y Lectores en la España de los siglos XVI y XVII* also lists several other tournaments with "motifs" from *Amadís*. Among the most important are those held in Burgos in 1570 to receive Anne of Austria and those staged in Zaragoza on September 21, 1599, on the occasion of the king's visit to that city "en que se sucedieron encantamientos y desencantamientos en forma tal que, si hemos de creer a un cronista anónimo, 'parecía ficción de los libros de *Amadís* o *Esplandián*.'"[2]

Amadís' chivalric ideals and virtues, as well as his deeds, became sublimated not only in the way of life and activities of the upper-class civilian society, but also in the ideology and way of life of a number of ecclesiastics and religious orders. For instance, San Ignacio de Loyola, who called himself "the Knight of Christ," organized "his order

---

[1] *Crónica de don Francesillo de Zúñiga* (Biblioteca de Autores Españoles), XXXVI, p. 49.

[2] Maxime Chevalier, Lectura y Lectores en la España de los siglos XVI y XVII (Madrid: Ediciones Turner), pp. 85-7.

according to the principles of the moral code of chivalry,"[1] and in his autobiography dictated by him to Fr. Camara, we read that

> in the household of the Catholic King . . . [h]e was much given to reading certain worldly and fictitious books known as caballerías: "Amadís of Gaul" and similar romances . . . And his mind became filled with the adventures these books related that he used to imagine himself facing hazards and performing great deeds, like the knights he read of . . .[2]

His autobiography also tells us that "since his whole mind was full of those things, *Amadís* and other novels, some things similar to them entered his mind,"[3] and so watching all night and praying before the holy Virgin's statue he decided to stand watch over his arms "in the manner that those who are about to be armed as knights stand watch."[4] Moreover, "recalling how novice knights were wont to be consecrated and dedicated for battle, he resolved to imitate them by devoting himself to God's service."[5]

Outside of Spain, Amadís de Gaula, in Italian, French, and English translations, not only was the source of inspiration of many great literary works, but also was

---

[1] Arnold Hauser, *The Social History of Art*, 2 vols. (New York: Vintage Books, 1957), p. 144.

[2] Quoted in Mary Purcell, *The First Jesuit, St. Ignatius Loyola* (Westminster, Maryland: The Newman Press, 1957), p. 17.

[3] Pedro Leturia, *Íñigo de Loyola*, trans. Aloysius J. Owen (Syracuse: Le Moyne College Press), p. 142.

[4] *Ibid.*

[5] Leturia, *Íñigo de Loyola*, p. 142.

used as a reference text on court rituals, customs, knightly conduct, and polite speech among royalty. We know that Amadís was a very popular reader at the court of dei Medici and that in France it became *le breviare* of the court of Henry II.[1] François de la Noue, an old soldier in the court of Henry II, lamented the habit of many noblemen who were trained to *amadiser de paroles,*[2] In France, themes from Amadís were used in a series of tournaments held in Bayonne in 1565 in which

> se trata de rescatar una dama que guardan cautiva peligroso encantamiento y fiero gigante. Muchos son los franceses, y de los más ilustres, que participan en el juego: el rey de Francia, el rey de Navarra, el duque de Orléans, el duque de Guise, el duque de Nemours y el duque de Langueville.[3]

Tournaments with characters from *Amadís* were also staged in England in the town of Binche in 1549 as part of a ceremony organized by Mary of Hungary to celebrate

---

[1] Edward Bourciez, *Les moeurs polies et al litterature de cour sous Henri II* (Paris, 1886), p. 81.

[2] W. W. Wiley, *The Gentleman of Renaissance France* (Cambridge: Mass., 1954), p. 116. The influence of *Amadís* was particularly felt in the court of Francis I, who commissioned Nicholas de Herberay "Seigneur des Essarts" to translate the romance for the edification of the ladies and gentlemen of his court. On the French and English translations, see the excellent analysis of John J. O'Connor, pp. 131-47. On *Amadís* in France, see also Hugues Vaganey, *Amadís en Français* (Florence, 1906). In Italy *Amadís* is said to have inspired the *Amadigi* of Bernardo Tasso and the *Orlando Furioso* of Ludovico Ariosto. In Portugal Gil Vicente wrote for the theater a *Tragicomedia de Amadís de Gaula*. On the above, see Maxime Chevalier, p. 76 and Al. Cioranescu, pp. 22-29.

[3] Chevalier, p. 85.

the meeting of Prince Philip and his father Charles V. In reference to this event, Maxime Chevalier says:

> Las decantadas justas organizadas en Bins en el mes de agosto de 1549 son adaptaciones de varios episodios de *Amadís de Gaula* y los caballeros que entran en ellos llevan los nombres de los héroes más gloriosos de Montalvo.[1]

Similarly, we read that in England the earls of Essex and Cumberland, in 1592, issued a dual challenge that on February 25 they would maintain that their mistress was "most worthyest and most fayrest, quoth *Amadís de Gaule*."[2] Finally, what *Amadís* really meant to the court society of the sixteenth century is, perhaps, best summarized by John J. O'Connor:

> First, it was read as a book of war, a record of valor in action, of exemplary deeds done by right-minded knights in the face of overwhelmingly physical odds. Second, it was read, especially by ladies, as a book of love, a history of the joys and vicissitudes of lovers of all sorts, and the key to the indecipherable mysteries of the heart. Third, it was read as a courtesy book, a guide to proper behavior and polite manners of knights and ladies in peace and in war, and a compendium of speeches, challenges, letters, and rhetorical flourishes for different occasions. Finally, it was read as a wonderful

---

[1] Chevalier, p. 82.

[2] Strong, p. 255.

treasury of stories, exciting and varied, which ran the gamut from tragedy to farce.[1]

"Amadís": An Evaluation

This analysis of Montalvo's text as a courtesy book indicates that for the most part the action of *Amadís* is limited to the chivalric and the sentimental. It does not yet enter in the realm of the intellect. Amadís is a well-born, valiant, polished knight, but he is not exceptionally learned. Intellectual pursuits and instruction in literature are not stressed in his training as a knight. Courtesy manuals, in fact, up to the fifteenth century are quite "narrow in scope"[2] and make almost no mention of the requirement of erudition for the knight, and so go as far as discouraging noble youngsters who wish to enter the order of chivalry from being overenthusiastic in seeking knowledge not directly related to their knightly profession. William Worchester, for example, in his *Boke of Noblesse* recommends that the young aristocrat should not "wastyn gretlie their tyme in nedelese besinesse . . . as to lern to practique of law or custom of lande or civile matier." [3]The same thought is more or less expressed in the *Crónica de don Pedro Niño:* "El que ha de aprender a usar arte de caballería no conviene despender luengo tiempo en escuela de letras."[4]

---

[1]   O'Connor, p. 23.

[2]   Arthur B. Ferguson, *The Indian Summer of English Chivalry* (Durham, North Carolina: Duke University Press, 1960), p. 183.

[3]   John Nichols, ed., *The Book of Noblesse* (London: Nichols, 1860), p. 77.

[4]   Blanco-Gonzalez, *Del Cortesano al Discreto . . .* , p. 218.

Reflecting the views expressed in chivalric manuals, the knights in *Amadís de Gaula* do not seem overly concerned with education. It is true that Amadís demonstrates some poetic talent in his "Villancico" to Leonoreta and shows some scant knowledge of Greek in his remarks to Queen Menoresse of Greece, but it was later in the proliferous sequel of *Amadís* that we find heroes of considerable intellectual accomplishment. The later progeny of Amadisian descendants are usually cultured gentlemen, proficient in foreign languages, versed in the study of government, expert musicians, ingenious writers, philosophers, and poets, as well as great conversationalists and platonic lovers. The emphasis on these new acquired proficiencies and pursuits in the *Amadís' Cycle* is normally coupled with constant reminders of the civilizing influence of culture on politeness of manners and gentlemanlike behavior with women. In book 7, the Knight of the Burning Sword is presented as an accomplished linguist. He is proficient even in the most exotic languages like Chaldean and Arabic. Rogel, the hero of book 11, is sent to the best tutors to be instructed in the principles of government so that he may become a good ruler. In book 17, Arlanges displays unusual familiarity in matters of theology and presents himself as both a great knight and a scholar.[1] The intellectual attainments of these knights suggest that scholarship is not incompatible with the profession of arms, but that it rather complements traditional knightly interests. The recognition and acceptance of erudition as an essential component of the system of chivalric ideals open a new horizon for the knight and offer him the possibility of pursing and acquiring glory, social

---

[1]   O'Connor, pp. 74-5.

distinction, and advancement by means of learning and scholarly accomplishments. The new conception of the knight is representative of the gradual change in court ideology, political reality, and perception of the individual that characterize the transition from the culture of the Middle Ages to the culture of humanism and Renaissance. It becomes increasingly apparent by the beginning of the sixteenth century that the traditional knightly ideal had become an anachronism and that it was most unsuited to the more culturally enriched Renaissance aristocracy. The emergence of the soldier-scholar, whose new pathway to virtue was learning, had arrived. "Virtue," as Ferguson points out, "had always occupied a primary place in the chivalric ideal, but it was virtue sought within the scope of the Renaissance to link virtue with learning as well as with the innate character of man."[1] In the sixteenth century it will be *Il Cortegiano* of Baldassare Castiglione that will embody these new attitudes and currents of thoughts.

---

[1]   Furguson, p. 199.

CHAPTER II

Il Cortegiano Of Castiglione In Spain: A Study Of Its Ideal And Of Its Affinity And Contrast With *Amadís De Gaula*

The Spanish Influence in the "Courtier"

When *Il Cortegiano* of Baldesar Castiglione was published in Venice in 1528, *Amadís de Gaula* had already been widely circulated in the courts of Europe. The first mention of *Amadís* in Italy is found as early as 1512 in a letter written by Pietro Bembo, one of the interlocutors of the *Courtier*, to his friend Ramusio.[1] In this letter, Bembo refers to Valerio, a close acquaintance of Castiglione, as totally "engrossed" in the reading of *Amadís*. On or about the same time, Montalvo's text is also mentioned in a checklist of books that comprised the library of Duque Federico of Montova, also a good friend of Castiglione. Moreover, there are in the *Courtier* direct references to *Amadís* such as the mention of *Isola Firma* and *l'arco dei leali innamorati*.[2] From these clues there is sufficient reason to believe that Castiglione was familiar with the text of *Amadís* when he began to write the *Courtier* in 1514. Therefore, one cannot exclude the possibility that the *Amadís'* ideal of the knightly gentleman was present in Castiglione's mind and played a part in the fashioning of the *cortegiano*.

There has never been a meeting of minds among critics on Castiglione's purpose in writing the *Courtier*. The most obvious assessment derived from the author's declared intention *di formar con parole un perfetto Cortegiano*[3] is that the *Courtier* is a rule book of behavior designed to improve the manners of contemporary Europe, which until the beginning of the sixteenth century had relied for its standards of conduct on a few tersely formulated precepts set down in the writings of learned ecclesiastics and in documents, in various languages, from the courts of chivalrous societies.[4]

---

[1] Baldesar Castiglione, *Il Cortegiano*, ed. Vittorio Cian (Firenze: G. C. Sansoni, 1929), fn. 11, p. 380.

[2] *Ibid.*, p. 381.

[3] Baldesar Castiglione, *Il Cortegiano con una scelta delle Opere minori*, ed. Bruno Maier (Torino: Unione Tipografico-Editrice Torinese, 1964). Bk. I, chap. xii, p. 100. All quotations from the *Courtier* are from this edition.

[4] J. R. Woodhouse, *Baldesar Castiglione: a Reassessment of the "Courtier"* (Edinburg University Press, 1972), p. 2 discusses some of the critical

Since the twelfth century, books such as *De institutione novitiarum* by Hugh of St. Victor (d. 1141), *Disciplina Clericalis* of the baptized Spanish Jew Petrus Alphonsi, and *Morale Scolarium* (1241) by Johannes von Garland aimed at setting the standards of behavior and manners among members of the Latin-speaking clerical society.[1] Similarly, the *Breviari d'Amor* of Matfre Ermengaud, the *Ziquanta Cortesie da Tavola* of Fra Bonvicino da Riva, and *Tesoretto* of Brunetto Latini, among a few others, served to establish the rules of etiquette among the secular upper classes of Provence and Italy.[2] More recent books on behavior, ranging from Russel's *Book of Nature* to Erasmus' *De civilitate morum puerilium* and Dalla Casa's *Galateo*, do not differ substantially from earlier texts:[3] they all list detailed sets of practical rules dealing with table manners, physical appearance, and conversation; and

---

interpretations of Catiglione's work. His own conclusion is that the *Courtier's* true purpose is to teach "survival and security in an hostile world." Vittorio Cian, *Un illustre nunzio pontificio del Rinascimento: Baldassar Castiglione* (Città del Vaticano: Biblioteca Apostolica del Vaticano, 1951), p. 229, considers the *Courtier* as a book of personal memories, "un libro di ricordi vivi, vissuto, rampollato, a dir cosi, spontaneamente dalla vita." Antonio Corsano in *Studi sul Rinasciemento* (Bari: Adriatica Editrice, 1949), pp. 70-1, sees the *Courtier* as "un ampio, caldo, fluente elogio della pace."

[1]   Norbert Elias, *The Civilizing Process: The History of Manners*, trans. Edmund Jephcott (New York: Urizen Books, 1978), p. 60.

[2]   Thomas F. Crane, *Italian social customs of the sixteenth century and their influence on the Literature of Europe* (New Haven: Yale University Press, 1920), pp. 325-251.

[3]   For an analysis of the difference between the *Courtier* and "courtesy books" in general, see Alexander Corbin Judson, "Spenser's Theory of Courtesy," *PMLS* XLVII (1923), pp. 122-36. A study of differences between the *Courtier* and *Il Galeteo* of Giovanni Della Casa can be found in Hilary Adams' analysis of "*Il Cortegiano* and *Il Galateo*" in *Modern Language Review*, No. 42, 1947, pp. 457-66.

some descend even to such trifles as the use of the napkin, personal apparel, the avoidance of immodest topics, and blowing one's nose.

Although *Il Cortegiano* can be properly classified within the traditional definition of etiquette manual, it would not do justice to appraise it solely as a book of behavior and a mere summary of the refined manners of the Renaissance. As Wayne A. Rebhorn points out, interpreting Castiglione's work essentially, if not exclusively, as a book of etiquette "lessens it by reducing its many complex concerns to a single one and ignoring Castiglione's interests in defining an ideal type, depicting an ideal society in operation and creating a memorial befitting the men and women of Urbino."[1]

The *Courtier*, like *Amadís de Gaula*, besides dealing with many questions of tact and propriety, also embraces a whole gamut of questions concerning human dignity, ethical behavior, and personal responsibilities. Because of its thoroughness, Castiglione's text, together with Montalvo's *Amadís* and Spenser's *Fairie Queene*, can be properly considered one of the most ambitious "courtesy books" ever written: it represents both the medieval and the renaissance conceptions of the perfect gentleman.

That the *Courtier* should fare preeminently in the study of the trends and changes in the ideal of courtliness in Spain is dictated by historical, literary, and social considerations. "The connection of Spain with *Il Cortegiano* was more direct than that of the rest of Europe,"[2] says Pauline Marshall, and Leonard Mades states:

---

[1] Wayne A. Rebhorn, *Courtly Performances* (Detroit: Wayne State University Press, 1978), p. 13.

[2] Pauline Marshall, Edition with Introduction and Notes to *El Caballero Perfecto* by Alonso Gerónimo de Salas Barbadillo, University of Colorado

Castiglione played a key role in Spanish affairs during a highly critical period of history. No account of the events of those times, in which Spain was so deeply involved, can be complete without reference to him. His diplomatic reports and his letters constitute important historical documents. His presence in Spain influenced that country's spiritual and social history as well as its foreign affairs.[1]

According to A. von Reumont, Castiglione came to Spain for the first time in 1519, six years before he was assumed as *nunzio pontificio* in the court of Charles V on October 5, 1524.[2] If such an early visit took place, says Menéndez y Pelayo, some revisions and passages of the *Courtier* could well have been written in Spain;[3] Spanish customs and ideas could have easily influenced Castiglione's thinking and writing of *Il Cortegiano,* whose final redaction, the Laurentian Codex, was signed in Florence in 1524.[4]

Studies: Languages and Literature, No. 2 (Boulder, Co.: University of Colorado Press, 1959), p. ix.

[1] Leonard Mades, *The Armor and the Brocade: A Study of "Don Quijote" and the "Courtier"* (New York: Las Americas Publishing Company, 1968), p. 9.

[2] Vittorio Cian, *Un illustre nunzio pontificio del Rinascimento: Baldessar Castiglione* (Città del Vaticano: Biblioteca Apostolica del Vaticano, 1951), p. 254, calls "infontate" the belief that Castiglione visited Spain prior to 1524.

[3] Juan Boscán, *Antología de poetas líricos castellanos*, Vol. XIII, p. 96. A. Giannini in "La carcel de amor y el *Cortegiano* de B. Castiglione," *Revue Hispanique*, XLVI (1919), p. 547, states about Castiglione's supposed visit, "podemos aseguarar que algunos trozos fuéronle sugeridos por aquel ambiente en que vivía, y aún no vacileremos en afirmar que a tal influencia se debe cuanto escribió de España y de los Españoles."

[4] Mades, p. 16.

The Spanish element in Castiglione is of "considerable importance," says Prof. Mades: "it is no exaggeration to say that if not for his acquaintance with the Spaniards the character of the *Courtier* might well have been different. It is hard to imagine the book without its many Spanish ingredients."[1]

Castiglione's familiarity and admiration for Spanish history, culture, and letters are manifest in many passages of the *Courtier*. He points to the Spaniards as *maestri della cortegiania,* defends them against the charges of presumptuousness of Calmeta, eulogizes Queen Isabella as *esempio di vera bontá* and *cortesia,* and applauds *la magnanimitá* and *il sapere* of Gonzalo Fernándex of Cordoba. Moreover, he repeatedly alludes to the affinity of Spanish and Italian manners and temperament, suggests to the Italians the natural ease and composure of the Spanish character, and recommends the study of Spanish as a foreign language. He even goes as far as using numerous Castillian derivatives, e.g. *sforzato* and *disinvoltura,* to describe many of the courtier's essential qualities.[2] Finally, in a letter to Alfonso Valdés in 1528, he declares himself

---

[1] Mades, p. 16.

[2] In the *Courtier* direct references to Spain and the Spaniards are found as follows: Bk. I, chaps. xxi. Bk. II, chaps. xxi, xxii, xxxi, xxxvii, xiil, lxv, lxxii, lxxiii, lxxiv, lxxvi, lxxviii, lxxxii, lxxxv, xiic. Bi. III, chaps. xxxv, xil, liv. Bk. IV, chap. xxxviii. A detailed study of the language of the *Courtier* is made by Margherita Morreale, *Castiglione y Boscán: El ideal cortesano en el Renacimiento expañol* Boletín de la Real Academia Española, Añejo I; Madrid, 1959). Cian discusses the use of Spanish derivatives in the Italian language in B. Castiglione, *Il Cortegiano* (4th ed., Florence: Sansoni, 1947), p. 83n. Benedetto Croce also reviews the extensive use of hispanisms in the Italian language in *La Spagna nella vita Italian durante la Rinascenza* (Bari: Laterza, 1949), pp. 154-80.

to be no less Spanish than Italian: "Io non mi riputeró giammai di essere meno Spagnolo che Italiano."[1]

The Spaniards, likewise, admired and esteemed Castiglione. The Duque of Sessa, in a letter dated 1524, says of Baldesar: "era caballero muy honrado de muy buenas letras y que no había dado menos cuenta de si en las armas." [2]And Charles V, who kept a copy of the *Courtier* by his bedside and often consulted Castiglione on questions of politics and diplomacy, upon hearing the death of Castiglione in Toledo on February 7, 1529, said to his courtiers: "yo os digo que es muerto uno de los mejores caballeros del mundo."[3]

The circumstances by which *Il Cortegiano* was introduced in Spain are narrated by Juan Boscán in a letter to Doña Geronima Palova de Almogavar:

> No ha muchos días que me envió Garcilaso de la Vega este libro llamado *El Cortesano*, compuesto en lengua italiana por el conde Baltasar Castellon. Su título y la autoridad de quien le enviaba. me movieron a leelle con diligencia. Vi luégo en el tantas cosas tan buenas, que no pude dejar de conocer gran ingenio en quien le hizo. Demás de parecerme la invinción buena y el artificio y la dotrina, perecióme la materia de que trata no solamente provechosa y de mucho gusto, pero necesaria por ser de cosa que traemos

---

1   Bruno Maier, ed. *Il Cortegiano*, p. 693. See also Baldasar Castiglione, *Letters*, ed. P. Serassi (Padova: G. Comino), p. 198.

2   Antonio Marichalar, "*El Cortesano* en el centenario de Boscán," *Escorial: Revista de Cultura y Letras*, December 1942, p. 298.

3   Julia Cartwright, *Baldassare Castiglione: The Perfect Courtier* (New York: P. Dutton, 1908), II, p. 14, p. 418. See also Cian, *Un illlustre nunzio pontificio*, pp. 127-8.

siempre entre manos. Todo esto me puso gana que los hombres de nuestra nación participasen de tan buen libro y que non dejasen de entendelle por falta de entender la lengua, y por eso quisiera traducille luégo.[1]

Juan Boscán's translation of the *Courtier* appeared in Spain in 1534. Soon after its publication, says Menéndez y Pelayo, *"El Cortesano* entró en el gusto español como si aquí hubiese nacido sirviendo de modelo para otros libros análogos."[2] The humanist Ambrosio de Morales writes: *"El Cortesano* no habla mejor en Italia donde nació que en España."[3] And a more contemporary writer, Carmelo Bonet, states: *"El Cortesano* merced a esa traducción ha tomado carta de ciudadanía en la literatura española."[4] The great popularity of Castiglione's work among the Spanish-reading public is further attested by the thirteen editions of *El Cortesano* redacted between 1534 and 1588[5] as compared to eleven editions of *Amadís de Gaula* during the same period (1533-1586).[6] It is not difficult, therefore,

---

[1]   Baltasar de Castiglione, *El Cortesano*, trans. Juan Boscán (Barcelona: Editorial Bruguera, S. A., 1972), p. 55.

[2]   Marcelino Menéndez y Pelayo, "Estudio sobre Castiglione y *El Cortesano*" in B. Castiglione, *El Cortesano*, trans. Juan Boscán (Madrid: Revista de Filología Española, Añejo XXV, 1942), p. L.

[3]   *Obras del maestro Fernán Pérez de Oliva* (Madrid: Benito Cano, 1787), vol. I, p. XLI.

[4]   Carmelo Bonet, "El arte de escribir: la lección del *Cortesano*" in *Despuntes críticos* (Buenos Aires: Academia Argentina de Letras, 1969), p. 200.

[5]   Margherita Morreale, *Castiglione y Boscán*, vol. I, p. 19.
Leonard E. Opdyke, who published his English translation of the *Courtier* in 1908, lists eighteen Spanish editions of the Italian text; see Joseph Mazzeo, *Renaissance and Revolution* (New York, 1965), pp. 131-2.

[6]   Place, ed. *Amadís de Gaula*, Vol. I, pp. XX-XXIV.

to form a mental picture of the wide appeal and the interest with which the *Courtier* was read in Spain.

The purpose of the following analysis is to examine Castiglione's *Courtier* and explore how the ideal it embodies relates to Montalvo's portrayal of the knightly gentleman already traced in the first chapter of this study. It also aims at appraising what new perspectives and attitudes are at the center of Catiglione's view of *cortegiania* and how these sentiments are echoed in the Spanish conception of *el caballero perfecto* of the sixteenth century.

The Qualities of the Courtier

The courtier's first requisite is that he be of good lineage and of distinguished family: "Voglio adunque che questo cortegiano sia nato di nobile e di generosa famiglia."[1] Ludovico Canossa, one of the interlocutors of *Il Cortegiano*, gives two basic reasons for this essential requirement in the courtier. First, noble breeding is a guarantee of courage and virtue: "La nobiltá accende e sprona alla virtú . . . interviene quasi sempre che e nelle arme e nelle altre virtuose operazioni gli omini piu segnalati sono nobili." [2]Second, the nobly born are placed under greater obligation to emulate the virtuous conduct and the great deeds of their ancestors, "perché molto men si desdice a un ignobile mancar di far operazioni virtuose, che ad un nobile il qual se desvia del cammino dei sui antecessori."[3]

---

[1]   Bk. I, chap. xiv, p. 103.

[2]   Bk. I, chap. xiv, p. 103.

[3]   *Ibid.*

This line of reasoning by Ludovico provokes the anger of Gaspar Pallavicino, another interlocutor, and a firm believer in Natural Law and men's equality. He argues that high birth need not be the determining factor in achieving great goals and perfection.[1] But in spite of his eloquent and animated discourse, Gaspar's objections are overruled and the requirement of noble ancestry remains, as it did for Amadís, the distinguishing mark of the "renaissance gentleman." "Para Castiglione," says Margherita Morreale, "'nobiltá' es en sentido específico nobleza de linaje . . . condición que de hecho considera imprescindible para el cortesano."[2]

As it stands, it is clear that Castiglione's view of noble birth as a necessary prerequisite for the courtier and his belief that good breeding is the "seed" and "stimulus" to virtue add nothing to the traditional doctrine of inherited nobility. Rather, it falls within medieval patterns of thought and has a parallel and a precedent in the general principles of hereditary nobility outlined in *Amadís de Gaula*.

The second most important requisite for the courtier is that he excels in military skill and virtue: "Estimo che la principale e vera profession del Cortegiano debba esser quella dell'arme; la qual sopra tutto voglio che si faccia vivamente, e sia conosciuto tra gli altri per ardito e sforzato e fedele a chi serve." [3]Here, once again, the soldierly qualities that Castiglione ascribes to the courtier—prowess, courage, and loyalty to his lord—seem to be, at least in theory, very close to Montalvo's conception of military virtue. Even the courtier's honor

---

[1]   Bk. I, chap. xv, pp. 106-7.

[2]   Morreale, *Castiglione y Boscán*, p. 129.

[3]   Bk. I, chap. xvii, p. 109.

in battle is directly related as in *Amadís* to the avoidance of cowardice and to the degree of valor he displays in combat:

> La fama d'un gentilom che porti l'arme, se una volta in an minimo punto si denigra per coardia . . . sempre resta vituperosa al mondo e piena d'ignominia. Quanto piú adunque sará eccellente in nostro Cortegiano in questa arte, tanto piú sará degno di laude.[1]

The courtier must also be bold, fierce, and among the first in battle. In any other place, he must be modest, gentle, and reserved, avoiding, above all, self-praise and ostentation:

> Sia adunque . . . dove si veggon gli inimici, fierisimo, acerbo, e sempre tra i primi; in ogni altro loco, umano, modesto e ritenuto, fuggendo sopra tutto la ostentazione e lo impudente laudar se stesso.[2]

In like manner, Amadís is often described as *valiente, acometedor, esforzado, feridior de espada,*[3] but also as *humilde, modesto, piadoso,*[4] or with expressions such as "Amadís ouo della gran duelo que las lagrimas le vinieron a los ojos," and "Amadís los miraba auiendo muy gran duelo de los ver tan maltrechos."[5]

---

[1] *Ibid.*

[2] Bk. I, chap. xvii, p. 111.

[3] I, xviii, 73 and 162.

[4] III, comienco, p. 661; I, xviii, 167.

[5] I, xix, 175.

In body figure, the courtier is gracefully handsome, "dotato da natura di bella forma di volto e di persona, con quella grazia che lo facesse cosi amabile."[1] He is well-built and shapely of limb. He is endowed with strength and agility and displays great skill in every sort of bodily exercise, and in handling all types of weapons both on horse and on foot:

> Voglio che egli sia di bona disposizione e de' membri ben formato, e mostri forza e leggerezza e discioltura, e sappia de tutti gli esercizi di persona, che ad uom di guerra s'appartengono; e di questo penso il primo dover essere maneggiar ben ogni sorte d'arme a piedi ed a cavallo.[2]

In *Amadís* the same concerns for bodily countenance are expressed with the terms, *su gran hermosura por marauilla era mirada, tan apuesto e tan fermoso, membrudo algun tanto*[3]; and to describe his physical prowess, the words *fuerça, ligereza, ardimento, andar valiente e ligero* are used.[4]

In the realm of physical education and courtly diversion, the courtier shares with Amadís the same interest in horsemanship and also the fondness for hunting for its similarity to war: "Voglio che il nostro cortegiano sia perfetto cavalier d'ogni sella."[5] "Sono ancor molti altri

---

[1]   Bk. I, chap. xix, p. 113.
[2]   Bk. I, chap. xx, p. 115.
[3]   I, iii, 31 and 32.
[4]   I, iii, 38; I, xxxv, 283; I, sviii, 170.
[5]   Bk. I, chap. xxi, p. 117.

esercizi . . . e tra questi parmi la caccia esser de' principali, perché ha una certa similitudine di guerra."[1]

Like Amadís, the *cortegiano* is also polished in love. In fact, the same romantic portrayal of the knight and the same postulates of "courtly love" found in Montalvo's text are also repeated, almost exactly, in the *Courtier*. As in *Amadís*, love is the most powerful source of refinement and the fountain of all goodness. The courtier must serve his lady and be sensitive to her wishes, and if possible, become one with the beloved. As in the code of *amour courtois*, he must also protect his lady's reputation and keep his love secret:

> Quello che comincia ad amare deve ancora cominciare a compiacere ed accomodarsi totalmente alle voglie della cosa amata e con quelle governar le sue; e far che i proprii desideri siano servi e che l'anima sua istessa sia come obediente ancella, ne pensi mai ad altro che a transformarsi, se possibil fosse, in quella della cosa amata, e questo reputar per la sua somma felicitá . . . Pero se 'l nostro cortegiano volesse usar del mio consiglio, io lo confortarei a tener secreti gli amori suoi.[2]

Amadís is often admired and praised for his fine diction and manner of speaking. In his speech, he is described as *bien hablado, discreto, cortés, de graciosa habla y donaire.*[3] These same attributes are also desirable in the courtier:

---

[1] Bk. I, chap. xxii, p. 118.
[2] Bk. III, chap. lxiii, pp. 426-7.
[3] IV, cxxiii, 1216; I, xxi, 194; I, xx, 185.

> Nel conversare con omini e con donne d'ogni
> qualitá, nel giocare, nel ridere e nel motteggiare
> tiene una certa dolcezza e cosí graziosi costumi,
> che forza é che ciascun che gli parla . . . gli resti
> perpetuamente affezionato.[1]

Four other qualities of Amadís—*discreción, bondad, fortaleza,* and *mesura*[2]—sum up the essential attributes of the courtier: "diremo in poche parole attendendo al nostro proposito, bastar che egli sia . . . omo da bene ed intiero, ché in questo si comprende la prudenzia, bontá, fortezza e temperanza."[3]

From the foregoing analysis, it is obvious that the basic characteristics that define Castiglione's concept of *cortegiania* are consistent and not essentially different from those that define the concept of courtliness and chivalry in *Amadís de Gaula.* In fact, seen from an historical and social perspective, Castiglione's idea of the perfect man—distinguished in birth, skilled at arms, refined in love, polished in manners, and graceful in appearance—stands almost entirely within the medieval tradition of *courtoisie* of which Amadís is the outstanding literary example. Yet a closer look at these two perfect models point to fundamental differences in attitude, perceptions of reality, and philosophy of life.

---

[1]   Bk. I, chap. xvi, p. 105.

[2]   III, lxvi, 698; II, xliiii, 368; III, lxxi, 776.

[3]   Bk. I, chap. xli, p. 156.

The Courtier vs. the Knight

There are several traits that distinguish Catiglione's model from the Amadisian ideal and call attention to the new tendencies that reflect the process of transformation and the diverging paths of these two prototypes. It should be noted, however, that Castiglione's profile and prescription for the perfect gentleman is not earmarked by a plea for new rules as opposed to old ones, but by the eagerness to elaborate the details of the *courtois* tradition and redefine the chivalric code in relation to the social and political realities and the climate of intellectual and artistic sophistication that prevailed in the courts of Italy during the beginning of the sixteenth century. Undoubtedly, the revival of humanistic culture and spirit, the growth of a very intricate court bureaucracy, the availability of more leisure time, the more frequent human contacts, the increasing exposure and participation of courtiers in public functions, the individual's strife for social eminence and political power on grounds of artistic and literary merits rather than on military prowess warranted a more elaborate and intellectually-oriented set of guidelines by which the courtier could tactfully and effectively function in the new sphere of influence, power struggle, and personal relationships at the palace of great lords.

For example, in the field of bodily exercises and knightly diversions, Castiglione adds to Montalvo's list: swimming, running, leaping, throwing stones, playing tennis, and vaulting on horseback.[1] He also recommends that in riding horses the courtier be among the best Italian cavalrymen; in tourneys and in the art of

---

[1]   Bk. I, chap. xxii, p. 118.

defense and attack, be distinguished among the French; and in stickthrowing, bullfighting, and in the casting of darts, prominent among the Spanish.[1] But even more significantly, while Castiglione acknowledges the usefulness of these skills in the physical conditioning of the body and particularly in the training of the warrior, he takes special interest in emphasizing the "graceful" performance of these exercises in public as a unique opportunity for the courtier to impress his audience and win the praise of his peers and superiors: "ma sopra tutto accompagni ogni suo movimento con un certo bon giudicio e grazia, se vole meritar quell'universal favore che tanto s'apprezza."[2]

Thus it becomes apparent from the very start that Castiglione's main preoccupation is not the performance of the deed itself, but the aesthetic appeal[3] of physical

---

[1] Bk. I, chap. xxi, p. 117-8.

[2] Bk. I, chap. xxi, p. 118.

[3] Although it was not before the latter part of the eighteenth century that the term "aesthetic" was adopted with the meaning now commonly recognized: the philosophy of the beautiful as a distinct province of theoretical inquiry, the principles that regulate the appreciation of beautiful objects and the practice of the fine arts had already been the subject of discussion and speculation among Greek, Roman, and medieval writers. During the Renaissance the philosophy of the beautiful had considerable influence on art and literature and also on man's idea of self-formation and cultivation. The idea of formation and cultivation became very important during the period of German Classicism and was expressed in the word *Bildung*, a term that according to Hans-Georg Gadamer "is intimately associated with the idea of culture and designates primarily the properly human way of developing one's natural talents and capacities" and it also involves the ability "to distinguish between the beautiful and the ugly, good and bad qualities." The above quotations from Gadamer are from the pages 11 and 17 of his work *Truth and Method* (New York: The Seabury Press, 1975). For a compete discussion of the concept of *Bildung*, the doctrine of the ideal beauty, the concept of taste, tact,

education and bodily movements. Castiglione was, indeed, following an already established tradition. As Jakob Burckhardt points out, bodily exercises and gymnastics, apart from "military training and mere amusement," were probably first taught by Vittorino da Feltre, the renowned educator of the court of Giovan Francesco Gonzaga at Mantua, often acclaimed in the early fifteenth century as the "chosen school of the aristocratic world."[1] After this time, Burckhardt states "not only strength and skill, but grace of movement was one of the main objects of physical training and became essential to the complete education" of the gentleman.[2]

No such aesthetic consideration or concern, on the other hand, seems to be of any significance in the physical education of Amadís, whose skills and abilities were primarily geared to warfare. Nor is there in Montalvo's text any strong suggestion that the physical conditioning and development of the knight must be complemented by the fostering of the knight's mental abilities, a notion heavily stressed in the life-long preparation of the *cortegiano*. In Italy the idea of the harmonious development of both body and mind had been a goal of the gentleman's education much before Castiglione's time. It is treated in San Bernardino's *Prediche* in the late thirteenth century and during the following decades, notably in *De Educatione liberorum clarisque eorum moribus* by Maffeo Vegio and in *De ingenuis moribus* by Pier Paulo Vergerio.[3] Aneas

---

aesthetic judgment, aesthetic consciousness, aesthetic pleasure, and aesthetic education, especially as they are seen in the writings of Kant, Schiller, Hegel, and Helmholtz, see also pp. 10-90.

[1]   Jakob C. Burckhardt, *The Civilization of the Renaissance in Italy* (New York: Oxford University Press, 1968), p. 108.

[2]   *Ibid.*

[3]   Woodhouse, p. 42.

Piccolomini, almost a century before Castiglione, writes that "these two elements of which we are constituted must be developed side by side." He then gives the rules on the discipline of the body, stresses the need of noble youth to receive military training, and suggests the type of reading best suited for that purpose. He later proceeds to recommend the teaching of eloquence, both in speaking and in writing, as well as stressing the value of a liberal education.[1]

Castiglione elaborates these ideas even further. He specifically urges the courtier to study the humanities and to be proficient both in Latin and Greek as well as in French and Spanish: "Voglio che nelle lettere sia piú che mediocramente erudito, almeno in questi studi che chiamano d'umanitá, e non solamente della lingua latina, ma ancor della greca abbia cognizione."[2] "Il medesimo intervien del saper diverse lingue; il che io laudo molto nel cortegiano, e massimamente la spagnola e la franzese."[3] The pursuit of letters, however, although essential, must not be an end in itself, according to Ludovico Canossa, but an ornament to the courtier's true profession which is that of arms: "mostrando sempre e tenendo in effetto per sua principale professione l'arme e l'altrre bone condizioni tutte per ornamento di quelle."[4]

This assertion by Ludovico provokes, among the interlocutors of *Il Cortegiano*, a dispute on the relative advantage of arms and letters, a topic much debated in classical and Renaissance literature. In Roman antiquity

---

[1]   A. G. Dickens, *The Courts of Europe: politics, patronage and royalty 1400-1800* (New York: McGraw-Hill, 1977), p. 40.

[2]   Bk. I, chap. xliv, p. 162.

[3]   Bk. II, chap. xxxvii, pp. 248-9.

[4]   Bk. I, xliv, p. 164.

Cicero's viewpoint *cedant armae togae* was a slogan often repeated by "those who wore the toga and who did not bear arms."[1] In the Middle Ages "the hypothetical contraries were personified by the knight and the clerk; and while it was normal to argue that both were necessary to society, it was difficult, in the face of learning endemic in the warrior class, to postulate their perfect union."[2] Lull's *Order of Chivalry* was partially an attempt to place the knight on an equal footing with the cleric. The knight, however, judging the pursuit of letters unsuitable to his profession and damaging to his warrior-image, remained "armed and unscholarly."[3]

Amadís, Lancelot, Tristan, and other chivalric heroes, although not antagonistic to the values of culture and learning, fell within this tradition and upheld the dignity of their profession by noblesse, gallantry, and by force of arms to the exclusion of "letters." During the Renaissance, the theme of arms and studies appears in Boiardo, Ariosto, Rebelais, Spenser, and Cervantes, but the theme *sapientia et fortitudo*, according to Ernest Curtius, entered the Renaisssance "in the didactic writings on courtly ideals (Castiglione)."[4]

In the *Courtier*, it is Ludovico Canossa, who despite Bembo's arguments on the contrary,[5] eloquently upholds the supremacy of the military profession over that of

---

[1]   Dickens, p. 38. |

[2]   Dickens, p. 38.

[3]   *Ibid.*

[4]   Ernst Curtius, *European Literature and Latin Middle Ages* (New York: Pantheon Books, 1920), p. 178. Cian notes that the theme of "arms and letters" was treated before Castiglione in the works of Flavio Biondo, *De Literis et armis comparatio* (1460) and Cristoforo Lafranchino, *Tractatulus seu Quaestio utrum preferendus sit miles an doctor* (1497).

[5]   Bk. I, chap. xlv, pp. 164-5.

letters and enthusiastically defends the merit of combining scholarship with prowess of arms. He tells of ancient heroes like Alexander who admired Homer and studied philosophy under Aristotle, Cesar whose writings bear witness to his love for study, and Hannibal who had an excellent knowledge of literature and Greek language.[1] Pointing to these outstanding examples, Canossa argues that the combination of literary and military interests is especially desirable in the courtier:

> Tengo che a niun piú si convenga l'esser litterato che a un om di guerra; e queste due condizioni concatenate e l'una dall'altra aiutate, il che é convenientissimo, voglio che siano nel nostro cortegiano.[2]

The courtier, thus, becomes an idealization of the supportiveness of "arms and letters" and of the union between the knight and the clerk, the soldier and the scholar—the end result of serious military training and classical education.

To further foster the courtier's refinement Count Ludovico suggests that the courtier be also an accomplished musician. Besides understanding and being able to read notes, he must be able to play various instruments. Music restores the soul, lifts the spirit, pleases the ladies, and enhances the image of the courtier who can skillfully perform:

> Non mi contento del cortegiano s'egli non é ancor musico e se, oltre allo intendere ed esser

---

[1]   Bk. I, xliii, pp. 159-161.
[2]   Bk. I, xlvi, p. 166.

> sicuro a libro, non sa di varii instrumenti,
> perché, se ben pensiamo, niuno riposo di
> fatiche e medicina d'animi infermi ritrovar si
> pó piú onesta e laudevole nell'ocio, che questa;
> e massimamente nelle corti, dove . . . molte
> cose si fanno per satisfar alle donne, gli animi
> delle quali, teneri e molli, facilmente sono
> dall'armonia penetrati e di dolcezza ripieni.[1]

Ludovico's view is supported by Magnifico Giuliano who emphasizes that for court music is not only an "ornament" but a necessity: "Estimo . . . esser la musica no solamente ornamento, ma necessaria al cortegiano."[2]

No such sense of urgency in learning music, on the other hand, is apparent in *Amadís*. In fact, music plays no role in the education of the knight, and even when music is played at the court of King Lisuarte it serves only to enhance the atmosphere of festivity and relaxation and it is in no way thought of as an element of culture or refinement. Similarly absent from Amadís' knightly education is the study of art and the skills of drawing and painting. These abilities, however, play an important role in the fashioning of the courtier. "Il saper disegnare ed aver cognizion dell'arte propia del dipingere,"[3] says Ludovico, should not be omitted from the courtier's education. This knowledge is both useful in war such as when drawing places, sites, rivers and the like, and also in developing one's aesthetic sensibility.[4] It also serves to increase one's appreciation of other forms of art such as

---

[1]   Bk. I, chap. xlvii, p. 168.

[2]   Bk. I, chap. xlviii, p. 171.

[3]   Bk. I, xlix, p. 172.

[4]   Bk. I, chap. xlix, p. 173.

sculpture, and it helps toward a better understanding of the beauty of the human body itself.[1]

Another interlocutor, Federico Fregoso, recommends that the courtier be good at dancing, which he should do with "grace" and "dignity": "Sono alcuni altri esercizi, che far si possono . . . come e il danzare . . . danzando parmi che si gli convenga servare una certa dignitá, temperata pero con leggiadra ed aerosa dolcezza di movimenti."[2] And Gaspar Pallavicino suggests singing as a means of entertaining and winning the ladies: "Bella musica parmi il cantar bene a libro . . . e con bella maniera . . . ma sopra tutto conviensi in presenzia di donne."[3]

The courtier should also perform skillfully at public functions, attract the interest of the spectators, earn the respect of the audience by his composure and ingenuity, but especially by the garments he wears.[4] Federico suggests darker colors and reserved rather than showy style for ordinary wear, although brighter colors are more appropriate at festivals, masquerades, and tournaments. In general, however, Spanish reserve in dress is to be preferred.[5]

In jesting and telling pleasant stories, a topic that Castiglione treats extensively, the courtier should be witty yet discreet. He should bring about laughter at the proper time and place, seeing that it makes for excitement and cheerfulness, and that it wins for him the goodwill of those whom he seeks to entertain.[6] The Spaniards, according to

---

[1] *Ibid.*

[2] Bk. II, chap. xi, p. 205.

[3] *Ibid.*

[4] *Ibid.*

[5] Bk. II, chap. xxvii, p. 232.

[6] Bk. II, chap. xliii, p. 256-7.

Federico, have a special talent at jesting and provide the best model in this activity: "Pare ancor che ai Spagnoli sia assai propio il motteggiare."[1]

Turning to the subject of games, Gaspar Pallavicino points out that it is not improper for the courtier to play cards, provided that it is not done for the sake of earning money. Even more amusing and inventive, says Gaspar, is the game of chess, and here again the Spaniards are praised for their outstanding ability at this game and many others: "Molti Spagnoli trovansi eccellenti in questo ed in molti altri giochi."[2]

The incessant preoccupation of the interlocutors of the *Courtier* to train the *cortegiano* in a wide range of leisure activities contrasts dramatically with the stamp of social life in *Amadís*. Although we often find Amadís participating in *muchas danças y juegos*, appropriately dressed, *ricamente armado e atauiado*, gracefully taking part *en burla* and *reyr* as in the episode of Leonoreta, *jugando al axedrés* with Oriana *en el patín de los hermosos árboles*,[3] these glimpses of festivities and idleness are presented in *Amadís* only as an interlude in between battles—a time for restoration of the body and the spirit, and also an opportunity for the recognition of valor at arms. In *Il Cortegiano*, these same skills and activities are a way of life and serve a different purpose: they aim mainly at perfecting an art for its own sake and at enhancing the courtier's public image and prestige in the eyes of his peers and superiors. In addition, they underscore the climate of playfulness and the constant search for amusement, which are at

---

[1]   Bk. II, chap. xlii, p. 255.

[2]   Bk. II, chap. xxxi, p. 239.

[3]   I, xxxi, 252; II, liv, 644-5; II, lvi, 471.

the center of Castiglione's work. For the courtier, as for Schiller's "aesthetic man" two centuries later, "the play-impulse" dominates all aspects of living.[1] As a result it is not surprising that the uninhibited urging of the enjoyment of the present moment is often cited as one of the most distinctive features of Castiglione's *Courtier*. There is, in fact, throughout the text a sense of urgency to enjoy the present because all vanishes quickly. This perception of time and the limitations that it imposes on human happiness and pursuits most often appears in the Renaissance man's obsession and frenetic search for the most superficial pleasures, as long as they offered some type of aesthetic experience or stimulated the senses.

The art-conscious atmosphere that prevailed in Italy during the Renaissance and the vogue to look upon social life as an art are the theme and focus of interest of some of Burckhardt's best pages: "This society," he says, "at all events at the beginning of the sixteenth century, was a matter of art."[2] He points to Italy as a nation where "even serious men . . . looked on an handsome and becoming costume as an element in the perfection of the individual.[3] And where more than any other "country of Europe since the fall of the Roman empire so much trouble was taken to modify the face, the colour of skin and growth of the hair."[4] All aspects of religious, cultural, and social life—from the performance of the Mysteries and secular drama to singing and dancing—were submitted to "an

---

[1]   Friedrich Schiller, *On the aesthetic education of man*, trans. Elizabeth M. Wilkinson and L. A. Willoughby (Oxford: The Clarendon Press, 1967), p. 107.

[2]   Burckhardt, p. 198.

[3]   *Ibid.*, p. 191.

[4]   *Ibid.*, p. 192.

artistic method of treatment"[1] whose theoretical and practical soundness was determined and judged by the beauty and the richness of the spectacle and the effects it produced rather than by its substance.

Such emphasis on appearance and on image in daily living was not out of context. It was, in fact, reflective of certain aesthetic tendencies that prevailed in the arts since the Middle Ages. Benedetto Croce, for instance, quotes both Dante as saying in his *Convivio* in reference to the meaning of art, "Bellezza più che bontá sará in grado"; and the Marqués de Santillana in *Prohemio al Condestable de Portugual* defining poetry as "un fingimiento de cosas útiles, cubiertas ó veladas con muy fermosa covertura, compuestas, distinguidas é escondidas, por cierto cuento, pesso é medida."[2] These views and attitudes not only were later reflected in various ways in the art of Leonardo, Michelangelo, and Rafael, among many others, and in the treatises on art and aesthetics by Luca Paciola, Lomazzo, and Pellegrino Morato, but also found easy transfer into the realm of human behavior.[3]

The courtier is the legitimate heir of this aesthetic orientation of Renaissance life and culture. Thus to be successful in the milieu of "transparent deception"[4] and artistic refinement of the time, it was necessary for the courtier to learn not just the principles of mere etiquette, but also how to feign with tact, skillfully plan his moves, and perform all actions as to achieve certain artistic effects and practical ends. In the pursuit of these aims, Castiglione's text provided the courtier with both a list of

---

[1]   *Ibid.*, p. 208; p. 209.

[2]   Benedetto Croce, *Estetica* (Bari: Laterza & Figli, 1958), p. 194.

[3]   *Ibid.*, pp. 196-7.

[4]   Burckhardt, p. 192.

prescriptive details of tact and propriety and, more notably, with a specific well-organized set of aesthetic principles by which he could mold his character and fashion his personality.[1]

As a result of defining in terms of art and in details the courtier's essential characteristics, Castiglione created in his *cortegiano* a human stereotype and a conventionalized model that stands in marked contrast with the less stylized figure of the knight presented in *Amadís*. In fact, while Castiglione aims at a complete formalization of the courtier's behavior and personality by explaining, as he himself declares in Book I, "Tutte le condicioni e particular qualitá che si richieggono a chi merita questo nome,"[2] Montalvo offers in *Amadís* guidelines of a more general nature flexible enough to allow for individual freedom and expression. As he states in his *Prólogo*, he merely wants to give a series of "enxemplos y doctrinas . . . porque assí los caualleros mancebos como los más ancianos hallen en ellos lo que a cada vno conuine."[3]

It is clear that due to the more formalized and more exacting nature of Castiglione's prescriptions, as well as prohibitions, the courtier is undoubtedly placed under a greater degree of restraint than the knight of chivalry. When compared to the free play of emotions, the flexible self-control, and independence of Amadís' character, the courtier appears very much deprived of his freedom and spontaneity. He is often reminded that true virtue, together with the ability to properly spur a horse, handle a lance,

---

[1]   Schiller, p. xliii. Schiller also conceives the progressive ennoblement and refinement of personality only through art. In Schiller's theory man's progress is from the physical through the aesthetic to the moral.

[2]   Bk. I, chap. xii, p. 100.

[3]   Place, ed. *Amadís de Gaula*, Bk. I, pp. 9-10.

and gallantly court the ladies, consists in learning to exercise greater control of oneself, namely adjusting one's conduct, manners, language, glances, gestures, and even the smallest signs or winks, and also in being constantly aware of "il loco ove si trova ed in presenzia di cui."[1]

It appears, as Wayne Rebhorn points out, that the social idealism of Castiglione consists essentially in "playing a series of roles, each entertaining certain predetermined attitudes and modes of activity, status relationship, and types of dress and deportment—in other words, each having its appropriate figurative mask."[2] This mask, states Prof. Rebhorn, "provides a way of suppressing the everyday social self and freeing oneself for definite kinds of self-transformation.[3] One of the peculiarities of the individual from the Renaissance onward, says Norbert Elias, is the displacement of the "self" from the "other" and the discrepancy between the inner reality and the image he projects outwardly.[4] For the courtier, however, such defense mechanism and projections of the self did not result in alienation or in the agonistic conflict typical of many characters of the early twentieth century novel; rather, it became a convenient means of identification as well as a way to achieve self-stylization and perfection.

No such mask or problems of self-perception are apparent in Amadís. Montalvo's knightly gentleman, in fact, seems to be closer to Rousseau's romantic portrayal of *l'homme de la nature* than Castiglione's *l'homme de l'homme*. Unlike the courtier, Amadís' refinement of

---

[1]   Bk. II, chap. viii, p. 201.

[2]   Rebhorn, p. 14.

[3]   *Ibid.*, p. 17.

[4]   Norbert Elias, *The Civilizing Process: The History of Manners*, trans. by Edmund Jephcott (New York: Urizon Books, 1978), pp. 257-8.

manners and chivalric conduct are a reflection of inner worth. His interpersonal relationship are founded on a system of chivalric honor, trust and loyalty. Amadís' self-assertive drive is sublimized in action by his physical and moral superiority and by his feats of arms rather than by artistic talent or beautiful performances. In whole, Castiglionie's courtier presents himself essentially as an actor able to manipulate his appearances; he is a man on display who seeks the favor and the admiration of an appreciative audience.

The court is both the field of action and the stage for role playing. Whatever the courtier is engaged in—conversation, entertainment, bodily exercises, or love pursuits, his identity is defined through art. Interestingly enough, this art consists in concealing all art or in showing great mastery in what Castiglione calls *sprezzatura*, commonly translated in English as "nonchalance," a quality characterized by the appearance of natural ease and the hiding of conscious effort in performing even the most difficult tasks: "Si po dir quella esser vera arte che non pare esser arte" "E ció é . . . usar in ogni cosa una certa sprezzatura, che nasconda l'arte e dimostri ció che si fa e si dice venir fatto senza fatica e quasi senza pensarvi."[1] This studied "nonchalance" can only be accomplished by avoiding the flaw of affectation: "Trovo una regola universalissima, la qual mi par valer circa questo in tutte le cose umane che si facciano e dicano piú che alcuna altra, e ció é fuggir . . . l'affettazione."[2] From the avoidance of affectation comes *grazia*, described by Castiglione as the universal seasoning without which all other properties and good qualities are of little value.

---

[1]   Bk. I, chap. xxvi, p. 124.

[2]   *Ibid.*

Behind Castiglione's concept of *grazia* and *sprezzatura* lies a large system of theoretical material that is connected to the idea of man as an imitation of nature. The Artistotelian concept *omnis ars naturae imitanda est*[1] was an ideal already established in Italy since the fourteenth century in the works of Dante and later in those of Boccaccio and Petrarch. "It became a further application of the belief that man is an earthly god who rivals and disputes with nature or even excels her by adding to her qualities of his own mind,"[2] in the writings of Alberti, Vasari, Dolce, and Leonardo.[3] In the typical *trattato del Cinquecento*, the concept of *grazia*, in its application to art, was defined as an elusive simplicity of design, a somber calm and harmony of the parts. These artistic qualities were associated essentially with the aesthetic elements that distinguished Raphael's paintings.

Translated into behavioral patterns, the concept of *grazia* referred to a refined style of civility and culture which had as its principle characteristics the unaffected elegance and refined simplicity of painting—both the qualities of a work of art.[4] Bruno Maier says, "La' grazia' é, secondo Castiglione, il fondamento della *cortegiania*,"[5] and Edward Williamson in his study "The concept of grace in the work of Raphael and Castiglione," states: "In the *Courtier* 'grace' is translated into conduct by a sense

---

[1] Croce, *Estetica*, p. 188.

[2] Robb, p. 222.

[3] For some interesting thoughts on "the return to nature" and its application to art see Leonardo Da Vinci, *Notebooks*, ed. I. A. Richter (Oxford: University Press, 1952), p. 218. See also Giorgio Vasari, *Lives*, ed. W. Gaunt (London, 1963), Vol. II., p. 164.

[4] Rebhorn, pp. 41-3.

[5] Maier, ed. *Il Cortegiano*, p. 121.

of appropriateness that fits each act to the occasion which calls it forth."[1]

The application of *sprezzatura*, "unaffectedness," and *grazia* to human behavior is hardly Castiglione's invention, and although the cultivation of these qualities in the individual belonged to the hall rather than the battlefield, they were also a source of virtue for the courtly knight. These attributes of the courtier were in fact akin in many respects to the concept of chivalric "franchise,"[2] the natural demeanor and effortlessness that distinguished the cultivated knight.

Certainly not the attitude, but the principle of Castiglione's *sprezzatura* finds a close equivalent and a precedent in Amadís' *mesura, gracia,* and *buen comedimiento.*[3] For instance, one of the main features of the concept of *grazia* in Castiglione is that it emanates from God and that it has the power to generate both the greatest admiration and affection for those who possess it, and a sense of awe and wonder in those who witness it.[4] It is interesting to note how almost the same idea is expressed in King Perión when he remarks to Esplandián:

> Miró el rey a Esplandián que le nunca viera,
> e fue mucho murauillado en ver criatura tan
> hermosa y tan graciosa . . . mas el rey le abraçó y
> le dixo, Donzel mucho deuéys gradecer a Dios la
> merced que vos fizo en darvos tanta hermosura

---

[1] Italica, XXIV (1947), p. 321.

[2] A. G. Dickens, The Courts of Europe, politics, patronage, and royalty 1400-1800 (New York: McGraw-Hill, 1979), p. 41.

[3] IV, lxxxv, 973.

[4] Bk. I, chap. xv, p. 107: "Quella grazia che al primo aspetto sempre lo faccia a ciascun gratissimo."

e buen donayre, que sin conoscimiento atraéys a
todos que vos amen e vos precien.[1]

Similarly the fashioning of the individual as a work
of art, which is generally associated with Castiglione's
work, is not strictly a Renaissance phenomenon. In theory,
the aesthetic delineation of the individual existed in the
Socratic aim and consumation of all education, "the love
of loveliness," and in real life, in the *Kalos Kagathos*,
the Athenian ideal of the perfect citizen.[2] Reflecting
the aspirations of an essentially intellectual society and
aesthetic culture, the Hellenistic complete man, chiefly
because of his dissatisfaction with the government and
the unstable political conditions forced upon Greek
civilization by Alexander and his successors, sought
self-identification primarily by way of learning and art
rather than by "political association with a state or ruler."[3]
Moreover, the belief that the pursuit of knowledge was a

---

[1]   IV, cxii, 1, 132.

[2]   Harold Nicolson, *Good Behavior* (Garden City: Doubleday & Company, Inc.,
      1956), pp. 44-7.

      Werner Wilhelm Jaeger points out that the Greeks were "the first to recognize
      that education means deliberately moulding human characters in accordance
      with an ideal," and that "the greatest work of art they had to create was
      Man." Prof. Jaeger adds that "the German word 'Bildung' clearly indicates
      the essence of education in the Greek, the Platonic sense; for it covers the
      artist's act of plastic formation as well as the guiding patterns present to his
      imagination, the 'idea' or 'typos.'" "In Greece," he states, "the process of
      education is aimed at 'forming an ideal man as he ought to be. 'Utility' is
      neglected." The essential element was "the cultivation of the Beautiful."
      For these quotations and a description of what constituted the ideal man in
      ancient Greece, see pp. xxiii, and 1-12 of his classic study, *Paideia: The
      ideals of Greek culture*, trans. Gilbert Highet, 2nd edit. (3 vols.: New York:
      Oxford University Press, 1965).

[3]   Rebhorn, p. 26.

vehicle for happiness and health on earth and immortality in the afterlife often added to the perception of art both as a goddess and as a religoin.[1]

In Roman antiquity, these ideas and attitudes were reflected in various ways in the works of Quintillian, Plutarch, and Cicero. But while these writers recognized intellectual activity and aesthetic discernment as useful in the education of *homo liberalis*, even more emphatically they stressed achievement in the art of war, public administration, engineering, and service to the state.[2] The Roman preoccupation with learning as an end in itself and as a means of acquiring practical skills, coupled with the Roman ideal of *humanitas*—which comprised the concept of "decorum," the virtue of propriety and good taste; *comunitas*, the Roman idea of social conscience; and *gravitas*, a dignified attitude toward life—became later, together with Christian moralism, the basis of medieval and Renaissance thought on education and the background for the appearance of *l'uomo universale*, the living embodiment of the union of aesthetic qualities and practical skills.[3]

As early as the twelfth century we find that the Greek and Roman perceptions of the perfect gentleman had become part of the ideals of chivalry and courtliness, put forward in the "Roman *courtois*" of Chrétien de Troyes. He writes:

---

[1]   *Ibid.*, p. 27.

[2]   Harold Nicolson, *Good Behavior* (Garden City: Doubleday and Company, Inc., 1956), p. 69.

[3]   *Ibid.* For some ideas on the contribution of the Greek and Roman period on the educational and intellectual ideals of the Middle Ages and the Renaissance, see chapter 7, "The New Education" in Edward Kennard Rand, *Founders of the Middle Ages* (Harvard University Press, 1969), pp. 218-50.

Our books have informed us that the pre-eminence in chivalry and learning once belonged to Greece. The chivalry passed to Rome together with the highest learning which has now come to France. God grant that it may be cherished here, and that it may be made so welcome here that the honour which has taken refuge with us may never depart from France.[1]

In explicit terms, however, Hellenistic aestheticism, Roman *humanitas*, and religious morality is nowhere during the Middle Ages reflected in better form than in Dante's idea of the perfect gentleman. In his *Monarchia*, he urges man to fully develop his human potential. In the *Divina Comedia*, Virgil emerges as the "gentle sage" who knows it all and is the true symbol of the perfect *humanitas*. In *Convivio* Dante sketches the complete gentleman, assigning him the qualities of *gentilezza*, *bontá*, and *grazia*. Specifically, in his youth he is to give proper attention to his body that it may be sound and beautiful. In his prime of life, courtesy is especially becoming, and in his maturity he should strive to excel in "wisdom," the hallmark of the counselor, statesman, or just the simple citizen. Later in life, he should be of "meditative repose" and pious devotion.[2]

Dante's idea of man's perfectability through knowledge and the recognition of man's ability to seek in this life the fulfillment of his human potential were soon to be

---

[1]   Chrétien de Troyes, *Cliges*, trans. W. W. Comfort (London, 1914), p. 91.

[2]   Jefferson B. Fletcher, *Literature of the Italian Renaissance* (Port Washington, N. Y.: Kennikat Press Inc., 1934), pp. 32-4.

       Plato suggests that at the age of fifty man should begin to devote his life to the pursuit of contemplation of the Good. See Edward K. Rand, p. 224.

pioneered by Petrarch, often referred to by critics as "the precursor of the modern world."[1] In his *Secretum Meum,* an intimate self-confession and an imaginary dialogue with St. Augustine, Petrarch bluntly retorts to the theologian who is urging him to attend to the care of his soul rather than producing "rare and distinguished works" and squandering his life in "transitory pursuits"[2]:

> My principle is that, as concerning the glory which we may hope for here below, it is right for us to seek while we are below. One may expect to enjoy that other more radiant glory in heaven, when we shall have there arrived. . . . Therefore, as I think, it is in the true order that mortal men should first care for mortal things.[3]

Besides calling attention to this worldliness and presenting a more dynamic conception of man's nature, Petrarch, heedless to a long-established tradition of Aristotelian thought, also aimed at restating and combining in his philosophical writings the precepts of Augustinian voluntarism and self-knowledge with stoic ideals of life, Roman *humanitas,* and Neoplantonic aesthetic doctrine.[4] From the elucidation and fusion of these ideas emerged the vision of man as an active force in the universe "in a continual process of self-creation consciously and deliberately undertaken."[5]

[1]   George Voight, *The revival of classical antiquity* (Berlin: Reimer, 1859), pp. 80-1.

[2]   Harold H. Blanchard, *Prose and Poetry of the Renaissance in Translation* (London: Longman, Green and Co., 1958), p. 52.

[3]   *Ibid.*

[4]   Robb, p. 19.

[5]   *Ibid.,* p. 27.

Centeral to Petrarch, conception of the perfecting of the human character is the acquisition of knowledge and artistic sensibility by the study of the classics. In this activity, Plato and Cicero became for Petrarch and his successors the new symbols of culture and learning. Plato's political, social, and aesthetic ideology and tenets, together with those of Neoplatonic writers, especially Plotinus and Porphyry and the so-called Latin Platonists, Cicero and St. Augustine, soon became the favorite topics of discussion in the courts, in the homes, and in literary circles.[1] The literary academies of the fifteenth and sixteenth centuries, in particular those of Ficino in Florence, Pomponio Leto in Rome, and Pontano's in Naples, all of which later served as models for similar institutions in France and in Spain,[2] provided an opportune forum for debating and disseminating the Neoplatonic philosophy that influenced the intellectual background of the time in two ways: by its theory of beauty, and even more importantly, by the universality of man.[3]

The same questions, thoughts, and interests of the academies were also expressed in a number of treatises. Giannozzo Manetti, for one, in his *De excellentia et dignitate hominis*, rejects the medieval point of view of man's helplessness and assigns him a unique place in the universe.[4] Likewise, Pico Della Mirandola, in his *Oration on the Dignity of Man*, enthusiastically affirms man's

---

[1] Robb, p. 31.

[2] Crane, p. 42.

[3] G. Tiraboschi, *Storia della Letteratura Italiana* (Florence, 1905) Vols. V and VI provides an excellent account of the questions debated and the activities of Italian academies during this period.

[4] A study of Manetti's work can be found in Giovanni Gentile, *Giordano Bruno ed il pensiero del Rinascimento* (Florence, 1929).

potentiality "to be reborn into higher forms, which are devine."[1]

That man has the responsibility to arrive at such ideal perfection is well put by Schiller in his writings on the education of the "aesthetic man." He declares: "Every individual human being, one may say, carries with him, potentially and prescriptively, an ideal man, the archetype of a human being, and it is his life's task to be, through all his changing manifestations, in harmony with the unchanging unity of this ideal."[2]

Finally, the reverence for man's ability is reflected in the whole humanistic conception of education and especially in the works of Paulo Vergerio and Maffeo Vegio, whose writings, previously mentioned in this chapter, called for the human development of body and mind by alternating physical activity and learning, but most of all insisted on the training of the individual as a citizen capable of serving his community in peace and in war. These guidelines and the idea of combining action and thought emerged in the sixteenth century as the underlying principles and inspiration for Erasmus' *De civlitate morum puerilium*, Ellyot's *Governor*, and Della Casa's *Galateo*.

In this tradition of humanistic education earmarked by the union of intellectual attainment and practical deeds, it was soon obvious to Castiglione, who until the end of *Book III* had sketched his courtier strictly as a work of art and limited his activity solely to the realm of aesthetics, that the ideal he proposed could not fare well in a courtly society preoccupied not just with

---

[1]   Pico Della Mirandola, *Oration on the Dignity of Man*, quoted in Peter Burke, *The Renaissance* (Longmans, 1967), p. 24.

[2]   Schiller, p. 18.

the beautiful but also with the pragmatic. Castiglione skillfully remedies this inherent weakness in his fourth and final book of *Il Cortegiano*. In fact, now that through the laboring of a long series of dialogues and the efforts of many participants the courtier's claims to noble birth, grace, virtue, social refinement, physical prowess, arms, and letters have been stipulated, Castiglione, through the words of Signor Ottaviano, raises the worrisome question of whether the whole enterprise of attending to the courtier's perfection constitutes anything but triviality and wasted effort:

> Se con l'esser nobile, aggraziato e piacevole ed esperto in tanti esercizi il cortegiano non producesse altro frutto che l'esseser tale per se stesso, non estimerei che per conseguir questa perfezione di cortegiania dovesse l'omo ragionevolmente mettervi tanto studio e fatica.[1]

The courtier's efforts and endeavors concludes Ottaviano are to be praised only if they are diverted toward some useful and serious goals: "Ma se le operazioni del cortegiano sono indirizzate a quel bon fine che debbono e chi'io intendo, parmi ben che no solamente non siano dannose o vane, ma utilissime e degne d'infinita laude."[2] Ottoviano himself finds that there is, indeed, such purpose. In his own words, the true aim of all perfection or *cortegiania* in the courtier is the exertion of a beneficial influence on the prince he serves: "Pero yo estimo che . . .

---

[1]   Bk. IV, chap. iv, p. 450.
[2]   *Ibid.*

lo indurre o aiutare il suo principe al bene e spaventearlo dal male, sia il vero frutto della cortegiania."[1]

Castiglione believed that by means of acquiring good traits, by wit, by practical knowledge and familiarity with letters, and by cultivating in oneself all other gentlemanlike qualities, the courtier could win the good will and esteem of the prince, and thus, without fear of falling out of favor, he could draw the prince away "da ogni intenzion viciosa ed indurlo al camin della virtú."[2] It is then, in the service of giving advice and instructing the prince, that Castiglione endeavors to find a definite purposiveness for the courtier's artistic development and wisdom. It seems, however, that Castiglione's effort, more than being an encouragement for a more active participation in social and political affairs, is a real attempt to attach a specific function and find a definite application for the courtier's education in the liberal arts, which until then had been frowned upon, especially by the warrior class. In Renaissance Italy, says Lionel Trilling, "one could speak plain to sovereign power only if one possessed knowledge and trained perfection of grace and charm."[3] Francesco Guicciardini, a century before Castiglione, points out how the possession of great qualities "opens the way to the favours of princes and for those who abound in them it may be the beginning or cause of immense profit and promotion."[4]

---

[1] Bk. IV, chap. v, p. 451.

[2] *Ibid.*

[3] Lionel Trilling, *Sincerity and Authenticity* (Cambridge: Harvard University Press, 1973), p. 22.

[4] *History of Italy and History of Florence*, trans. Cecil Grayson (New York: Washington Square Press), p. 1. Also see Dickens, p. 43.

Certainly giving advice and instruction to the prince are not goals in the education of the knight. Amadis neither receives nor seeks education in the liberal arts. His training is geared almost exclusively toward the art of combat. His life purpose, as outlined in the chivalric code and mission of knight-errantry, is mainly to serve the needy and the weak. Moreover, in his warrior role Amadís is far more detached from the court of his king than the courtier from that of his prince. His usefulness to his king is mostly in the quality of military service he is capable of rendering. Amadís, however, like the courtier, enjoys a close relationship and binding sense of loyalty to his lord. Interestingly, at the end of his career Amadís becomes himself a prince; the courtier on the other hand is still left to pursue even greater perfection in courtliness. Perhaps only an active life in the practice of arms can lead to a greater honor, and is in Montalvo's view the proper background for effective kingship. It is true that in *Il Cortegiano* the practice of arms is likewise considered the principal profession of the courtier, but there is hardly any mention of how one performs in battle or handles a weapon. The courtier is only a knight in theory; in practice his status and honor are expressly related not to his prowess as a warrior but to the level of culture, refinement, and wisdom he can master and exhibit at court.

Honor is what the courtier constantly seeks. For the courtier honor is not a code of behavior or a set of principles but the good opinion of his peers and superiors: "quell'universal favore che tanto s'apprezza,"[1] "il consorzio degli omoni nobili."[2] These same beliefs and thoughts are also reflected in many treatises of the period,

---

[1] Bk. I, chap. xxi, p. 118.
[2] Bk. I, chap. xix, p. 114.

notably in *Dialogo dell'onore* by Giovanni Possevino, who perceives "honor" not as a quality inherent in the human condition but derives from "l'opinion de gli huomini"[1]—a view that stands in direct contrast with the Judian-Christian concept of personal honor stressing moral character and inner worth. Castiglione goes as far as discouraging the courtier from performing "notable" and "brave" deeds unless other great men, especially the prince, are there to witness them:

> Dee discretamente procurar di appartarsi dalla moltitudine e quelle cose segnalate ed ardite che ha da fare, farle . . . al cospetto di tutti i piú nobili ed estimati omini . . . e massimamente alla presenzia e, se possibil é, inanzi agli occhi proprii del suo re o di quel signore a cui serve . . . estimo che . . . sia male defraudar se stesso del debito onore e non cercarne quella laude, che sola é vero premio delle virtuose fatiche.[2]

In addition, sounding very much like Machiavelli, Castiglione urges the courtier to follow the way of the fox and employ all his arts or any other means he deems necessary to create a favorable impression and thus win honor and praise:

> Consideri ben cosa é quella che egli fa o dice e 'l loco dove lo fa, in presenzie di cui, a che tempo, la causa perche lo fa, la etá sua, la professione, il fine dove tende e i mezzi che a quello condur

---

[1] Giovanni Battista Possevino, *Dialogo dell'honore* (Vinegia: Gabriel Giolito de Ferrari, 1556), p. 11.

[2] Bk. II, chap. viii, pp. 200-1.

lo possono; e cosí con queste avvertenzie s'accomodi discretamente a tutto quello che fare o dir vole.[1]

In his *Prince*, Machiavelli gives a similar formula for success:

It is unnecessary for a prince to have all . . . good qualities . . . but it is very necessary to appear to have them. Therefore it is necessary . . . to have a mind ready to turn itself accordingly as the winds and variations of fortune force it, yet as I have said above, not to diverge from good if he can avoid doing so, but if compelled, then to know how to set about it . . . Men judge generally more by the eye than by the hand. . . . Everyone sees what you appear to be, few really know what you are, and in the actions of all men and especially of princes, which is not prudent to challenge, one judges by the result.[2]

Leonard Mades, calling attention to Messer Federico's statement "In dishonorable things, we are not obliged to obey anyone,"[3] insists that Castiglione does not altogether fail to recognize honor as a code of behavior. John S. White argues convincingly that "even this line of reasoning based on ethical considerations . . . is seen exclusively from the perspective of public opinion, for

---

[1] Bk. II, chap. vii, p. 200.

[2] Niccoló Machiavelli, *The Prince and the Discourses* (New York: The Modern Library, 1950), p. 65. The translation of this passage is taken from Mortimer J. Adler & Charles Van Doren, *Great Treasury of Western Thought* (New York: R. R. Bowker Co., 1977), p. 69.

[3] Mades, p. 171.

Castiglione stresses in this context particularly that 'good' and 'bad' are relative values."[1]

The conception of honor as a quality external to the individual and stemming from universal acclaim rather than from intrinsic worth is connected, as Burckhardt explains, to the spirit of competition, deep-rooted individualism, and great "passion for fame" of the Renaissance man. Honor perceived as fame was a view also prevalent among ancient and medieval thinkers but it could not be pursued to the detriment of one's moral character. Plato, for one, states, "He who is really good (I am speaking of the man who would be perfect) seeks reputation with, but not without the reality of goodness."[2] Aquinas also says. "Honour is given to man on account of some excellence in him and consequently it is a sign of testimony of the excellence that is in the person honoured."[3] Castiglione, however, seems to be unaffected by these and other precedents. His statement in *Book II* that "many things which are evil seem at first sight good and many seem evil and yet are good,"[4] appears to be less in harmony with traditional thought and more in line with Machiavelli's doctrine of "the effectual truth of things,"[5]

---

[1] *Renaissance Cavalier* (New York: Philosophical Library, 1959), p. 20.

[2] Plato's Laws, XII, 950A. Quoted in Mortimer J. Adler & Charles Van Doren, *Great Treasury of Western Thought*, ed. cit. p. 65.

[3] *Summa Theologica*, I-II, 2, 2. Quoted in Mortimer J. Adler & Charles Van Doren, p. 69.

[4] "Vero é che molte cose paiono al primo aspetto bone, che sono male, e molte paiono male e pur son bone" (Bk. II, chap. xxiii, p. 226). Machiavelli expresses the same thought with the following words: "If one considers well, it will be found that some things which seem virtues would, if followed, lead to one's ruin, and some others which appear vices result in one's greater security and wellbeing." (Machiavelli, p. 57)

[5] *Ibid.* See also Cian, ed. *Il Cortegiano*, fn. p. 171.

a view with which Castiglionie was more familiar and was more fitting to patterns of Italian culture during that period. For Castiglione as for Machiavelli, it is the outcome, not the intention or the means, that validates any action or performance. Their recommended path to success is not based on any objective order but on flexible standards of ethics, whose soundness is validated by the "effective results," and especially in the case of the courtier, by the praise and recognition he can muster irrespective of inner worth or "virtue."

In contrast, the concept of honor in *Amadis* combines both worldly fame and inherent goodness. In the first place, "honor" in *Amadís*, like in the *Courtier*, is tied to the idea of good reputation, but in the Amadisian romance it is recognition arrived through individual prowess in arms rather than a series of beautiful appearances and it is kept alive only by ongoing activity and service. This message comes clearly across when Amadís, living a life of temporary idleness in the *Insola Firme*, similar in many ways to the life of dignified otiosity of the courtier, fears for the possible loss of his good name:

Quedó en la Insola Firme Amadís con su señora al mayor vicio y plazer que nunca cauallero, estuuo . . . a cabo de algún espacio de tiempo, Amadís tornando en sí, conosciendo que ya aquello por suyo sin ningún contraste lo tenía, començó acordarse de la vida passada, quánto a su honrra y prez fasta allí auía seguido las cosas de las armas, y como estando mucho tiempo en aquella vida se podría escurescer y menoscabar su fama, de manera que era puesto en grandes congoxas, no sabiendo que fazer de sí.[1]

Secondly, "honor" in *Amadís* is associated with inner worth, unrelated to the esteem and judgment of others. When a group of knights say to Beltenebros: "Paréscenos, cauallero que essas vuesstras armas mas son defendidas con palabras fermosas que con esfuerço del coraçon," he answers, "Uos me tened por qual quisierdes . . . que por cosa que me digáys no me quitades la bondad si alguna en mí ay."[2]

In brief, both concepts of honor—1) as "worldly fame," the remuneration of good deeds, and 2) as an immanent God-given quality that manifests itself outwardly through man's moral conduct—are amply mirrored in Montalvo's test. In the *Courtier*, on the other hand, honor is perceived chiefly as the praise of others, regardless of the means used to achieve it, a view that mirrors currents of political thought and the intellectual milieu of Italy of the time. Moreover, Amadís' idea of honor as a possession more important than life itself, "más le valdría la muerte que en vergüença buiir,"[3] later a constantly recurring theme in the drama of the Golden Age,[4] is equally absent in Castiglione's text.

---

[1] IV, cxxvii, pp. 1, 244. See also María Rosa Lida de Malkiel, *La idea de la Fama en la Edad Media Castellana* (México: Fondo de Cultura Económica, 1952), p. 261.

[2] I, lv, 456.

[3] I, iv, 40. See also p. 27 of this sgudy.

[4] Americo Castro in "Algunas observaciones acerca del concepto del honor en los siglos XVI y XVII," *Revista de Filología Española*, Vol. III (1916), p. 3, says: "el honor y la fama son idénticos; la pérdida de la honra es análoga a la pérdida de la vida consistiendo la honra en la buena fama, para conservarla hay que sigilar los actos que puedan motivar mala reputación."

The *Courtier's* close adherence to the cultural currents of the age is even more revealing if one considers Castiglione's philosophical treatment of the love theme. As it was noted earlier in the chapter, the tenets of *amour courtois* enunciated in the *Art of Courtly Love* by Andreas Capellanus are central to the concept of love in both the *Courtier* and *Amadís*. In both of these texts, as in Andreas', "love" is perceived as a source of inspiration, ennoblement, and self-worth.[1] Castiglione, however, carries these ideas somewhat further in the last pages of his *Fourth Book* of the *Courtier* by superimposing to the theoretical enunciations of Andreas' doctrine, the Neoplatonic philosophy of love and beauty that by the beginning of the sixteenth century, mainly through the works of Ficino and Pico, had become pervasive in all aspects of Italian culture and artistic life. Interestingly, Montalvo in *Amadís* had also modified and reconciled Capellanus' doctrine with Spanish moral standards by superimposing to the lax morality of the *Art of Courtly Love* Christian ethics and attitude. But while in *Amadís* love is exalted consistently throughout the text as the foundation of social order, family life, and union in marriage, in the *Courtier's* final discourse and summation it becomes nothing more than a sheer aesthetic experience, leaving no possibility of union between the lover and his lady.

In the words of Pietro Bembo, one of the most distinguished interlocutors of *Il Cortegiano*—often referred to by critics as the "highest priest of Renaissance Platonism"[2] and author of *Gli Asolani*, a Renaissance

---

[1]   See chapter 1 of this study, pp. 35-55, for a discussion of "courtly love."

[2]   Sir Thomas Hoby, *Baldassare Catiglione, The Book of the "Courtier"* from the Italian with introduction by Walter Raleigh (New York AMS Press, Inc., 1967), p. lxix.

courtly imitation of Plato's Symposium—"love" is but a
certain desire to enjoy Beauty: "Amor non é altro che un
certo desiderio di fruit la bellezza."[1] For the courtier, he
says "love" is only the starting point for his ascent toward
greater perfection and the physical beauty of the beloved,
the nexus et colligation, with beauty itself the very essence
of God:

> Vorra servirsi di questo amore com d'un grado
> per ascendere ad un altro molto più sublime. . . .
> Non più la bellezza particular d'una donna,
> ma quella universale che tutti i corpi adorna,
> contemplará.[2]

> E rapita dal splendor di quella luce comincia ad
> infiammarsi e tanto avidamente la segue, che quasi
> diviene ebria e fuor di se stessa, per desiderio
> d'unirse con quella, parendole aver trovato l'orma
> di Dio, nella contemplazione del quale, come nel
> suo beato fine, cerca di riposarsi.[3]

Once the courtier has reached such a state of perfection,
the beloved has no more purpose or meaning in his life:
"Onde offuscato da questo maggior lume, non curerá
il minore, ed ardendo in piu eccellente fiamma, poco
estimará quello che prima avea tanto apprezzato."[4]

---

[1] Bk. IV, chap. 11, p. 514. On "Beauty" and "Love" see Schiller, pp. 56, 113-15,
   124, 125. See also Edmund Burke, *A Philosophical Inquiry into the Origin
   of our Ideas of the Sublime and the Beautiful*, ed. J. J. Bouton (London:
   Routledge; New York: Columbia University Press, 1958).
[2] Bk. IV, chap. 67, p. 534.
[3] Bk. IV, chap. 67, p. 536.
[4] Bk. IV, chap. 67, p. 535.

During the Renaissance, the Platonic philosophy of love, states Walter Raleigh, "had become part of the common inheritance of knowledge; from Florence the cult of Plato spread all over Italy. . . . And of all Plato's works the *Dialogues* concerning Love and Beauty were strongest in their appeal to the mind of the Renaissance."[1] The doctrine of love and beauty set forth in Plato's *Dialogues*, especially the *Symposium* and the *Phaedrus*, was elaborated first in Plotinus' *Enneads*[2] in the third century, and was later assimilated in various ways and to various extents in the poetry of Guinizelli, Cavalcanti, Dante, and Petrarch. In the fifteenth century it found its best expression in Ficino's *Commentary* on Plato and Pico's *Commentary* on Benivieni's *Canzone dell'Amore Celeste e Divino*. Ficino's and Pico's ideas became then the basis for the sixteenth century *trattato d'amore* of which Bembo's *Gli Asolani, Dialoghi d'Amore* of Leon Ebreo, and Mario Equicola's *Libro di Natura d'Amore*, among many others, are classic examples.[3] Castiglione's *Il Cortegiano* is not a *trattato d'amore* per se; indeed, its main purpose was to frame the perfect courtier, but it contains the leading arguments and conventional attitudes outlined in the typical sixteenth-century love treatise. It appears, nonetheless, that his treatment of the Platonic philosophy is not one of personal conviction but one of applied art.

In the *Courtier*, the pragmatic application of the Platonic doctrine is implicit in Bembo's assertion that mystical love should be another adornment in the

---

[1] Sir Thomas Hoby, p. lxx.

[2] Albert Hofstadter, ed., *Philosophies of Art and Beauty: Selected Readings from Plato to Heidegger* (New York: The Modern Library, 1964, p. 141.

[3] Robb, p. 198.

perfection of the gentleman, a beautiful solution, so to say, to the expression and sublimation of sensual love, especially in the elderly courtier.[1] Bembo's eloquent speech on platonic love and his suggestion that such love without "mixture of bitterness or regret" be heeded by the experienced and knowledgeable courtier, advanced in years and adviser to the prince, is in fact an aesthetic yet conveniently applicable solution to both Ottaviano's plea that the elderly courtier not be deprived of the happiness of loving,[2] and to Gaspar's concern that *il cortegiano non giovane* might be faced with mockery and contempt if he should display with the ladies courtesies and refinements attractive in the young yet unbecoming in the elderly.[3]

That the author of the *Courtier* is entertaining the idea of platonic love strictly from an artistic point of view rather than from personal perspective is even more apparent if one considers his qualified approval and excuse of sensuality in the young: "Io estimo che, benché l'amor sensuale in ogni etá sia malo, pur ne' giovani meriti escusazione, e forse in qualche modo sia lecito . . . purché in esso mostrino gentilezza, cortesia, e valore."[4] Undoubtedly Castiglione's effort to assign the Platonic doctrine an appropriate role in the courtier's final drive for self-stylization has contributed much to giving the figure of the courtier an air of irreality, a feature that contrasts with the more human and earthly portrayal of the lover embodied in Amadís. This process also underscores the lack of serious commitment on the part of Catiglione to explore the human significance and the social relevance

---

[1]   Bk. IV, chap. 1, p. 513.
[2]   Bk. IV, chap. 49, p. 512.
[3]   Bk. IV, chap. 49, pp. 511-2.
[4]   Bk. IV, chap. 54, p. 519.

of the sentimental relationship between the sexes. The treatment of love in the *Courtier* thus appears to be narrow in scope; it lacks the pervasiveness that the sentiment has in *Amadís* where in the words of Menéndez y Pelayo love is "centro de la vida, el inspirador de toda obra buena."[1]

The study of the love theme in *Il Cortegiano* would be incomplete without some mention of the ideal lady envisioned by Castiglione and her constructive role in the development of the courtier's personality. Cesar Gonzaga states that there could be neither court nor courtier without court lady:

> Corte alcuna, per grande che ella sia, non pó aver ornamento o splendore in se, né allegria senza donne, né cortegiano alcun essere aggraziato, piacevole e ardito, né far mai opera leggiadra di cavalleria, se non mosso dalla pratica e dell'amore e piacer di donne.[2]

As to her physical and moral characteristics, basically the same qualities embodied in Oriana: beauty, natural grace, tenderness, faithfulness in love, noble birth, prudence, discretion, refinement of manners are also ascribed by the *magnifico* to the *dona di palazzo*. In his words, the perfect lady must excel in "la nobiltá, il fuggir l'affettazione, l'esser aggraziata da natura . . . l'esser di boni costumi, ingeniosa, prudente, non superba, non invidiosa."[3] She must also distinguish herself in "magnanimitá, continenzia . . . l'esser bona e discreta" and must possess "una certa affabilitá piacevole, per la

---

[1] Origenes de la Novela, pp. 353-4.

[2] Bk. III, chap. 3, p. 340.

[3] Bk. III, chap. v, p. 343.

quale sappia gentilmente intertenere ogni sorte d'omo con ragionamenti grati ed onesti."[1] Like Oriana, the courtier's lady displalys *mesura*, a certain golden mean of reserve and tact being neither too bold nor too bashful, gracious yet not too gracious, easy yet not too easy: "Le bisogna tener una certa mediocritá difficile e quasi composta di cose contrarie, e giunger a certi termini a punto, ma non passargli."[2]

The *magnifico*, repeating almost exactly the same warnings of Montalvo to the ladies and damsels of *Amadis* says, no woman "yet unmarried" should allow herself to fall in love unless there is a definite possibility of marriage, and he adds that physical gratification outside the boundaries of marriage is forbidden if a woman wishes to protect "quella fama d'onestá che tanto importa."[3]

Where the *donna di palazzo* differs from Oriana and the ladies of chivalrous romances in general is in her intellectual and artistic preparation. Like the courtier, she is well versed in literature, music, painting, and in the entertaining arts: "Voglio che questa Donna abbia notizia di lettere, di musica, di pittura, e sappia danzar e festeggiare."[4] In her education, greater emphasis is also placed on aesthetic refinement and conscious control of impulses, dissimulation, and the use of *sprezzatura*:

---

[1] ??

[2] Bk. III, chap. 5, p. 343. An analysis of how the idea of the "golden mean: became part of the concept of the "perfect gentleman" during the Middle Ages and later in the Renaissance period is given in the study of A. D. Menut, "Castiglione and the Nicomachean Ethics," *PMLA*, Vol. LVIII (1943), pp. 309-21.

[3] Bk. III, chap. 56, p. 418.

[4] Bk. III, chap. 9, p. 349. On the feminine qualities of Oriana, see chapter 1, pp. 53-54 of this study.

deve questa donna aver iudicio di conoscer quai
sono quegli abiti che le accrescon grazia . . .
conoscendo in se una bellezza vaga ed allegra,
deve aiutarla coi movimenti, con le parole e con
gli abiti . . . e tenendosi delicata e polita mostrar
sempre di non mettervi studio o diligenza
alcuna.[1]

In addition, her vocation as housewife and mother
is subordinate, to a greater degree than the women of
Amadís, to her role of lady of society. Typically, Signora
Emilia Pio, described by Castiglione as *maestra di tutti*
for her wit and discretion fiercely protests against the
fashioning of an ideal woman whose attention centered
mainly on "cooking and spinning": "Che non sappia far
altro che la cugina e il filare."[2]

Although less cultured and somewhat more restrained
than the ladies of the *Courtier*, on the whole the women
of Lisuarte's court show also considerable intelligence,
knowledge, and charm, and do not limit their activities
strictly to domestic tasks. For instance, in *Amadís* we
often find Queen Brisena gracefully and intelligently
entertaining the company of men and enjoying their
esteem and admiration:

Fablaba con ellos en mulchas cosas; mostrándoles
amor como aquella que sin falta era una de las
dueñas del mundo que más sesudamente hablaba
con hombres buenos, por causa de lo cual muy
preciada e amada era no solamente de aquellos
que le concocían, mas aun de los que le nunca

---

[1]   Bk. III, chap. 8, p. 348.

[2]   Bk. II, chap. 99, p. 332.

> vieran, que esta tal preeminencia la humanidad
> en los grandes tiene, sin que otro gasto en ello
> pongan mas de los que la virtud y la nobleza a
> ello les obliga.[1]

Thus, except for somewhat higher degree of intellectual sophistication and aesthetic refinement of the *donna di palazzo*, there seems to be little difference between the ideal of the lady portrayed in the *Courtier* and the one portrayed in *Amadís*. There is, however, one trait that distinguishes the Amadisian model from her Italian counterpart, and that is her deep-rooted religious sentiment. Expressions such as *plugo a Dios, assí Dios me ayude, Dios mande que sea por bien, en vuestro querer y voluntad pongo y dexo todos mis trabajos y angustias*[2] are recurring terms in the diction of Oriana, and by and large are representative of the fervent devotion toward God that characterizes the damsels and ladies of Montalvo's novel.

The same attitudes and feelings of religiosity are not less alive in the knights and princes of *Amadís*. There is rarely a page in the text or a remark made by Amadís in which the name of *Dios* does not appear either in form of an invocation or in thanksgiving. Amadís often prays: "Hizo su oración ante el altar rogando a Dios."[3] He has faith and fears God. He says to Arcaláus: "Mi muerte . . . está en la voluntad de Dios, a quien yo temo"[4] upon entering the arch of "los leales amadores, santiguóse e encomendóse a Dios."[5] He is devoted to the Virgin Mary:

---

[1]   I, xxiii, 108.
[2]   I, xxxviii, 297; I, xvii, 154; II, lvi, 471; IV, cxiii, 1, 121.
[3]   I, iv, 45.
[4]   I, xviii, 170.
[5]   IV, cxxv. 1. 231

"Fincados los ynojos en tierra . . . dixo, Señora Virgen Maria . . . me encomiendo que me accoráys con vuestro glorioso Fijo."[1] Even his brother Galaor, less orthodox in matters of religion and morality, shows himself to be a good Christian. He says, "Hoy he oido misa e vi el verdadero cuerpo de Dios."[2]

In the *Courtier*, references to theological or religious concepts are by far fewer than in Montalvo's text. In chapter 32 of the *Fourth Book*, Ottaviano Fregoso refers to piety as a quality desirable in all men but especially in the prince: "Direi come dalla giustizia ancora dipende quella pietá verso Idio, che é debita a tutti, e massimamente ai principi."[3] Castiglione then continues to elaborate on the need for religiousness in the prince but does not expand on or emphasize piousness in the courtier. The prince, he says, must love and honor God, and besides being truly religious, he should be watchful not to succumb to superstition or heed the influence of the supernatural, an element that is pervasive and often guides the action in *Amadís* and in chivalric romances in general:

> Non lasserei ancora di recordare al principe che fosse veramente religioso, non superstizioso, né dato alla vanitá d'incanti e vaticini, perché aggiungendo alla prudenza umana la pietá divina e la vera religione, avrebbe ancor la bona fortuna e Dio protettore, il qual sempre gli accrescerebbe prosperitá in pace ed in guerra.[4]

---

[1] II, xlv, 375.

[2] I, xi, 93.

[3] I, xi, 93.

[4] Bk. IV, chap. xxxii, pp. 487-8.

The above passage is at the basis of Cian's condemnation of those critics who tend to exaggerate the secular spirit of the *Courtier* or negate the existence of any religious sentiment among the intellectual elite of the Italian Renaissance. He says:

> Troppo si é esagerato e si continua ad esagerare nel discorrere dello scetticismo e perfino della irreligiositá degli Italiani nell'etá del Rinascimento. Che il sentimento religioso, nelle persone piu colte, nelle classi pui elevate e piu raffinate, nei circoli di corte e fra i letterati, non fosse profondo e vivo come nel Medio Evo, e che troppo vi si mescolasse la superstizione e il vano formalismo é indubitato; ma da questo a negarne l'esistenza o a vedere un generale scetticismo, ci corre.[1]

Wayne Rebhorn points out that another area of the *Courtier* which presents theological implications is the theme of *grazia* outlined in Bembo's Neoplatonic oration and the portrayal of the courtier as endowed with the possession of human qualities suggesting "moral wholeness and innocence" and "evoking harmony with the natural order." At the conclusion of his analysis, Rebhorn states that in spite of the "implicit power and suggestiveness" of these ideas, Castiglione's courtier, who lives in Urbino not the Garden Eden, "embodies all the characteristics peculiar to his culture and appears as a consummate artist and performer" more than "a natural man" or religious ideal.[2] Nevertheless, he continues, as a result

---

[1]   Cian, ed. *Il Cortegiano*, fn. 22, p. 444.
[2]   Rebhorn, p. 44.

of the image the courtier acquired in Bembo's discourse, he was able to affect the members of his culture, "men who were still deeply responsive to Christian archetypes and who might otherwise never have granted Castiglione's ideal the central place is assumed in their lives."[1]

From the preceding analysis it is clear that many of the traits that define the courtier also characterize the knightly ideal in *Amadís*. They are both of noble birth, handsome in appearance, and in perfect physical condition. They excel in handling weapons and horses and are fond of hunting. They also share the qualities of loyalty to their lord, discretion in speaking, courtesy, good manners, and gallantry with women. Other attributes common to both are modesty, humility, temperance, fortitude, courage, sense of honor, prudence, piety, and wisdom. Amadís, however, embodies certain characteristics that are distinctive of every Spanish *caballero*," whether medieval or of the Renaissance or of the Golden Age.[2] He has a deeper religious sentiment and a more marked sense of honor than the Italian counterpart. He also shows a tenderness of heart, an exuberant humanness, and a wealth of feelings that set him apart from Castiglione's ideal. The courtier, in contrast, is endowed with a broader education. He is a student of the classics; he speaks several languages; he is well versed in the sciences, history, and government; and he is the sage adviser of the prince. The courtier is also a platonic lover, a skilled painter, an accomplished musician; he plays various instruments and possesses a higher degree of aesthetic sensibility and refinement. Constantly engaged in a process of self-creation and perfecting, he is a master in the art of *sprezzatura* and a model of self-restraint and

---

[1]   *Ibid.* p. 45.

[2]   Marshall, p. L.

composure. Eminently individualistic and self-pleasing, he shows an intense interest in the enjoyment of life and in the world he believes to have inherited from above. He also displays an unmatched skill in telling witty jokes and stories, playing all types of parlor games, and entertaining with virtuosity all kinds of audiences and company.

The Presence of the "Courtier" in Spain

That the skills and ideals of the courtier will later, during the sixteenth century and during the Golden Age, become part of the Spanish conception of *el caballero perfecto* is evident from a survey of the courtly didactic literature that followed the arrival of *Il Cortegiano* in Spain. Although one cannot exactly determine the extent of the courtier's influence in the development of the Spanish prototype of the knight-gentleman-scholar, it appears that only after the publication of Castiglione's work there seemed to be in Spain sufficient interest in ascribing to the courtly gentleman the refinement of literary and artistic education.

In 1529, a year after the publication of the *Courtier* in Venice, Antonio de Guevara published *Libro del Emperador Marco Aurelio con Relox de Príncipes*. "Although nowhere in the work," says Pauline Marshall, "does the author choose one character and gives him ideal qualities, it is possible by becoming various characteristics which he records as admirable . . . to get a fair ideal of what Guevara's gentleman would have been."[1] Among the outstanding aspects of his education is that he "strive to learn all that sages know" and that he "study music,

---

[1] Marshall, p. xii.

grammar, eloquence, philosophy, law, painting, drawing, fencing, cosmography and the sciences."[1] In another work, *Despertador de Cortesanos* (1539), Guevara also views education as the distinctive quality of the gentleman. He says, "No hay en el mundo tan heroico, ni tan provechoso ejercicio como es el del hombre que se da al estudio."[2] This book, says Alvarez de la Villa in his introduction to the text,

> tiene su ascendiente literario inmediato en una obra del Conde Baltasar Castiglione. . . . Es una guia práctica del perfecto cortesano tal cual debe ser si ha de triunfar en la corte . . . Están reglamentados todas las cosas de cortesanía con los caballeros, las dumas, los eclesiásticos. Toda la galandería complicada y ultraexquisita de aquel tiempo caballeresco tiene su código en esta obra . . . Tiene por esta razón un gran valor de crónica, de cosa vivida y vista, tales como las prisas de los cortesanos por triunfar, los medios empleados, las maneras de aposentimiento.[3]

Another text of the epoch that attempts to define the gentleman-scholar is *El Scholástico* (1538) by Cristóbal de Villalón. Although in *Prohemio*, the author denies any imitation of Castiglione, his portrayal of *el perfecto caballero* is one of scholarly preparation. "El scholástico," he says, "deue ser adornado de saber muchas ciencias y

---

[1] Marhsall, p. xiii.

[2] Antonio de Guevara, *Despertador de Cortesanos* (Paris: Sociedad de Edicioines Luís Machaud), p. 44.

[3] *Ibid.*, p. 15.

artes,"[1] and "Tenga noticia de la música, de la pintura, de la architetura, de la cosmographía, agricultura y astrología."[2] He must learn law, medicine, theology, and eloquence, and avoid above all affectation in speaking.[3] Like the courtier, *el scholástico* must also place great emphasis on the art of feigning, on giving a good impression of himself, and on speaking at the proper place and time: "Se deue proueher de saber muchas cosas . . . por dar apariencia de grande estima."[4] He must learn "artes y sciencias para engendrar de si buena opinión"[5] and "deue hablar en el lugar y tiempo donde se requieren o se ofreçen los donaires y graçias."[6] He must also excel in "dezir motes y graçias sabrosas y apazibles y a decir cuentos fabulas y façeçias."[7] He must possess all of these qualities "para el augumento de su estima, utilidad y buena opinión."[8]

El Scholástico was soon to be followed by the publication in 1561 of *El Cortesano* by Luis Milán, who in his dedicatory letter to Philip IV openly declares to have imitated Castiglione's work:

> Este caballero armado cortesano que por presente doy, hize de la manera que diré: hablándome con ciertas damas de Valencia que tenían entre

[1] *El Scholástico* (Madrid: Clásicos Hispánicos, 1967), p. 208.
[2] *Ibid.*, pp. 208-9.
[3] *Ibid.*, p. 168.
[4] Antonio de Guevara, *El Scholástico*, ed. Alvarez de la Villa, p. 208.
[5] *Ibid.*, p. 208.
[6] *Ibid.*, p. 219.
[7] *Ibid.*
[8] *Ibid.*

manos el *Cortesano* del conde Baltasar Castillon
dizeron que me parescía del, yo les dije:

Mas querría ser vos conde
Que no don Luis Milán
Por estar en esas manos
Donde yo querría estar
Respondieron las damas:
Pues haced vos un otro, para que
Alleguéis a veros en las manos
Que tanto os han dado de mano.[1]

Milán, like Castiglione, presents his *cortesano* as *sabio y valoroso*,[2] adviser to the prince,[3] and unaffected in his speech,[4] but most of all, he reiterates, the traditional qualities of the Spanish *caballero*: he must avoid "todas las ocasiones por donde les puede venir deshonra"[5] and he must be truly religious, always remembering in Milan's own words, that "Omnis vita Christi actio nostra est."[6] As to the fidelity of Milan's work to the court life of the period, the following appraisal of his work is given in the introduction to the 1874 edition:

Es una exacta descripción de las costumbres
y maneras de vivir, de aquella epoca en el
palacio del duque de Calabria, pinta también, y

---

[1]   D. Luis Milán, *El Cortesano: Libro de Motes de Damas y Caballeros* (Madrid: Imprenta y Estoreotipia de Aribau, 1874), p. 15.

[2]   *Ibid.*, p. 461.

[3]   *Ibid.*, p. 459.

[4]   *Ibid.*, p. 460.

[5]   Milán, p. 452.

[6]   *Ibid.*, 451.

admirablemente por cierto, la sociedad de entonces haciendo figurar en su libro no personajes ficticios, sino lo más escogido de los nobles poetas valencianos; es en una palabra, la resurrección del siglo XVI, y hace pasar ante nuestra vista los saraos, fiestas y trajes de su tiempo.[1]

In addition to the texts already mentioned there are during this period a few other Spanish works in manuscript form that deal with the ideal gentleman. Among them are Francisco Manzon's *Del Perfecto Cortesano* and *El cortesano puesto en practica* by Francisco Fernández de Ixar.[2] From all indications, the impact of these and other minor works on the framing of a Spanish prototype of the sixteenth-century *caballero* seems to be quite negligible.

Apart from having given stimulus to this kind of literature and having thus contributed to a redefinition of the Spanish perfect gentleman, Castiglione's model also played an important role by its direct influence on the lives of many Spanish noblemen, some of whom eagerly strived to reach the heights of human perfection embodied in the courtier. One young aristocrat who translated Castiglione's ideal into a plan for living was Gracilaso de la Vega, often acclaimed by poets, historians, and critics as *el más perfecto caballero* of the Spanish Renaissance. In a letter to Doña Geronima Palova de Almogavar, Garcilaso recommends the *Courtier* to the most distinguished gentlemen and ladies of the time with these words:

Una de las cosas de que mayor necesitad hay, doquiera que hay hombres y damas principales,

---

[1] *Ibid.*, p. vi.

[2] *Ibid.,* p. 10. See also Marshall, fn. p. xvi.

es de hacer, no solamente todas las cosas que en aquella su manera de vivir acrecientan el punto y el valor de las personas, mas aun de guardarse de todas las que pueden abajalle. Lo uno y lo otro se trata en este libro tan sabia y tan cortesamente que me parece eque hay que desear en el sino vello cumplido todo en algun hombre y . . . en alguna dama.[1]

That Garcilaso was eager to fulfill within his own person the very ideal that he recommended to others is evident from a study of his life and works. He was himself a gentleman of noble birth. Among his ancestors were Fernan Pérez de Guzmán, author of *Generaciones y semblanzas*, and Don Íñigo López de Mendoza, Marqués de Santillana.[2] According to Fernández de Navarrete, his biographer, Garcilaso received the finest humanistic education: "Estudió las buenas letras y arte liberales y cultivó su lengua nativa con el auxilio de las lenguas sabias. Hablaba el griego mas culto y ático, el latín, el toscano, y el francés . . . desde los tiernos años de la ninez."[3] He was well-versed in music and played various instruments. Fernández de Oviedo in his *Batallas* calls Garcilaso *gentil músico de harpa*, and Herrera in his *Anotaciones* says "fue muy diestro en la música, en la

---

[1] Teresa Suero Roca, ed. *El Cortesano*, trans. Juan Boscán (Barcelona: Editorial Broguera, S. A.), p. 59.

[2] Fernández de Navarrette, *Vida del celebre poeta Garcilaso de la Vega,* in *Coleccion de documentos inéditos para la Historia de España*, XVI (Madrid): 1850), pp. 11-22. Garcilaso de la Vega, *Obras*, ed. Tomás Navarro (Madrid: Clásicos Castellanos, de "La Lectura," Tomo III, 1924), p. viii.

[3] Navarrete, p. 13.

vihuela y arpa."[1] He had a handsome appearance and good manners: "En el hábito del cuerpo tuvo justa proporción, porque fue más grande que mediano, respondiendo los lineamentos y compostura a la grandeza."[2] Cienfuegos in his biography of St. Francisco de Borja says of Garcilaso: "Era garboso y cortesano con no sé que majestad envuelta en el agrado del rostro que le hacía dueño de los corazones no más con saludarlos y luego entraban su elocuencia y su trato a rendir lo que su afabilidad y gentileza habían dejado por conquistar."[3]

Garcilaso was also skilled at arms and a great warrior in the emperor's army. Herrera calls him "exercitadíssimo en la disciplina militar."[4] And in the words of Navarrete, Garcilaso was especially able "en manejar la espada y sujetar un caballo."[5] Cienfuegos also describes him as "el más osado en arrojarse al peligro."[6] Garcilaso, himself, in the *Third Egloga*[7] alludes to his life of warrior and poet:

> Entre las armas del sangriento Marte,
> do apenas hay quien su furor contraste,
> hurte del tiempo aquesta breve suma,
> tomando, ora la espada, ora la pluma.

---

[1] Garcilaso de la Vega, *Obras con Anotaciones de Fernando de Herrera* (Seville 1850), p. 14. See also Marcelino Menéndez y Pelayo, *Antología de poetas líricos castellanos*, Vol. XIV, p. xv.

[2] Tamaio de Vargas, *Garcilaso de la Vega natural de Toledo*, príncipe de los poetas castellanos Madrid: 1622), p. 4.

[3] Alvaro Cienfuegos, *La heroyca vida de S. Francisco de Borja* (Madrid: 1917), p. 49.

[4] Herrera, *Anotaciones*, p. 14.

[5] Marqués de Laurencín, *Documentos inéditos referentes al poeta Garcilaso de la Vega* (Madrid: 1915), p. 15.

[6] Cienfuegos, p. 51.

[7] The following quotations are from *Obras*, ed. Tomás Navarro.

Like the courtier, Garcilaso is both a lover in the tradition of *amour courtois*:

> El amor me aflige y me tormenta,
> y en el ausencia crece el mal que siento,
> > (Elegía II, vv. 71-2)

> Por vos nací, por vos tengo la vida,
> por vos he de morir y por vos muero.
> > (Soneto V, vv, 13-4)

> Mirad bien que el amor se desgrada
> deso, pues quiere que el amante viva
> y se convierta a do piense salvarse.
> > (Canción I, vv. 17-9)

and also a platonic lover:

> ¡Oh bienventurado, que sin ira
> sin odio, en paz estás, sin amor ciego
> con quien acá se muere y se sospira;
> y en eterna holganza y en sosiego
> vives, y vivirás cuanco encendiere
> las almas del divino amor el fuego!
> > (Egloga I, vv. 289-294)

> Gracias al cielo doy ya del cuello
> del todo el grave yugo he sacudido
> y que del viento el mar embrevecido
> veré desde la tierra sin temello.
> > (Soneto XXXIV, vv. 1-4)

Garcilaso is also master of *sprezzatura*. From Naples Bembo writes to Garcilaso, who had invited him to comment on some of his poems: "Nada he leído en nuestros días que haya sido escrito con más elegancia, sencillez y pureza, ni ciertamente con más sublimidad."[1] But no writer has left us with a better and more complete picture of Garcilaso, the perfect courtier, than Tamayo de Vargas:

> La trabazón de los miembros igual, el rostro apacible con gravedad, la frente dilatada con majestad, los ojos vivísimos con sosiego, y todo el talle tal, que aun los que no le conocían, viéndole le juzgaran facilmente por hombre principal y esforzado, porque resultaba de una hermosura verdaderamente viril; era prudentemente cortés y galán sin afectación y naturalmente sin cuidado, el más lucido en todos los generos de ejercicios de la corte y uno de los caballeros más querido de su tiempo; honrado del Emperador, estimado de sus iguales, favorecido de las damas, alabado de los extraneos y en todos en general.[2]

Another area in which Castiglione might have influenced Spanish courtly society is in the sphere of social diversions. One of the distinctive features of Spanish life during the second part of the sixteenth century is the rapid growth and popularity of the *academias* as a means of social entertainment. It appears that the festive aura and playfulness that permeate the meetings of Spanish literary academies during this period, many of which eagerly sought and encouraged the presence and participation of women, seem at least to have some connection with the

---

[1]   Menéndez y Pelayo, *Antología de poetas líricos castellanos*, Vol. XIV, p. lix.

[2]   Tomayo de Vargas, *Garcilaso*, p. 4.

atmosphere of conviviality and the debating techniques entertained by the interlocutors of the *Courtier*. The idea of a group of ladies and gentlemen forming a sort of union and gathering for the purpose of amusing themselves in debating various questions, either as an academic exercise or as a social diversion, is not new. It has its precedents in the *Filocolo* and in the *Decameron* of Boccaccio.[1] But the fact that the same questions wittingly debated in the *Courtier*—e.g., Who loves more, the young or the old? Are all the things beautiful also good? Can love exist without jealousy? What is the right kind of entertainment? What games are most suitable? And many more—began shortly after the publication of *Il Cortegiano*, to be similarly entertained and methodically treated in the discussions and debates at the meeetings of "Los Nocturnos" at Valencia and "Los Humildes," "El Parnaso," "La Selvaje," "La Imitatoria," and "La Peregrina" at Toledo, Seville, and Madrid,[2] point to the real possibility that the *Courtier* did have a significant impact on the cultural climate of the Spanish academies during the second half of the sixteenth century and afterward.

Another indication of Castiglione's influence on Spanish forms of social diversions is apparent in the fact that many details in the *Courtier* dealing with the topic of *facezie* were incorporated in several manuals of behavior of the time and in particular in the *Galateo Español* by

---

[1] Thomas F. Crane. *Italian Social Customs of the Sixteenth Century and Their Influence on the Literature of Europe* (New Haven: Yale University Press, 1920), p. 592.

[2] For an account of the activities and the impact of the Italian academies on the Spanish *academias* see *Boletín de la Real Academia Española*, Tomo I, Cuaderno I, Feb. 1914. Also see chap. 6, "Academias," in D. Felipe *Picatoste, Estudios sobre la Grandeza y decadencia de España* (2 vols.; Madrid: Imprenta de la Viuda de Hernando Y Cª, 1887), Vol. I, pp. 91-106.

Gracián Dantisco, a text that enjoyed wide popularity among Spanish fashionable society.[1] Particularly those chapters of *Galateo Español* dedicated to "los 'motes y burlas' y 'al hablar continuado,'" says Margherita Morreale, coincide with "los avisos de comportamiento social" outlined by Castiglione.[2] Moreover she adds, "los capítulos del *Galateo* dedicados a la materia de la risa han de colocarse en la línea de la influencia del *Cortesano*."[3]

But the real influence of the *Courtier* on Spanish culture, says Leonard Mades, is not to be sought in the area of social customs and manners but in the field of literature and ideas in general. The *Courtier*, in Mades' words,

> contributed to the tendency of Spanish novelists, including Cervantes, to indulge in moral digressions in their works. It was an important source for Spanish treatises and dialogues on love and the Renaissance cult of women. It was a major influence on Spanish poetry. It left its mark on the drama. The poet Herrera's commentary on the poetry of Garcilaso and Boscán reveals that the discussion of love and beauty in the *Courtier* is the key to his love poems. Boscán's poetry—*La historia de Leandro y Hero*, for example—shows the influence of the golden mean as expounded in the *Courtier*. Torres Naharro's *Comedia Aquilana* has been

---

[1] Lucas Garcían Dantisco, *Galateo Español* ed. Margherita Morreale ("Consejo Superior de Investigaciones Científicas," Madrid: Clásicos Hispánicos, 1968), p. 1.

[2] *Ibid.*, pp. 29-30.

[3] *Ibid.*, p. 48.

shown to have been influenced by Bembo's speech. Some of Lope de Vega's plays, among them *La cortesía de España* and *El príncipe perfecto*, portray the Spanish gentleman in ways strongly reminiscent of the *Courtier*.[1]

Several other critics have addressed themselves to the question of the *Courtier's* influence on Spanish letters. Among them, Arturo Marasso in *Cervantes: la invención del "Quijote"* points to *Il Cortegiano* as the model of Spanish lyric poets and mystics.[2] Otis Green studies the Platonic echoes of Castiglione in *Boscán*.[3] Pauline Marshall examines the impact of the *Courtier* on the drama of Lope de Vega and on Salas Barbadillo's *El Caballero perfecto*.[4]

The influence of the *Courtier* was also heavily felt in other countries of Europe. In England, for example, "The court of Gloriana modelled itself on the famous company of Urbino."[5] Sir Thomas Hoby, the distinguished translator of the *Courtier* and a model gentleman himself, calls Castiglione's text "a storehouse of most necessarie implements for the conversation, use, and trayning up of man's life with Courtly

---

[1] Mades, p. 17.

[2] Arturo Maraso, *Cervantes: la invención del "Quijote"* (Buenos Aires: Biblioteca Nueva, 1947), p. 205.

[3] Otis H. Green, "Boscán and *Il Cortegiano*: The Historia de *Leandro y Hero*" in the *Literary Mind of Medieval and Renaissance Spain* (Lexington, Ky.: The University Press, 1970), pp. 133-140.

[4] Marshall, pp. xi-li.

[5] Wilhelm Schenk, "The *Cortegiano* and the Civilization of the Renaissance," *Scrutiny*, XVI (1949), p. 100.

demeaners,"[1] and Dr. Johnson calls it "the best book that was ever written on good breeding."[2] In France, *Il Cortegiano* had a similar success. Its first translation, attributed to J. Chaperon, appeared in 1537, and it has been shown to have contributed much to the definition of *bonne grace* and the concept of *l'honnete homme* of the seventeenth century.[3] Pauline Smith says:

The *Cortegiano* enjoyed a very considerable success in French court circles during the latter half of the reign of Francois I. In an apologia of court life presented to the king in 1543, the *Discours de la Court*, the author Claude Chappuys echoes approvingly, confident no doubt of the approval of those for whom his work was intended, certain precepts laid down by Castiglione for the guidance of the would-be perfect courtier, while during the reign of Henri II, a flourishing court society tended more and more to the ideal of social politeness—l'honnetêté in the seventeenth-century parlance—implicit in the *Cortegiano*.[4]

Another critic, Thomas F. Crane states that "it is impossible to mention the multitude of works which were

---

[1]   Lawrence Lipking, "The dialectic of *Il Cortegiano*," *PMLA*, 81 (1966), p. 355.

[2]   Crane, p. 206.

[3]   Pauline Smith, *The Anti-Courtier Trend in Sixteenth-Century French Literature* (Genéve: Librairie Droz, 1966), p. 26.

[4]   *Ibid.*, p. 124.

called into existence by the *Courtier*."[1] It is often cited as being the cornerstone for Spenser's *Fairie Queene* and Henry Peachman's *Compleat Gentleman*. Other authors often mentioned to have been inspired in a number of ways by Castiglione are Shelly, Marlow, Corneille, Schiller, Lessing, and Ibsen. Perhaps the most fitting commentary to Baltesar Castiglione are the words of Torquato Tasso in a passage of his *Dialogo della Corte*: "Mentre dureranno le Corti, mentre dureranno i principi, le donne e i cavalieri insieme si raccoglieranno, mentrre valore e cortesia avranno albergo negli animi nostri, sará in pregio il nome del Castiglione."[2]

Anticourtier Trends

But just as there were those who enthusiastically welcomed Castiglione's ideal of courtliness, there were those who vehemently condemned it for its lack of touch with reality. The *Courtier* portrayed a world that stood in dramatic contrast with "the background of violence and insecurity, of lawlessness in ill-lit streets, of murder, bloody riots, and open prostitution"[3] of the epoch. Even the very entertainment of court society at this time, states John R. Hale, was often characterized by merciless slaughter and inhumanity:

> Broken limbs were commonplace in the tournaments and mock fights were popular diversions in city squares and even death was

---

[1]   Crane, p. 206.
[2]   Cian, ed. *Il Cortegiano*, p. v.
[3]   John H. Hale, *Renaissance* (New York: Time Inc.), p. 58.

not unusual. It was a time of savage torture, of public manglings of criminals; more than one chronicler describes football games played with heads of executed prisoners of war. Combats between wild beasts were popular spectacle . . . When on one occasion in Florence, a stallion was loosened in a group of mares, some of the tens of thousands of spectators were indignant, but one diarist wrote that "this was the most marvelous entertainment for girls" . . . Lorenzo de Medici himself wrote obscene carnival songs and fresco painters decorated the palaces of great patrons with scenes that would raise most modern eyebrows.[1]

Beautiful as it was, the courtier's ideal could not remain unchallenged in this climate of duplicity, of "violence and refinement," of "coarseness and reserve."[2] In fact it soon became one of the major targets of satire within an already copious literature of protest against the courtly way of life that was thought to be pretentious and hypocritical.[3]

In Italy the first denunciation of the *Courtier* came in *La Cortegiana* (1534) by Pietro Aretino. In this satirical comedy, the author portrays Messer Maco, a foolish and wealthy gentleman from Siena who travels to Rome with the intention of becoming a cardinal and meeting a fine mistress. He soon falls in love with Camilla, a courtesan who was being kept by a Spanish lord, and concludes

---

[1] *Ibid.*

[2] *Ibid.*

[3] Benedetto Croce discusses the anticourtier literature in Italy in "Libri sulle Corti," in *Poeti e Scrittori del pieno e del tardo Rinascimento* (Bari: Laterza, 1958), pp. 198-205.

that only if he were a master in the art of courtship could he win her. In this, Maco seeks the help and instruction of Maestro Andrea, a charlatan who claims to be a consummate courtier. Andrea, reading from a textbook on courtly manners in an apparent allusion and mockery of Catiglione's *Courtier*, teaches Messer Maco to deceive, to flatter, and to feign.[1]

A similar attack on the *Courtier* was also launched in France by Phylibert de Vienne in his work *Le Philosophe de Court*. He mocks the courtier and describes the civility and courtesy of the Italian as "nothing other than the perfection of the art of dissimulation and the unscrupulous control and concealment of all ambitions and emotions."[2]

The anticourtier trend in European literature, says Pauline Smith, has its literary precedents and thematic background in the satirical and moral writings of classical antiquity, mainly in the *Eunuchus* of Terence and Lucian's *De Parasito* and *Rhetorum Praeceptor*.[3] This tradition was later continued during the early Renaissance, notably in *De Curialium Miseriis Epistola* by Aeneas Piccolomini and in *Aula Dialogus* by Ulrich von Hutten.[4] In the period following the publication of Castiglione's text, the attacks on the courtier became even more frequent and intensified. This hostility, however, seems to derive more from historical and political events than the influence of literary precedents. The greater demand for military manpower during the Italian campaigns, conducted at this time by Francis I and Charles V, had brought about a

---

[1] Pietro Aretino, *The Courtesan*, trans. Samuel Putnam (New York: Charles Scribner's Sons, 1926)

[2] Dickens, p. 50.

[3] Smith, p. 13 and 19.

[4] Smith, p. 20.

large increase in what was previously considered a small and select group of courtiers. These newcomers, many of whom were adventurers motivated by greed and even simple mercenaries, "combined the faults and vices of both the courtier and the soldier and their presence was obnoxious to the populace between campaigns when the army was idle and were equally redundant at court. Frequently insolvent, they lived on gifts and pensions from the king."[1] In addition, the acceleration of the trend toward absolutism of the French and Spanish monarchies, the consolidation of the central authority in the figure of the king, the institution of stricter rules of protocol, and the formalization of public functions and ceremonies, had made court life, during this period in particular, dependent on a large entourage of courtiers, many of whom served no useful function and contributed nothing to the economy.

The presence of this rapidly expanding class of privileged beings, who were often accused of engaging in lavish entertainment subsidized by the king at the expense of the poorer working class, fuelled even more anticourtier feelings and resentment. The fact that women began to be viewed as an essential adornment of the court and that the arts and literature and many frivolous pastimes, rather than the administration of government and justice, became increasingly a primary activity of the courts of great monarchs and princes of the Renaissance provided additional reasons for the mocking of both the courtier and the court.[2]

---

[1]   *Ibid.*, p. 58.

[2]   For an account of the social and economic conditions of Spain during this period, see chap. 7, "King and Court" and chap. 7, "Splendor and Misery" in J. H. Elliot, *Imperial Spain*, ed. cit., pp. 245-264; 281-316.

It is apparent that *Il Cortegiano* could not have reached the public at a worse moment. Torquato Tasso pointed to the courtier's main weakness when he remarked that there existed a wide discrepancy and found almost no direct connection "tra i cortegiani della realitá e l'ideal di Castiglione."[1] Giuseppe Toffanin, in his study *Il Cinquecento*, states that Castiglione was a romantic more than a humanist, and in his assessment of *Il Cortegiano* he often alludes to what he calls "l'elemento chimerico," "l'astratta cortigiania" of the *Courtier* and "la creazione di un ideale estraneo ai grandi problemi del suo tempo."[2]

Undoubtedly Castiglione's recommendation that the courtier use all his skills and knowledge to enhance his reputation and that he employ whatever other means he had at his disposal to achieve success in his endeavors underscored the selfish utilitarian nature of his character and helped to make the courtier's ideal even more suspect. Similarly Castiglione's view of the art of dissimulation and its application in promoting an "impression" of inner worth and graciousness where none existed also contributed to make the courtier's ideal readily identifiable with the ambiguous political morality advocated in Machiavelli's *Prince*. Finally Castiglione's strong suggestion that the courtier show great flexibility—that he adjust his taste and accommodate his whole personality to the prince's wishes—must have helped to establish for the courtier an unpleasant connotation of duplicity and servility. These thoughts and perceptions undoubtedly served to place the courtier under an unfavorable light.

In Spain the main criticism of the courtier and his profession, as well as the condemnation of the vices,

---

1   Croce, *Poeti e Scrittori*, p. 204.

2   Giuseppe Toffanin, *Il Cinquecento* (Miltano: Vallardi, 1950), pp. 235-245.

discomforts, and dangers of court life are found in Antonio de Guevara's *Menosprecio de Corte y Alabanza de Aldea* (1539), a work that enjoyed great popularity in Italy[1] and especially in France where in the period between 1542 and 1568 there were no fewer than twenty-six editions.[2]

In *Menosprecio* Guevara contrasts the life of the courtier at court with that of the country gentleman and praises the retirement and the bucolic setting in which the latter lives. There are in Guevara's text constantly recurring references to Horace's "beatus ille" in the form of reflections such as "O quám bienventurado es aquel," "O Bendita tú, aldea, y bendito el que en ti mora," "O felice vida de la aldea,"[3] but most of his remarks and comments are directed at condemning the "physical degeneration and the moral regression which court life promotes and encourages."[4] He portrays the court as the place where "es la virtud muy trabajosa de alcanzar y muy peligrosa de conservar" and where "más dan al chocarrero porque dixo una gracia, al truhán porque dixo a la gala, á la gala, al bien hablante porque dize una lisonja, á una cortesana porque da un favor . . . que á un criado que sirve toda su vida."[5]

In his prologue and dedicatory he says to have personally witnessed what he describes in his book:

---

[1]   Croce, *Poeti e Scrittori*, p. 198.

[2]   Smith, p. 33.

[3]   Guevara, *Menosprecio* (Madrid: Ediciones de "La Lectura," 1539) pp. 106, 122, 126.

[4]   Smith, p. 34.

[5]   Guevara, *Menosprecio*, pp. 148, 167.

He dado esta cuenta á vuestra Alteza, muy alto
príncipe, para que sepáis que todo lo que dizere
en este vuestro libro este, vuestro siervo no lo ha
soñado ni aún preguntado sino que lo vió con sus
ojos, paseó con sus pies, tocó con sus manos y
aún lloró en su coraç'on; por manera que le han
de creer como á hombre que vi lo que escribe y
experimentó lo que dize.[1]

Guevara also describes his total transformation at court
from a man of integrity to a man of vices and sins:

Fui a la corte inocente y tornéme malicioso, fuí
sincerisimo y tornéme doblado, fuí verdadero
y aprendí a mentir, fuí humilde y tornéme
presumptuoso, fuí modesto y hízeme voraze, fuí
humano y tornéme inconversable, finalmente
digo que fuí vergonçoso y allí me derramé y fuí
muy devoto y allí me entibié.[2]

The denunciation of court life and the anticourtier trend
in Spanish literature continued unabated during the second
half of the sixteenth century as the economic conditions
of the country deteriorated and the social discontent
increased. The criticism and satire of the court and its
courtiers continued in the seventeenth century and became
an essential part in Cervantes' *Don Quijote*, which will be
the subject of the next chapter.

---

[1]   *Ibid.*, p. 41.
[2]   *Ibid.*, p. 235.

CHAPTER III

The Courtier And Courtliness
In *Don Quijote*

The Critics' Appraisals

Cervantes, in his works, never mentions by name either Castiglione or *Il Cortegiano*, yet there is considerable agreement among critics that Castiglione's work played an essential part in Cervantes' writings in general, and in *Don Quijote* in particular.

It was Américo Castro who perhaps first among modern scholars called attention to specific thematic links between the two authors. Castro attributes to the influence of the *Courtier* much of Cervantes' doctrinal material and treatment of topics including those dealing with the subject of "arms and letters," Neoplatonic philosophy, the fashioning of the perfect prince, the avoidance of affectation, and prudence over emotions.[1]

In discussing Cervantes' position and attitude toward fencing, Castro writes: "Tal doctrina es típica del Renacimiento, y la hallamos en el *Cortesano* de Castiglione repertorio maravilloso de temas renacientes,

---

[1]   Americo Castro, *El Penamiento de Cervantes* (Madrid: Herando, 1925), pp. 144, 148, 154, 180, 213, 217, 223, 224, 317, 343.

cuya acción sobre Cervantes fué muy sensible aunque nadie lo haya estudiado."[1] This statement by the Spanish critic was both point of departure and stimulus for the study of Ernesto Krebs, who uncovered substantial evidence in *Don Quijote* of what he calls *el espíritu* that is at the basis of the *Courtier*'s argument and discussion. Krebs' findings outlining the various points of contact and dissimilarities between the two authors are gathered in his study *"El Cortesano" de Castiglione en España* in which he makes approximately more than fifty references to Cervantes, most of them to *Don Quijote*.[2]

Another critic, Joseph Fucilla, in *The Role of the Cortegiano in the Second Part of Don Quijote*,[3] after concisely reviewing Prof. Krebs' analysis, also seeks to establish some parallels between Cervantes' and Castiglione's text. Fucilla's short commentary centers for the most part on the connection between the theme of *burle* in the *Courtier* and the *burlas* played on Don Quijote and Sancho at the ducal palace, which are, in his view, a reenactment of the *Courtier*'s doctrinal material. In addition, he traces certain content relationships between the advice imparted to the prince in the *Courtier* and Don Quijote's admonishments to Sancho before and during his mock government in the island of "Barataria." At the conclusion of his study, Fucilla remarks: "The stimulus of the Italian treatise is more or less continuously present, moulding the narrative and exerting powerful influence

[1]   *Ibid.*, p. 61.
[2]   Ernesto Krebs, "El Cortesano de Castiglione en España," *Boletín de la Academia Argentina de Letras*, vol. VIII, 1940, pp. 93-146, 423-35; IX, 1941, pp. 135-42, 517-43; X, 1942, pp. 53-118, 689-748.
[3]   Joseph Fucilla, "The Role of the Cortegiano in the Second Part of *Don Quijote*," *Hispania*, XXXIII (1950), pp. 291-6.

in the elaboration of a goodly section of the great masterpiece."[1]

Arturo Marasso also believes that the *Courtier* was a source of inspiration for Cervantes. He refers to the theme of *burlas* and to the Platonic doctrine of love as basic common grounds for the two authors.[2] In his mention of the episode at the palace of the *duques*, he states: "*El Cortesano* de Castiglione ofrece un elegante código palaciego a Don Quijote. No lo olvida siquiera para señalar una palabra mal sonante, caída en desuso."[3]

Some connection between the *Courtier* and *Don Quijote* is also alluded to by E. C. Riley in *Cervantes: teoría de la novela*.[4] Specifically he cites Don Quijote's effort to mold, like the courtier, his personality, and translate his own life into a work of art by imitating Amadís' behavior and deeds. Riley calls Don Quijote's *instinto artístico* one of the prime movers of his heroism.[5]

At present, the most extensive and up-to-date analysis of the relationship between *Don Quijote* and the *Courtier* is found in *The Armor and the Brocade* by Leonard Mades. In his study, Prof. Mades deals extensively with those aspects of *Don Quijote* "which come to light when we compare it with the *Courtier*" and with "the underlying relationship between the two works as they relate to some of their central themes."[6] As the author himself states, his work is "concerned principally with those elements in *Don*

---

[1]   *Ibid.*, p. 295.

[2]   Arturo Marasso, Cervantes: *La invención del "Quijote"* (Buenos Aires: Colección Academus, 1947), pp. 126, 203.

[3]   *Ibid.*, p. 116.

[4]   E. C. Riley, *Cervantes: teoría de la novela* (Madrid: Taurus, 1962), pp. 28, 111, 176, 226, 241, 320, 335.

[5]   *Ibid.*, p. 71.

[6]   Mades, p. 7.

Quijote and the *Courtier* which are antagonistic" since "it is these which have chiefly suffered neglect."[1]

The present chapter is an attempt to focus on Cervantes' attitude toward courtiership and particularly toward the courtier's pursuits, aspirations, and lifestyle. It also aims at providing at least a partial analysis of how the courtier's proverbial talents and stereotyped characteristics and his fame of mind are reflected and also satirized in many of Don Quijote's assumed courtly postures and behavioral patterns.

Don Quijote as a Courtier

That Cervantes in *Don Quijote* is concerned with expressing his feelings toward courtship is evident from the many direct references and allusions to courteous behavior and courtly qualities that he assigns, sometimes in jest and sometimes in earnest, to many characters of his novel. Although the first part of *Don Quijote* is not lacking in references to the courtier and his ideals, it is mainly in part 3 that there seems to be a constant and insistent preoccupation by the author to attribute to Don Quijote courtly traits and to portray him involved in situations or engaged in activities more descriptive of the stereotyped courtier than the typical knight-errant. It appears, in fact, that in part 2 Cervantes is deliberately pursuing the characterization of Don Quijote as a courtier-knight who has "temporarily forsaken the military life for that of the court."[2] Quite clearly the author's intention here, as it will be discussed later, is not to uphold the lifestyle and

[1]   *Ibid.*, p. 22.
[2]   *Ibid.*, p. 228.

aspirations of the courtier, but to satirize the fundamental premises upon which the courtier bases his existence and profession.

Although Cervantes does not frown at Don Quijote's courteous disposition and gentlemanly behavior, it is by and large in a fictitious manner and with the purpose of achieving certain ironic and artistic effects that he repeatedly and persistently presents the hidalgo as overflowing with courtesy. For instance, Don Quijote is again and again described as "comedido y cortés," "con gentil continente y denuedo," "con gentil donaire y gallardía," "con gentil continente y donaire."[1] Sancho calls him "el más cortés bien criado caballero que hay en toda la cortesanía."[2] The curate describes him as "la flor y la nata de la gentileza."[3] Oriana, in a sonnet to Dulcinea, praises him as "comedido hidalgo."[4] The author also takes special interest in emphasizing that Don Quijote answers to the plea of Micomicona with "mucha cortesía y comedimiento," he holds the reign of the duchess' palfrey "de puro cortés y comedido," he greets Doña Cristina, the wife of the Gentleman of the Green Coat, "con mucha cortesía," and exchanges "muchas cortesías" with Álvaro Tarfe.[5]

---

[1] Miguel de Cervantes Saavedra, *Don Quijote de la Mancha*, ed. Martín de Riquer (Barcelona: Editorial Juventud, 1958). I, xxix, 295; I, iv, 59; I, xxiii, 224; II, xvii, 663. All quotations from *Don Quijote* are from this edition. Other editions consulted in this study are those of Diego Clemencín, Rodolfo Schevill and Adolfo Bonilla, and Rodríguez Marín. For complete entries see bibliography.

[2] II, xxxviii, 812.

[3] I, xxix, 297.

[4] I, Elogios, 31.

[5] I, xxix, 295, II, xxxiv, 790; II, xviii, 662; II, lxxii, 1054-5.

Moreover Don Quijote's courtliness is recognized by all who come in contact with him. Cardenio tells him "os agradezco las muestras y las cortesías que conmigo habéis usado," and the duchess remarks to Sancho, "Habéis aprendido a ser cortés en la escuela de la misma cortesía; bien parece . . . que os habéis criado a los pechos del Señor Don Quijote que debe ser la nata de los comedimientos y la flor de las ceremonias."[1]

From the tone, the form, and the context in which these remarks are made, it is quite obvious that Cervantes makes a deliberate effort to fictitiously assign to Don Quijote not just the military prowess generally associated with the knight-errant or Amadís, whose example and life the hidalgo wants to emulate, but also those qualities that more properly characterize the courtier-knight. Of particular interest in this connection is Don Quijote's unusual fickleness and preoccupation with his image as a courteous knight at the beginning of part 2. In his remarks to Sancho, Don Quijote emphatically asks his squire not only what people thought of his valorous deeds, but also of his "courtesy": "Dime, Sancho amigo: ¿ Qué es lo que dicen de mi por ese lugar? ¿ En qué opinión me tiene el vulgo, en qué los hidalgos y en qué los caballeros? ¿ Qué dicen de mi valentía, qué de mis hazañas, y qué de mi cortesía?"[2]

On the whole, when contrasted to part 1 of the novel, where allusions to the courtier and to courtliness are more "sporadic and incidental,"[3] it is not difficult to see that the author in part 2 unveils the picture of a more fashionable Don Quijote, increasingly concerned and absorbed in the

---

[1]   I, xxiv, 225; II, xxxii, 781.

[2]   II, ii, 554-5.

[3]   Fucilla, p. 295.

role and activities of the *caballero cortesano*, and less involved in the typical pursuits of the knight-warrior. Although in spirit Don Quijote remains, even in the second part of the novel, always committed to the defense of chivalric principles and fulfillment of his knightly obligations, the feats of courage and noble deeds that mark the action and control the pace in part 1, seem to be considerably diminished. Apparently, in the second part of the novel Cervantes is intentionally presenting Don Quijote with a distinct and more controlled set of circumstances and with a lack of opportunity for military involvement for the purpose of separating him, at least in part, from the knights of his fantasy and bringing him in close contact with the more down-to-earth brand of courtiership practiced by courtier-knights of the real world in which he lived and moved.

Interestingly, as Don Quijote gradually escapes the rigors of knight-errantry and meets the real-life knights of his time—represented to a degree in the characters of Don Diego in whose house "cuatro días estuvo don Quijote regaladíssimo,"[1] Basilio who treated both Don Quijote and Sancho "como cuerpos de rey,"[2] Don Antonio "caballero rico y discreto y amigo de holgarse,"[3] and most notably in the person of the *duque*, whose palace or *castillo* is more than once referred to as "casa de placer"[4]—his image as a knight-warrior seems to tarnish considerably and weaken. Indeed, it appears, especially during the visit at the ducal palace, as if Don Quijote were suffering from a loss of will and as if he were hastily and almost inadvertently

---

[1]   II, xviii, 669.

[2]   II, xxii, 696.

[3]   II, lxii, 998.

[4]   II, xxxi, 761.

swept into his hosts' lifestyle, sometimes with ironic and unexpected results.

Moreover, as Don Quijote becomes a participant in the leisure activities and courtly games staged by his new acquaintances, and as he does in more than one occasion exhibit traits or assume postures typical of *un caballero cortesano*, he also becomes quite obviously a parody of the courtier's pretentiousness and vanity, as well as a vehicle for Cervantes' social criticism. In view of the more chivalric content of *part 1* and the shift to a more courtly content in *part 2*, it is not unreasonable to conclude that Cervantes in the second part of his novel, more than pursuing the satire of Don Quijote's fantasies of heroic life, intended to stress the negative aspects of courtliness. In addition, without rejecting the gentleman's intellectual attainments and good manners, perhaps he also wanted, through the depiction of Don Quijote's newfound interest and naive acquiescence to courtly triteness and mannerisms, to ridicule the courtier's *raison d'etre* and the excess amateurism of his profession.

Cervantes' portrayal of Don Quijote as *caballero cortesano* is particularly highlighted in the description of the knight's visit with the *duque's*. From the very start of the episode, Don Quijote assumes the posture of a typical courtier: "Se gallardeó en la silla, púsose bien en los estribos y . . . con gentil denuedo fue a besar las manos de la duquesa."[1] Later, upon his arrival to the courtyard of the palace, two beautiful maidens threw a "cloak of sumptuous scarlet cloth"[2] upon his shoulders,

---

[1] II, xxx, 757.

[2] Miguel de Cervantes Saavedra, *The Ingenious Gentleman Don Quizote de la Mancha*, trans. Samuel Putnam (2 vols.; New York: The Viking Press, 1949), p. 709.

and others spilled scented water all over his body. He is then taken into a richly decorated room and he is helped by six damsels to disarm. Shortly after, Don Quijote, dressed in courtly garments, appears in the great hall, where following an elaborate predinner ritual he proceeds to wash his hands. Received in the dining hall with truly regal pomp by the *duque*, the duchess, and the ecclesiastic, Don Quijote participates first in an exchange of formalities and mutual compliments, and then, at the insistence of the duque, takes head of the table, while the bewildered Sancho watches in amazement the detailed ceremony and treatment to which his master most graciously submits himself.[1]

At the dinner table Don Quijote is so overtaken by the solemn procedures and so concerned with observing all matters of propriety and tact that as soon as Sancho opened his mouth and uttered a few words, he began to tremble and "púsose de mil colores,"[2] for fear of embarrassment. Thereafter, fearing further embarrassment by his squire, he begged the *duque* to "throw the fool out for he will continue to talk all kinds of nonsense."[3]

An even more striking and also humorous representation of Don Quijote as "the courtly gentleman" is given in the description of the elaborate after-dinner bathing, during which the knight, believing that to be the custom of the land, obediently stretches out his whiskers and allows several damsels not only to wash his beard in place of his hands but also to lather and to scrub his entire face with soap. As a result, "quedó Don Quijote can la

---

[1]   II, xxxi, 762-3.

[2]   II, xxxi, 768.

[3]   Cervantes, *Don Quixote*, ed. Samuel Putnam, p. 713.

más extraña figura y más para hacer reír que se pudiera imaginar."[1]

Seemingly, the mannerisms, vanity, and submissiveness to court formalities displayed by Don Quijote at the ducal palace thus far are more descriptive of the courtly gentleman than they are of the knight-errant or Amadís, Don Quijote's example and model. There are, however, other peculiar traits and patterns of behavior manifested by Don Quijote during his visit with the *duque* and the Duchess that set him apart from the heroes of chivalric romances and identify him more readily with the courtly gentleman. Undoubtedly the intellectual ability and vast learning exhibited by Don Quijote in his various conversations with his noble hosts bear him a closer resemblance to the courtier than to the knightly models of his choice. For instance, in his dialogue with the *duque* and also in his animated exchanges with the ecclesiastic, Don Quijote displays considerable familiarity with classical art and literature. He speaks of the brushes of Parrhasius, Timanthes, and Apelles, and of the chisel of Lysippus, as well of Ciceronian and Demosthene eloquence.[2] He also shows considerable versatility and knowledge in matters of philosophy, rhetoric, and language, all of which are further evidence of his erudition and distinguish him from the less book-learned and less cultured Amadís.

Another attribute distinctive of the courtier that Don Quijote flaunts at the *duque's* palace is the ability for poetic improvisation. He composes and recites his own poetry. The author takes a special interest in underscoring Don Quijote's poetic talent by offering an example of his

---

[1]   II, xxxii, 773.
[2]   II, xxxii, 775.

virtuosity as a poet: "Cantó el siguiente romance, que él mismo aquel día había compuesto:

-Suelen las fuerzas de amor
sacar de juicio a last almas
tomando por instsrumento
la ociosidad descuidada . . .[1]

No less remarkable is Don Quijote's musical skill and aptitude for singing. In a typical courtly posture, he plays the lute and serenades Altisodora.[2]

Equally reminiscent of *Il Cortegiano* and the courtier's lifestyle, types of entertainment, and actions are also Don Quijote's participation in the hunting trip in the immediate surroundings of the ducal palace and the time-worn allusion to the chase as "una imagen de la guerra."[3] Similarly, his open views on "arms and letters" expressed to the *duque* in the episode of "la Condesa Trifaldi,"[4] his remarks on duel and fencing formulated in response to the discourteous and sudden departure from the dinner table by the clergyman,[5] his self-portrayal as a platonic lover,[6] and his assumed role as adviser to Sancho,[7] the governor-to-be of "insula Barataria"—all call to mind the figure and profession of the courtier.

---

[1] II, xlvi, 867.

[2] II, xlvi, 867-8.

[3] II, xxxiv, 791.

[4] II, xxxvi, 809.

[5] II, xxxii, 772.

[6] II, xxxii, 770.

[7] II, xlii, 839-48. For some thoughts on Don Quijote's advice to Governor Sancho Panza see Donald W. Bleznick "Don Quijote's Advice to Governor Sancho Panza," *Hispania*, XL (1957), pp. 62-4.

It is worth nothing that Cervantes' depiction of Don Quijote as a courtly gentleman is not restricted to the episode at the ducal palace but it is also pursued, although less emphatically, in other parts of the text, and not always with the purpose of parodying the interests and accomplishments of the courtier. In effect, since the first chapter of the novel, the author attributes to Don Quijote the cultural characteristics and attainments of the Renaissance gentleman well trained in the *humanae litterae*.[1] Indeed, only a humanist and a true intellectual would have sold the land he inherited from his ancestors for the purpose of buying books. Don Quijote's library covered a wide range of subjects, which reflects the variety of his interests and his love for learning and culture. But even more representative of his passion for knowledge is the conversation Don Quijote held with "el Caballero del Verde Gabán," in which he eulogizes the study of languages and letters, "Las cuales tan bien paracen en un caballero de capa y espada, y así le adornan y honran y engrandecen como las mitras a los obisbos o como las garnachas a los peritos jurisconsultos."[2]

Don Quijote at different occasions also demonstrates considerable knowledge in the field of ancient and contemporary literature as well as proficiency in Greek and Latin, "reinas de las lenguas."[3] He easily recalls literary facts and refers to Homer, Virgil, Tasso, Garcilaso, Boscán, and other classical and current authors.[4] He

---

[1] Leo Spitzer calls Don Quijote a true "version of a frustrated humanistic scholar." See "On the significance of *Don Quijote*," *Modern Language Notes*, vol. 77 (1962), p. 118.

[2] II, xvi, 650.

[3] II, lxii, 998.

[4] II, i, 547; II, viii, 593; I, xxv, 237; II, xvi, 650; II, xxxii, 775; II, lxii, 998; II, lxx, 1045.

himself is a student of modern languages: he boasts to know "algún tanto del toscano"[1] and also recites some of Ariosto's poems in that language. Don Quijote's own poetic ability is widely known and it is not limited to the previously cited composition to Altisodora. In the second chapter of part 1 we already find him improvising and reciting a few verses at the damsels of the *venta*, and later in Sierra Morena "escribiendo y grabando por las cortezas de los árboles y por la menuda arena muchos versos, todos acomodados a su tristeza y algunos en talbanza de Dulcinea."[2] His skill in matters of poetry is also recognized by his niece, who says of him "mi señor es poeta,"[3] and the same Don Quijote, in his remarks to Sancho in chapter 67 of part 2, identifies himself as "algún tanto poeta."[4]

Other signs of Don Quijote's cultural sophistication and aesthetic sensibility that bears him close resemblance to the courtier are his commentary on the principles of poetic composition, comedy, and drama,[5] his unusually vast vocabulary, his flair for words and ability to organize sentences, his familiarity with the rules of rhetoric and oratory, and his concern and interest in questions dealing with language appropriateness and usage. No less remarkable is Don Quijote's knowledge of history: Sancho calls him "zahorí de las historias."[6] Just as notable is also

---

[1]   II, lxii, 998.

[2]   I, xxvi, 252.

[3]   II, vi, 582.

[4]   p. 1027.

[5]   II, xvi, 650; II, xii, 617. See also Bruce W. Wardropper, "Cervantes' Theory of the Drama," *Modern Philology*, 52 (1955), pp. 217-21.

[6]   II, xxxi, 762.

the knight's familiarity with topics of theology, science, astrology, and medicinal herbs.[1]

Apart from his humanistic background, Don Quijote also shows, like the courtier, excessive concern with feigning his status and image. For instance, he assumes the title of "don," a mark of distinction and a privilege extended to nobles, not to hidalgos. Sancho clearly reminds his master of it when Don Quijote asks him to comment on how the people of their native village perceived his noble status or *hidalguía*: "Los hildalgos—responded Sancho—dicen que no conteniéndose vuestra merced en los límites de la hidalguía, se ha puesto 'don' y se ha arremetido a caballero."[2] On another occasion Don Quijote begs Sancho to put a bridle on his tongue and to think over any word he is about to utter that might reveal the baseness of his nature since the indiscretions of the servants much too easily reflect on their master's image and reputation:

> Sancho, que te reportes, y que no descubras la hilaza de manera que caigan en la cuenta de que eres de villana y grosera tela tejido. Mira, pecador de ti, que en tanto más es tenido el señor cuanto tiene más honrados y bien nacidos criados . . . que si veen que tú eres un grosero villano, o un mentecato gracioso, pensarán que yo soy algún echacuervos, o algún caballero de mohatra.

Another description of Don Quijote that is more suggestive of the attitudes and activities of the courtier

---

[1] I, xviii, 167; II, xxix, 752.

[2] II, ii, 555.

than those of the knight-errant is the knight's portrayal at the dinner table of his host Don Antonio Moreno. Here, at first, Don Quijote is depicted as "hueco y pomposo"[1] and extremely delighted at seeing himself treated with great ceremony and courtesy. Later, the author gives us a glimpse of Don Quijote experimenting, at the insistence of two ladies, with the courtly art of dancing, an activity for which he shows no aptitude or fitness.[2]

But among the various manifestations of the attitudes and character of the courtly gentleman that Cervantes skillfully and in a fictitious manner representes in the figure of Don Quijote, no other aspect of the hidalgo's life brings to mind his close association with the courtier than his yearning and strife to become the embodiment of an ideal.

For the courtier the very essence of life consists in realizing within himself the ideal of the perfect human being by molding his personality to the principles of art. In this pursuit he dedicates his energies to emulate the lives of great historical figures who have fulfilled within themselves the aesthetic and social qualities of the model gentleman. Indeed, he feels intensely stimulated by such great men like Cesar, Alexander, Scipio, and Hannibal, whose mental and physical abilities and military prowess he amply admires. Don Quijote undertakes a similar endeavor. His uncontrolled aspiration is to fashion his life to the ideals of knight-errantry and thus bend his will to the imitation of the great Amadís, a fictional hero, who in

---

[1] II, lxii, 988.

[2] II, lxii, 992-3. See also Adolfo Salazar, "Música, Instrumentos y Danzas en las obras de Cervantes," *Nueva Revista de Filologís Hispánica*, II (1948), pp. 118-73. Additional insights on the subject can be found in Charles Haywood, "Cervantes and Music" *Hispania*, XXXI (1948), pp. 131-51.

Don Quijote's mind is both symbol and embodiment of spiritual and moral perfection as well as military virtue. In this ongoing process of transformation and imitation, Don Quijote, like the courtier, aims at creating within his own person a new self that conforms to the rules of art and to the heart and mind of Amadís, knight-errantry's most distinguished hero. As Riley points out,

> Don Quijote se ha lanzado a su empresa movido por el ejemplo de los héroes fabulosos que ha conocido en sus lecturas. No hay nada exesivamente insólito en que trate de imitar la vida de algún heroe ejemplar o quiera emular como cortesano las mejores cualidades de los modelos anteriores. Pero lo que es digno de ser notado es que su manera de obrar se halla también muy próxima a la del artista.[1]

In general, it is not an exaggeration to state that Don Quijote, in the guise of the courtier, stylizes his life according to the artistic principles outlined by Castiglione. The following remarks of Don Quijote to Sancho, which for their importance are here quoted to some length, accurately capture the concept of art and artistic imitation of the author of *Il Cortegiano*:

> Cuando algún pintor quiere salir famoso en su arte procura imitar los originales de los más únicos pintores que sabe; y esta regla corre por todos los más oficios o ejercicios de cuenta que

---

[1] Riley, pp. 111-12. See also Karl R. Frederick, "Don Quijote as Archetypal Artist and *Don Quijote* as Archegypal Novel" in *Adversary Literature* (New York: Farrar, Straus & Giroux, 1974), pp. 55-67.

sirven para adorno de las repúblicas, y así lo ha de hacer y hace él que quiere alcanzar nombre de prudente y sufrido, imitando a Ulises en cuya persona y trabajos nos pinta Homero un retrato vivo de prudencia y de sufrimiento, como también nos mostsró Virgilio, en persona de Eneas, el valor de un hijo piadoso y la segacidad de un valiente y entendido capitán, no pintándolo ni describiéndolo como ellos fueron, sino como habían de ser, para quedar ejemplo a los venideros hombres de sus virtudes. Desta mesma suerte, Amadís fué el norte, el lucero, el sol de los valientes y enamorados caballeros, a quien debemos imitar todos a quellos que debajo de la bandera de amor y de la caballería militamos. Siendo, pues, esto ansí, como lo es, hallo yo, Sancho aimgo, que el caballero andante que más le imitare estará más cerca de alcanzar la perfección de la caballería.[1]

It is interesting to notice in this context that Don Quijote's "surrender to art," like that of the courtier, is deliberately and consciously undertaken. He thinks a great

---

[1] I, xxv, 237. Compare this passage with the remarks of Castiglione on the subject of artistic imitation addressed to those who criticized him for having given the courtier models more readily found in the world of fiction than in the world of realty: "Si come . . . é la idea della perfetta republica a del perfetto ré e del perfetto oratore, cosí é ancora quella del perfetto cortegiano; alla imagine dello quale s'io non ho potuto approssimarmi col stile, tanto minor fatica averanno i cortegiani d'approssimarsi con l'opere al termine e meta . . . e se con tutto questo non potrán consequir quella perfezion qual che ella si sia, ch'io mi son sforzato d'esprimere, colui che piú se le avvicinará sará il piú perfetto." B. Castiglione, *Il Cortegiano*, ed. Bruno Maier (Torino, 1964), pp. 76-7.

deal before selecting appealing and pleasant-sounding names for himself, his lady, and his horse; he is art-conscious when he meticulously prepares the details of his penance in the Sierra Morena. No less art-minded is his concern with the effects and impact of his actions on others, and his preoccupation to duplicating Amadís' gestures and movements, as well as his obsession to experience within his own person the inner thoughts and feelings of the legendary hero. Obviously, Don Quijote's compulsive desire to mold his life to that of a fictional model is not less art-for-art's-sake than the courtier's adjusting of his character to the principles of art and beauty.

That Don Quijote's imitation of Amadís aims at perfecting an art is implicit as Riley points out "en que Don Quijote lleva a cabo su tentativa más rebuscada y desesperada de vivir la ficción literaria. La imitación de Amadís carece de todo propósito racional fuera de la imitación por la imitacion misma."[1] This is quite evident in Sancho's remarks to Don Quijote in Sierra Morena when his master, after considering various alternatives and examples, unveils his plan to imitate Amadís' form of penitence:

> Paréceme a mí—dijo Sancho—que los caballeros que lo tal ficieron fueron provocados y tuvieron causa para hacer esas necesitades y penitencias; pero vuestra merced, ¿ qué causa tiene para volverse loco? Qué dama le ha desdeñado, o que señales ha hallado que le den a entender que la señora Dulcinea del Toboso ha hecho alguna niñería con moro o critiano?[2]

---

[1]   Riley, p. 116.

[2]   I, xxv, 238.

Equally revealing is Don Quijote's answer to Sancho: "Ahí está el punto . . . y ésa es la fineza de mi negocio . . . el toque está desatinar sin ocasión . . . Así Sancho amigo, no gastes tiempo en aconsejarme que deje tan rara, tan felice y tan no vista imitación."[1]

Quite fitting in this connection is Riley's comment at the conclusion of his analysis of "Don Quijote" and "la imitación de los modelos." In Don Quijote, he says, "Se mezclan a gran escala y sin moderación la emulación heroica, y el afán propio del cortesano."[2]

René Girard points out that Don Quijote, by pursuing to the letter a literary imitation, "has surrendered to Amadís the individual's fundamental prerogative: he no longer chooses the objects of his own desire—Amadís must choose for him."[3] Like the courtier, in fact, Don Quijote suffers from the desire to be "another." His patterns of behavior and aspirations are suggested and determined by the model. Seen in this light, Don Quijote, like the courtier, lacks spontaneity and displays an absence of originality in response to most exterior challenges and situations. His life, as in the case of the courtier, becomes a typical example of amalgamation to artistic and literary molds: in short, a pure case of plagiarism.

Another area of activity in *Don Quijote* that comes close and relates to the field of action of the courtier is that of role-playing. Taking a part and masking one's own identity is a pervasive activity among many of *Don Quijote's* characters, for instance, the barber, the curate,

---

[1]   *Ibid.*

[2]   Riley, p. 116.

[3]   René Girard, *Deceit, Desire, and the Novel: Self and Other in Literary Structure*, trans. Yvonne Freccero (London: The Johns Hopkins Press, 1969), p. 1.

Sanson Carrasco, all take on masks in their effort to bring Don Quijote back to his senses and return him to his village. Don Quijote himself is often portrayed as taking considerable delight in assuming a variety of postures and shifting roles. Frequently during the course of the novel he frees his personality for many kinds of transformation and role-playing, each bearing its own peculiar marks and purposes. He is also quite effective at changing his performance and adjusting his act according to the place, the time, and the circumstances that confront him. One illustration of Don Quijote's ongoing transformation is the constant shifting of names. At the beginning of the novel, he is at first described by the author as an old-fashioned gentleman of La Mancha diligently occupied in managing his estate and bearing the possible surname of Quixada or Quesada or most likely Quixana.[1] Later we meet him as Don Quijote, the knight-errant, the self-proclaimed embodiment and disciple of Amadís de Gaula. Then he appears as "el caballero de la Triste Figura" obsessed with impersonating Beltenebros.[2] And subsequently, he is "el caballero de los Leones";[3] he is a courtier in the palace of the *duques*, and later he even aspires to be "el pastor Quijotiz"; finally, he is Alonso Quijano "el Bueno."[4] These name changes all reflect different roles and also the character's separation from the names previously assumed.

Critics have often suggested that Don Quijote shows great skill in the art of dissimulation. Giovanni Papini in *Don Chisciotte dell'Inganno* holds the view that

---

[1]   I, i, 36.

[2]   I, xxi, 199.

[3]   II, xxvii, 659.

[4]   II, lxxiii, 1060; II, lxxxiv, 1064.

Don Quijote feigned his madness to obtain freedom of self-expression so that he could mock the world around him.[1] A similar thought is entertained by Mark Van Doren. Don Quijote, he states, "was first and last an actor, a skillful and conscious actor."[2] Obviously such a perception and characterization of Don Quijote as a performer brings him very close to the figure of the courtier whose role-playing and masking are an essential part of his living and survival.

That Don Quijote is well aware of his play-act is evident when Pedro Alonso, a neighbor from his own village, finds him ill-treated at the hands of the merchants and bends over to help him out. Pedro, after removing the visor of Don Quijote's helmet, recognizes him and insists on calling him "Señor Quijana" and not Valdovinos as the knight-errant had told him. Don Quijote's response clearly indicates that he is artfully and consciously engaging in role-playing: "Yo sé quien soy . . . y sé que puedo ser no sólo lo que he dicho, sino todos los doce Pares de Francia, y aún todos los nueve de la Fama."[3] In the episode of "Las Cortes de la Muerte," Don Quijote not only declares that in his youth had his eyes fixed on the stage, but that he was very fond of masks: "Desde muchacho fui aficionado a la carátula, y en mi mocedad se me iban los ojos tras la farándula."[4] For Don Quijote, as for the courtier, taking a role or the wearing of different masks was a convenient means for the experimentation with human capability and potential, and thus served as a vehicle for self-knowledge

---

[1]   Quoted in Manuel Durán, *Cervantes* (New York: Twayne Publishesrs Inc., 1974), p. 134.

[2]   Mark Van Doren, *La Profesión de Don Quijote* (Mexico: D.F., 1962), p. 13.

[3]   I, v. 63-4.

[4]   II, xi, 613.

and growth. Don Quijote himself points out to Sancho soon after their encounter with "Las Cortes de la Muerte" that nothing like the art of the theater depicts all the varied aspects of man's life and "shows more clearly . . . what we are or ought to be than plays and players."[1] Needless to say, the portrayal of Don Quijote as a skilled performer capable of playing a variety of roles offered Cervantes a wide range of possibilities to experiment with his own potential as an artist and his ability to present many different perspectives.[2]

Without doubt, the critic can draw other parallels, besides those already mentioned, between the stereotyped personality traits of the courtier and Don Quijote's characterization as a "courtly gentleman" at various and distinct stages of the novel. I believe, however, that the main points of contact between the two figures are found in that both follow a similar process of self-identification and self-creation through art.

According to Renaissance aesthetic theory, the two main goals of the artist were fidelity to a model and simultaneous idealization of that model.[3] It appears that Don Quijote and Castiglione's courtier, in their attempt to turn every moment of their life into a work of art by the imitation and sublimation of an ultimate ideal, come very close to embodying these two goals.

---

[1]   Cervantes, *The Ingenius Gentleman Don Quijote de la Mancha*, ed. Samuel Putnam (New York: Viking Press, 1949), p. 579.

[2]   On the subject of "multiple perspectives" in Cervantes, see Leo Spitzer, "Linguistic Perspectivism in *Don Quijote*," *Linguistics and Literary History: Essays in Stylistics* (Princeton: Princeton University Press, 1967), pp. 41-85.

[3]   Erwin Panofsky, *Idea*, trans. Joseph Peake (Columbia: University of South Carolina Press, 1968), p. 49. Also Anthony Blunt, *Artistic Theory in Italy, 1450-1600* (Oxford: Clarendon Press, 1940), pp. 17-8.

Although Don Quijote's imitative zeal is more dramatically portrayed, quite obviously both figures succumb to the power of suggestion of artistic life and ideals. As a consequence, the more they strive to refine their existence, the more they become detached from reality. It is, indeed, this farthering from life and detachment from the real world, symbolized in many of Don Quijote's character manifestations and assumed roles, that Cervantes satirizes in his novel. If Cervantes mocks Don Quijote's intemperate passion for knightly adventures and his often borrowed courtly postures, it is not because he rejects the ideals of chivalry, or for that matter the principles of civilized behavior, or the intellectual achievements of the Renaissance gentleman. Rather, his satire is directed to those who, as in the case of Don Quijote, pursue unattainable goals or engage in activities unrelated to the sordid realities of the world as it exists, and who, as in the case of the courtier, waste their existence in refining tricks of behavior or take on postures that have little or no connection with man's civility, moral goodness, social progress, and human brotherhood. For Cervantes, art carried to such an extreme is vanity, idleness, self-deception. No man, in Cervantes' view, is a perfect artist and a creator. To resign oneself to such an illusion without proper cognizance of reality betrays and corrupts man's spirit.

Cervantes' Attitude toward the Courtier

The preceding analysis, for the most part, concentrated on examining specific aspects and episodes of Cervantes' novel where Don Quijote appears in the guise of the courtier. It also centered on how the figure of the hidalgo and that of the courtier seem to share to varying degree certain modes of behavior and various intellectual and artistic personality traits. In light of Cervantes' concentrated effort to paint Don Quijote, at different stages of the novel, as feigning many of the courtier's peculiar qualities, it is most opportune at this point to examine the author's reasons for having Don Quijote assume courtly postures, and at times even wear the mask of the courtier.

It has often been suggested that one of the problems the student is confronted with in assessing or interpreting Cervantes' views on art, political, and social philosophy; human behavior; and life as a whole is the constant presence in his works in general, and in *Don Quijote* in particular, of shifting planes of reality. In *Don Quijote*, says William Bryon, "everything is true and nothing is true."[1] Like in *Don Juan* and in *Faust*, Don Quijote, states Melveena McKendrick, "is a shifting symbol of something easy to recognize but difficult to define."[2] And although no one would argue with Gary McEóin's assertion that an essential literary trait of Cervantes is "to offer the reader with the reactions of a variety of characters to a particular set of circumstances without indicating which if any of the views he himself held,"[3] and that generally "one must be slow to attribute to Cervantes as his personal opinion every statement he puts in the mouth of one of his characters,"[4] it appears that he leaves no doubt as to what

---

[1]   William Byron, *Cervantes: A Biography* (Garden City, N.Y.: Doubleday and Co., 1978), p. 431.

[2]   Melveena McKendrick, *Cervantes* (Boston: Little, Brown and Company, 1980), p. 5. See also Manuel Durán, *La Amibigúedad en el Quijote* (Xalapa: Universidad Veracruzana, 1960).

[3]   Gary McEóin, *Cervantes* (Milwaukee: The Bruce Publishing Co., 1950), p. 105.

[4]   *Ibid.*, p. 134.

are his attitudes toward courtliness and the courtier. In studying Cervantes' feelings toward the courtier one need not struggle or unravel hidden meanings. There are, in fact, several obvious hints and also many direct statements in *Don Quijote* that clearly reflect the author's disliking for the courtier and what he stands for.

Cervantes mercilessly ridicules Don Quijote whenever he assumes the pose of *caballero cortesano*. For instance, when the knight in his real and first experiment in courtliness meets the *duque* and the duchess, no sooner does he draw himself up in the saddle and "with a graceful ease of manner [ride] forward to kiss the duchess' hands,"[1] that he suffers a most painful embarrassment as he is about to dismount from his horse:

> se le asió un pie en una soga de albarda, de tal modo que no fue posible desenredarle; antes quedó colgado del con la boca y los pechos en el suelo . . . Descargó de golpe el cuerpo y llevóse tras sí la silla de Rocinante que debía de estar mal cinchado, la silla y él vinieron al suelo no sin vergüenza suya.[2]

Then muttering a few curses in his teeth to Sancho, who had forgotten to properly fasten the saddle and did not hold his stirrup, Don Quijote, limping and shaken by the fall, manages to come close and kneel in front of the distinguished couple.

---

[1] Samuel Putnam, ed. *Don Quijote*, p. 706.
[2] II, xxx, 759.

The laughter of the author is also quite evident as he describes Don Quijote's gullibility[1] and self-deception in assuming and thinking of himself as a courtier-knight. After several damsels help him to remove his armor,

> quedó Don Quijote . . . en sus estrechos gregüescos y en su jubón de camuza seco alto, tendido con las quijadas, que por dentro se beseban la una con la otra: figura, que a no tener cuenta las doncellas que le servían con disimular la risa—que fue una de las precisas órdenes que sus señores le habían dado—reventaran riendo.[2]

Moments later, he allows himself to be lathered, much to the amusement of all present:

> Mirábale todo los que presentes estaban que eran muchos, y como le veían con media vara del cuello más que medianamente moreno, los ojos cerrados y las barbas llenas de jabón, fue gran maravilla y mala discreción poder disimular la risa; las doncellas de la burla tenían los ojos bajos sin osar mirar a sus señoras; a ellos les retozaba la cólera y la risa en el cuerpo, y no sabían a qué acudir: o a castigar el atrevimiento de las muchachas o darles premio por el gusto que recebían de ver a don Quijote de aquella suerte.[3]

---

[1]   Bruce W. Wardropper believes that Cervantes' principal target of satire in *Don Quijote* is man's gullibility and human credulity; for his ideas on the subject see "Don Quijote: Story or History?" *Modern Philology*, LXIII (August, 1965), No. I.

[2]   II, xxxi, 764.

[3]   II, xxxii, 774.

Cervantes' mocking of Don Quijote, however, becomes even more biting when the knight, upon returning to his room after the day's festivities, discovers a hole in one of his stockings: "Desgracia indigna de tal persona," exclaims scoffingly the author, "se le soltaron . . . hasta dos docenas de puntos de una media que quedó hecha celosía . . . Afligióse en estremo el buen señor y diera él por tener allí un adarme de seda verde una onza de plata."[1] The next day Don Quijote is left with no choice but to wear a pair of traveling boots left to him by Sancho.

Don Quijote also becomes a laughing stock when he endeavors to show his talent in the courtly art of singing and dancing. Before Don Quijote sings to Altisodora the ballad he himself composed, the author takes special interest in making it known that the knight first "escupió y remondóse el pecho"[2] and then "con una voz ronquilla"[3] begins his song. Later in the text, at the house of Don Antonio, Don Quijote brings into view his skill at dancing: "Era cosa de ver," pokes humorously Cervantes, "la figura de don Quijote, largo, tendido flaco, amarillo estrecho en el vestido, desairado y sobre todo nada ligero."[4] Moments later we find Don Quijote "en la mitad de la sala en el suelo molido y quebrantado de tan bailador ejercicio."[5] Even Sancho, much more aware of his limitations than his master, jokingly pokes fun at Don Quijote's pursuit of the courtly pastime:

[1] II, xliv, 852.
[2] II, xlvi, 867.
[3] *Ibid.*
[4] II, lxii, 992.
[5] II, lxii, 993.

> -¡ Nora en tal, señor nuestro amo, lo habéis
> bailado! ¿ Pensáis que todos los valientes son
> danzadores y todos los andantes caballeros
> bailarines? Digo que si lo pensáis, que estáis
> engañado; hombre hay que se atreverá a matar
> a un gigante antes que hacer una cabriola. Si
> hubiérades de zapatear yo supliera vuestra falta,
> que zapateo como un girafalte; pero en lo del
> danzar no doy puntada.

Obviously, the picture that Cervantes paints of Don Quijote whenever he poses as a courtier or participates in courtly exploits is not a pretty one. Judging mostly from the incidents that take place during the knight's visit at the ducal palace and at the house of Don Antonio, Don Quijote, far from being the embodiment of the youthful, handsome, and graceful courtier, is more his negation.

At the same time that Cervantes humorously flaunts Don Quijote's inability to properly function as a courtier he also lays bare the vanity, unproductiveness, and uselessness of courtly life. By way of contrasting Don Quijote's mad yet irreproachable behavior and Sancho's noble comportment as governor with the attitudes and conduct of the *duque* and duchess, the high representatives of the nobility, intensively occupied in playing elaborate and sometimes cruel jokes at the expense of their guests, Cervantes not only was able to achieve great mastery in literary craftsmanship, but also succeeded in taking on the mask of the social critic and commentator.

The mistreatment, the indignities, and even the physical abuses that Don Quijote and Sancho so graciously endured in their dealings with the *duques* and their servants are, in fact, a sad commentary on the character, amusements, and way of life of the Spanish high nobility during that time.

Thus, not undeservedly, many critics have assigned to Cervantes the laurel of historian of his period. Some have gone as far as labeling the pictures presented by Cervantes in his novel as "equivalent to the chronicles of the Spanish land,"[1] and others have seen in it "a social document portraying his epoch as a whole and in detail."[2]

There were, of course, personal and historical reasons that lead Cervantes to depict the vicarious structure of Spanish society of his time through some of the characters of his novel, and in particular to present the highest exponents of the Spanish aristocracy in an unfavorable light. Although he uses such artistic devices as literary parody, humor, irony, and comedy as instruments of his criticism, William Byron's statement that Cervantes "was an artist, not a political commentator"[3] and "that social criticism in his book became an element of style the texture of which a moral message is woven,"[4] might not be sufficient to explain the passion with which Cervantes pursues the satire of the noble class, their style of living at court, and the brand of courtiership they practiced. Cervantes, says Leonard Mades,

> lived in Spain at a time when, as a concomitant of the Counter-Reformation, there was an attempt to revive the chivalric spirit—an attempt coinciding with the increasing attacks of moralists on the courtier class. As a crippled war veteran, he would feel an understandable personal animosity toward courtiers. The latter, it

---

[1]   J. C. García, *Selección de Escritos* (Bogota: Editorial Gentro, 1935), p. 151.

[2]   Luis Marín Astrana, Estudio Crítico (Madrid: Editorial Castilla, 1947), p. vi.

[3]   Byron, p. 20.

[4]   *Ibid.*, p. 22.

must surely have seemed to him, were feathering their nests at court while he was risking his life for his country. His many difficulties following his return to Spain after an absence of ten years must have served to reinforce this feeling.[1]

Without going into a detailed description of the historical background and the social and political milieu in which Cervantes lived, a topic that has already been treated extensively in several studies dealing with the author's life and works,[2] suffice it to say that Cervantes' time was a period of vast insecurities and anxiety. "Bankruptcy," says J. H. Plumb, "was common place, sudden promotion could be overturned by sudden dismissal, affluence followed by destitution."[3] "It was a world too in which power was easily abused, far more easily abused than we can often grasp, and it was a world in which crime, violence—great and petty—flourished to a horrifying degree, and more often than not without redress."[4]

At the same time the aristocracy—"the chivalric tradition's titular occupant"—waged within its own ranks a fierce competition to determine which was "the most noble, the richest and most splendid."[5] Quite often, dukes,

---

[1] Mades, p. 23.

[2] For a study of Cervantes' life and the epoch in which he lived, see: Francisco Navarro Ledesma, Cervantes: *The Man and the Genius*, trans. Don and Gabriela Bliss (New York: Charterhouse, 1973); Sebastián Juan Arbó, Cervantes: *The Man and his Time* (New York: The Vanguard Press, 1955); Fernando Plaja-Díaz, *Cervantes* (Barcelona, 1974); Antonio Domín quez Ortiz, *La sociedad española en el siglo XVII* (Madrid, 1963); A. Arco y Garay, *La sociedad española en la obras de Cervantes* (Madrid, 1951).

[3] Foreword" to Melveena McKendrick's *Cervantes*, p. ix.

[4] McKendrick, *Cervantes*, x.

[5] Byron, p. 14.

marquises, and counts—for whom status and prestige were a matter of honor—pursued endless quarrels and "required the king's minister to spend precious hours" in attempts to determine and at times arbitrate claims of precedence and attribution of titles.[1] During the first decade of the seventeenth century, says John Eliot, the grandees and nobility of Spain "descended like birds of prey on the pickings of the court" and "vied with each other in the extravagance of their display and their lavish expenditures on clothes and jewelry."[2] This open exhibition of affluence contrasted dramatically with the large numbers of petitioners, place hunters, and *picaros* that crowded the streets and begged at the doorsteps of the royal palace and at the residences of the more affluent nobility.[3]

The same struggle for power, influence, and wealth that prevailed among the most distinguished representatives of the aristocracy is also found among the courtier class, whose members in large numbers filled the king's court and the mansions of the highest nobility, avoided any work that would entail hardship or deprivation, and served no other purpose except bearing witness to the magnificence of their patrons. These courtiers based their claims for special privileges and recognition at court—whose patronage they regarded as functions of their rank—on grounds of noble birth, gentlemanly appearance and manners, ability to handle weapons, and a certain flair to excel in artistic and literary activities. Interestingly,

---

[1] A. G. Dickens, *The Courts of Europe: politics, patronage, and royalty, 1400-1800*, p. 174.

[2] John H. Elliot, "Philip IV of Spain: Prisoner of Ceremony," in A. G. Dickens, *The Courts of Europe*, p. 176.

[3] On the activities of the Spanish nobility during Cervantes' time, see: Mauro Olmeda, *El ingenio de Cervantes y la locura de don Quijote* (México: Editorial Atlante, 1958), pp. 190-219.

Cervantes' attacks on the courtier centered mainly on the social ideals, claims of distinction, and display of personal qualities through which the courtier so proudly sought to establish his identity.

One of Cervantes' main indictment of the courtier is directed to his claim of excellence on the basis of noble birth. While the courtier considers noble ancestry as the spring of good character and the guarantor of all virtues, in *Don Quijote* the same attributes are tightly bound to one's own efforts and deeds. The brave man, remarks Don Quijote to Andres, carves out his own fortune, and everyone is the son of his works.[1] According to the knight, in fact what distinguishes one man from another are his actions: "No es un hombre más que otro si no hace más que otro."[2] True nobility lies in virtue, Don Quijote informs Sancho before he takes on the responsibility of his government: "Mira Sancho: si tomas por medio la virtud, y te precias de hacer hechos virtuosos, no hay para qué tener envidia a los que los tienen príncipes y señores; porque la sangre se hereda, y la virtud se aquista, y la virtud vale por sí sola lo que la sangre no vale.[3] Therefore, no one, insists Don Quijote, should be ashamed of his lineage no matter how humble: "Haz gala, Sancho de la humildad de tu linaje y no te desprecias de decir que vienes de labradores."[4] In a complete reverse of the courtier's tenets, Don Quijote tells the *duque* that it is virtue that improves the blood: "A eso puedo decir . . . que Dulcinea es hija de sus obras, y que las virtudes adoban la sangre y que en

[1] I, iv, 57.
[2] I, xviii, 167.
[3] II, xlii, 841.
[4] II, xlii, 840.

más se ha de estimar y tener un humilde virtuoso que un vicioso levantado."[1]

Noble birth does not entitle anyone to abuse another person's honor. That is the declaration of Dorotea to Don Fernando: "Tu vasalla soy, pero no tu esclava; ni tiene ne debe tener imperio la nobleza de tu sangre para deshonrar y tener en poco la humildad de la mía; y en tanto me estimo yo, villana y labradora como tú, señor y caballero."[2] Later in the text, Dorotea reiterates to Don Fernando: "La verdadera nobleza consiste en la virtud, y si ésta a ti te falta negándome lo que tan justamente me debes yo quedaré con más ventajas de noble que las que tú tienes."[3]

In the *Courtier,* the human condition, social as well as economical, is determined mostly by heredity. Cervantes, in his novel, presents a less stratified concept of society where social mobility is possible:

> Hay dos maneras de linaje en el mundo—affirms Don Quijote—unos que traen y derivan su descendencia de príncipes y monarcas, a quien poco a poco el tieimpo ha deshecho, y han acabado en punta, como pirámides puesta al revés; otros tuvieron principio de gente baja, y van subiendo de grado en grado, hasta llegar a ser grandes señores. De manera, que está la diferencia en que unos fueron que ya no son, y otros son, que ya no fueron.[4]

---

[1] II, xxxii, 777.
[2] I, xxviii, 282.
[3] I, xxxvi, 376.
[4] I, xxi, 200.

Reinforcing the same concept, Sancho states, "No todos los que gobiernan vienen de casta de reyes,"[1] and on another occasion he says, "Aunque pobre, soy cristiano y viejo, y no debo nada a nadie . . . y cada uno es hijo de sus obras; y debajo de ser hombre puedo venir a ser papa, cuanto más gobernador de una ínsula."[2]

Cervantes envisions several possibilities for progress on the part of the individual. Don Quijote explains these possibilities to his niece:

> A cuatro suertes de linaje . . . se pueden reducir todos los que hay en el mundo, que son éstas: unos que tuvieron principios humildes, y se fueron estendiendo y dilatando hasta llegar a una suma grandeza; otros que tuvieron principios grandes y los fueron conservando y lo conservan y mantienen en el ser que comenzaron; otros que aunque tuvieron principios grandes acebaron a punta como pirámides, habiendo diminuido y anguilado su principio hasta parar en monoda . . . otros hay, y estos son los más, que ni tuvieron principio bueno ni razonable medio, y así tendrán el fin sin nombre, como el linaje de la gente plebeya y ordinaria.[3]

Castiglione, on the other hand, limits the possibility of climbing the social ladder and restricts it to only a select few: almost exclusively to those whom nature endowed

---

[1]   II, xlii, 840.

[2]   I, xlvii, 480.

[3]   I, II, vi, 580.

with noble blood.[1] On the whole, it is obvious that the author of *Don Quijote* underplays the importance of noble birth, and that his view on the subject contradicts Castiglione's philosophy of hereditary nobility. Cervantes mocks the individual whose ambition is to achieve status, not by means of his actions, but by acquiring titles of distinction or aspiring to a career or to an office not suitable to his condition and rank.[2] The author, as it was pointed out earlier in the chapter, not only ridicules Don Quijote's self-attribution of the title of "don," but he also satirizes Sancho who left his village "sobre un jumento como un patriarca con sus alforjas y su bota, y con mucho deseo de verse ya gobernador de la ínsula que su amo le había prometido."[3] When finally Sancho reaches the position of governor on the "ínsula Barataria" and he is addressed by the *mayordomo* as Don Sancho Panza, fully conscious of the vanity of the ambition he once held—his attitude also being a reflection of Cervantes' criticism of the Spanish society's obsession for titles—he immediately informs the smooth-tongued courtier that there had been a "don" in his family and that he was plain *Sancho*. Then, brushing aside any further discussion on the topic, he remarks, "Yo imagino que en esta ínsula debe haber más dones que piedras."[4]

---

[1] "Perché la natura in ogni cosa ha insito quello occulto seme, che porge una certa forza e proprietà del suo principio a tutto quello che da esso deriva ed a sé lo fá simile." Maier, ed *Il Cortegiano*, Bk. I, chap. xiv, p. 104.

[2] For a discussion of the significance of titles of "don" in *Don Quijote*, refer to the study of John C. Dowling, "A Title of Distinction," *Hispania*, 41 (1958), pp. 449-56. See also Jose M. Chaves, *Intergroup Relations in Spain of Cervantes* (New York: Editorial Mensaje, 1974), pp. 166-197.

[3] I, vii, 79-80.

[4] II, xlv, 859.

Cervantes' satire of the Spaniards' uncontrolled passion for titles becomes even more pressing when Don Quijote, upon his arrival at the inn, insists that even the whores of that tavern—"la Tolosa" and "la Molinera"—take on titles of "doña."[1] But nowhere in the novel does the application of "don" to one's name assume a more humorous connotation than when the angry innkeeper calls Don Quijote "Don Diablo," and later in the text, Altisodora calls him "Don Bacallao." Don Quijote himself often uses similar expressions such as "Don Villano," "Don Bellaco," and in a moment of great anger, "Don Hijo de la Puta."[2]

Another indication of Cervantes' antithetical attitude toward the courtier can be found in the criticism of the courtier's pleasure-seeking and unproductive lifestyle. In his conversation with Vivaldo, Don Quijote states "el buen paso, el regalo y el reposo allá se inventó para los blandos cortesanos."[3] Later in the novel, in one of his many exchanges with the *duque,* Don Quijote again belittles the courtier and refers to him disparagingly as "perezoso cortesano que antes busca nuevas para referirlas y contarlas que procurar hacer obras y hazañas para que otros las cuenten o las escriban."[4] Then in a clear reference to the idle life of the court, Don Quijote tells the duchess "todo el mal nace de ociosidad cuyo remedio es la ocupación honesta y continua."[5] Sancho also criticizes the court's pastimes, and lectures the *duque* when he suggests

---

[1] I, iii, 53.

[2] I, xxxv, 363; I, xliv, 456; II, xxxv, 799; II, lxx, 1044; I, xxii, 212. See also Dowling, p. 450.

[3] xiii, 117.

[4] II, xxxvi, 809.

[5] II, lxx, 1045.

to him that upon becoming governor he take on "hunting" as a diversion:

> Eso no—respondió Sancho—el buen gobernador la pierna quebrada, y en casa. Bueno sería que viniesen los negociantes a buscarle fatigados, y él estuviese en el monte holgándose! Así en enhoramala andaría el gobierno! Mía fe, señor, la caza y los pasatiempos más han de ser para los holgazanes que para los gobernadores.[1]

Don Quijote clearly explains to his niece that there exists a wide disparity between the life of the courtier and that of the knight: "Los cortesanos, sin salir de sus aposentos ni de los umbrales de la corte, se pasean por todo el mundo, mirando un mapa sin contarles blanca . . . pero nosotros, los caballeros andantes verdaderos, al sol, al frío, al aire, a las inclemencias del viento . . . medimos toda la tierra con nuestros mismos pies."[2] In another allusion to the gradual disappearance of chivalrous and virtuous conduct among the *caballeros* of his time, Don Quijote remarks to the court clergyman "unos van por el ancho campo de la ambición soberbia; otros, por el de la adulación servil y baja; otros por la hipocresía engañosa, y algunos por el de la verdadera religión."[3]

By repeatedly upholding the ideals of chivalry and by calling attention to the contrast and to the diverse roles of the knight, as opposed to those of the gentleman of the

---

[1]   II, xxxiv, 792.
[2]   II, vi, 578.
[3]   II, xxxii, 770.

court, Don Quijote censures the courtier's public display of empty virtuosity:

> Buen parece un gallardo caballero, a los ojos de su rey, en la mitad de una gran plaza, dar una lanzada con felice suceso a un bravo toro; bien parece un caballero armado de resplandecientes armas, pasar la tela en alegres justas delante de las damas, y bien parecen todos aquellos caballeros que en ejercicios militares, o que lo parezcan, entretienen y alegran, y, si se puede decir, honran las cortes de sus príncipes; pero sobre todos éstos parece mejor un caballero andante, que por los desiertos, por las soledades . . . anda buscando peligrosas aventuras, . . . Mejor parece, digo, un caballero andante socorriendo a una viuda en algún despoblado que un cortesano caballero requebrando a una doncella en las ciudades.[1]

Don Quijote mockingly outlines to Don Diego what ought to be the proper responsibilities of the courtier: "Sirva a las damas el cortesano; autorice la corte de su rey con libreas . . . concierte justas, mantenga torneos, y muéstrese grande, liberal y magnífico . . . y desta manera cumplirá con sus precisas obligaciones."[2] In the words of Don Quijote to his niece, there is apparently one good reason that justifies the courtier's existence: he exists "para adorno de la grandeza de los príncipes y para la ostentación de la majestad real."[3]

---

[1]   II, xvii, 660.

[2]   *Ibid.*

[3]   II, vi. 578.

Cervantes not only denounces the lifestyle, the activities, and the questionable *modus operandi* of the courtier, but also ridicules courtly mannerisms and refinement. In an obvious parody of the courtier's stereotyped behavior, Don Quijote pokes fun at Sancho's unusually composed table manners while sitting at the dinner table in Don Antonio's house, by informing all those present that his squire "en el tiempo que fue gobernador aprendió a comer a lo melindroso tanto que comía con tenedor las uvas y aún los granos de la granada."[1] Don Quijote also derides Sancho's effort to speak eruditely and in the guise of the cultivated gentleman: "Rióse . . . de las afectadas razones de Sancho . . . puesto que todas las veces que Sancho quería hablar de oposición y a lo cortesano acababa su razón con despeñarse del monte de su simplicidad al profundo de su ignorancia."[2]

Both scholarship and pedantry, associated in seventeenth-century literary circles with the art and profession of the courtier, are also principal targets of satire by Cervantes. In the prologue to *part 1*, he scoffingly rejects the bookmadness of his time and the fascination of scholars to flaunt their erudition by the constant use of learned citations and direct references to the classics. Cervantes jokingly justifies the lack of such quirks in his novel by simply stating: "Soy poltrón y perezoso de andarme buscando autores que digan lo que yo me sé decir sin ellos."[3] The author of *Don Quijote*, says William Byron, "shows very little in his works of the formal dialectical structure that gave erudite writing of

---

[1] II, lxii, 989.

[2] II, xii, 618.

[3] I, Prologo, 21.

the day its surface of authority."[1] Rather, he often sneers at the impecunious profession of *l'homme de lettres*, a gentlemanly pursuit indeed, but not a serious occupation for a man of importance. Cervantes, for example, ridicules the young man who professes to be a humanist and whose main interest, by his own declaration, was

> hacer libros para imprimir y para dirigirlos a príncipes . . . libros . . . todos de gran provecho y no menos entretenimientos para la república . . . uno se intitulaba 'el de las libreas,' donde pinta setecientos y tres libreas, con sus colores, motes y cifras, de donde podían sacar y tomar lo que quisiesen en tiempo de fiestas y regocijos los caballeros cortesaños, sin andarlos mendigando de nadie, ni lambicando, como dicen, el cerbelo por sacarlas conformes a sus deseos e intenciones.[2]

The author of *Don Quijote* makes even a further travesty of the erudition of the young humanist as he portrays him vainly boasting about his writings, which again by his own mouth are "de invención nueva y rara, de grande erudición y estudio," "de gentil estilo," and where all major details are explained "al pie de la letra," and documented "con más de veinticinco autores."[3] More humor is added to this vignette when Sancho, impressed with the knowledge of the young intellectual, asked him, "¿ Quién fue el primer volteador del mundo?" He responded, "No me sabré determinar por ahora hasta que

---

[1]   Byron, p. 45.
[2]   II, xxii, 696-7.
[3]   II, xxii, 697.

lo estudie."[1] Sancho mockingly retorted not to bother with it since he had just thought of the answer.

An even better indication of Cervantes' attitude toward academic pretentiousness and the placing of excessive emphasis on scholarship as a prerequisite for high office is given in Sancho's remarks to the *duque* when he suggested to Sancho, the governor-to-be of *insula Barataria*, that he dress partly as a man of learning and partly as a captain since both arms and letters are equally important in discharging the responsibilities of the public servant. "Letras," responded Sancho, "pocas tengo porque aun no sé elabecé; pero bástame tener el 'Cristus' en la memoria para ser buen gobernador."[2] Nevertheless Sancho believes that the profession of arms is something worth heeding: "De las armas," he says, "manejaré los que me dieren, hasta caer, y Dios adelante."[3]

Cervantes agrees with Castiglione on the superiority of the profession of arms over that of letters. In Don Quijote's words, "No hay otro cosa en la tierra más honrada ni de más provecho que servir . . . especialmente en el ejercicio de las armas, por la cuales se alcanzan, si no más requezas, a lo menos, más honra que por las letras."[4] Moreover, he never leaves any doubt about his preference: "Lo que yo professo . . . es el ejercicio de las armas,"[5] declares Don Quijote to his squire. "Yo tengo más armas que letras,"[6] he

---

[1] II, xxii, 698.

[2] II, xlii, 839.

[3] *Ibid.*

[4] II, xxiv, 718.

[5] II, lviii, 954.

[6] II, vi, 581.

says to his niece. "Mis arreos son las armas,"[1] he proudly tells the innkeeper.

Don Quijote ridicules, however, the exercise of arms professed by the courtier and takes a special interest in drawing a distinction between the simulation of war and the reality of war, between the mock battles fought by courtiers and the real armed conflicts fought by true knights and soldiers, including himself:

> No solamente conocemos los enemigos pintados, sino en su mismo ser, y en todo trance y en toda ocasión los acometemos, sin mirar en niñerías, ni en las leyes de los desafíos si lleva, o no lleva, más corta la lanza, o la espada . . . si se ha de partir o hacer tajadas el sol, o no, con otras ceremonias desde jaez, que se usan en los desafíos particulares de persona a persona.[2]

Reflecting the author's feelings toward the pseudo soldiers of his time, Don Quijote also condemns the vanity and empty concerns of the courtier-knights: "Los más de los caballeros que agora se usan, antes les crujen los damascos, los brocados y otras ricas telas de que se visten, que la malla con que se arman."[3]

Cervantes' repudiation of the courtier and his lifestyle also comes in the traditional form of "desprecio de corte y alabanza de aldea." In a passage reminiscent of Guevara's

---

[1] I, ii, 45.

[2] II, vi, 578. On the theme of "arms and letters" in *Don Quijote*, see Olmeda, pp. 163-190.

[3] II, i, 547-8. On the attitude of the public toward chivalry and knights during Cervantes' time, see the study of Alberto Navarro González, *El Quijote Español del siglo XVII* (Madrid: Ediciones Rialp, 1964), pp. 189-229.

work, Sancho Panza tells Pedro Recio and the other officials of his mock government:

> Abrid camino, señores mios, y dejadme volver a mi antiqua libertad . . . Yo no nací para ser governador. . . . Mejor se me entiende a mí de arar y cavar, podar y ensarmentar las viñas . . . más quiero recostarme a la sombra de una encina en el verano y arroparme con un zamarro de dos pelos el invierno en mi libertad, que acostarme con la subjeción de martas cebollinas.[1]

Don Quijote shares similar thoughts upon leaving the palace of the *duques*:

> Sancho, . . . bien has visto el regalo, la abundancia que en este castillo que dejamos hemos tenido; pues en metad de aquellos banquetes sazonados y aquellas bebidas de nieve, me parecía a mí que estaba metido entre las estrechezas de la hambre, porque no lo gozaba con la libertad que lo gozara si fueran míos; que las obligaciones de las recompensas de los beneficios y mercedes recibidas son ataduras que no dejan campear al ánimo libre. ¡ Venturoso aquel a quien el cielo dio un pedazo de pan, sin que le quede obligación de agradecerlo a otro que al mismo cielo.[2]

Another area of interest that invites Cervantes' satire is the platonic of love that Castiglione in the *Courtier* had

---

[1] II, liii, 926.
[2] II, lviii, 952.

done much to promote. Don Quijote, like Amadís and the courtier, is presented as a faithful and virtuous admirer of womanly beauty, but in choosing to be a platonic lover he resolves to imitate the courtier rather than Amadís, whose loyalty, chastity, and passion for Oriana relate to the code of *amour courtois* but not to Platonism. "No soy de los enamorados viciosos sino de los platónicos continentes,"[1] says Don Quijote to the ecclesiastic. Sanson Carrasco, also refers jokingly to Don Quijote and Dulcinea's mutual attraction as "amores tan platónicos."[2] Don Quijote tells Sancho "mis amores y los suyos han sido siempre platónicos, sin estenderse a más que a un honesto mirar." Similarly, in the prologue to part 1, the author informs the reader that among the inhabitants of Montiel Don Quijote is known as "el más casto enamorado."[3]

Like a true platonic lover, Don Quijote portrays Dulcinea not as she is in reality but how she appears to his imagination:

> Básteme a mí pensar y creer que la buena de Aldonza Lorenzo es hermosa y honesta. . . . Y para concluir con todo, yo imagino que todo lo que digo es así, sin que sobre ni falte nada, y píntola en mi imaginación como la deseo, así en la belleza como en la principalidad.[4]

Although not quite clear at first, the parody of the Platonic doctrine becomes increasingly evident as the author wittingly calls attention to the humorous manner in

---

[1]   II, xxxii, 770.

[2]   II, iii, 559.

[3]   I, Prólogo, 25.

[4]   I, xxv, 246.

which Don Quijote resists the temptations of Maritornes, the advances of Altisodora, and the endearing expressions and *requiebros* of the two damsels who insisted on dancing with him during the courtly reception staged in his honor at the house of his host Don Antonio. The parody of the Platonic doctrine is also obvious if one considers the excessive mannerisms and the obsessive zeal with which Don Quijote seeks to project an image of abstinence and purity, a posture that stands in direct contrast with the lack of restraint, self-indulgence, and fickleness of the knights of the real world. Don Quijote himself in his poem to Altisodora alludes to the frivolousness of modern knights and courtiers:

> Los andantes caballeros
> y los que en la corte andan
> requiébranses con las libres;
> y con las honestas se casan.[1]

Prof. Mades states that Cervantes' satire of platonic love "is partly explicable on the basis of general procedure of confronting the ideal with the real."[2] Indeed, the courtier-lover in *Don Quijote* is not represented as a chaste devoted suitor but as an immoral, falsehearted double-dealer. In narrating the seduction of Antonomasia, La Dolorida describes how a noble lad with the qualities of the courtly gentleman was responsible for her misfortune as well as that of her mistress. The seducer of the young princess is presented as

---

[1]   II, xlvi, 857

[2]   Mades, p. 158.

un caballero particular que en la corte estaba,
confiado en su mocedad y en su bizarría, y en
sus muchas habilidades y gracias, y facilidad
y felicidad en ingenio . . . tocaba una guitarra
que la hacía hablar; y más que era poeta, y
gran bailarín. . . . Primero quiso el malandrín
y desalmado vagamundo de granjearme la
voluntad y cohecharme el gusto, para que yo,
mal alcaide, le entregase las llaves de la fortaleza
que guardaba . . . él me aduló el entendimiento
y me rindió la voluntad . . . y así, siendo yo la
medianera, él se halló una y muy muchas veces
en la estancia de la engañada Antonomasia.[1]

Finally it is with great disillusionment that Cervantes
looks at the courtier of his age, whom he holds responsible
for the economic and social evils of his country and the
loss of chivalric spirit and ideals. While Castiglione
regards his own age superior to other periods of history,
for Cervantes the golden age of chivalry has already been
buried: "Mas agora," remarks Don Quijote, "ya triunfa la
pereza de la diligencia, la ociosidad del trabajo, el vicio
de la virtud, la arrogancia de la valentía, y la teórica de la
práctica de las armas, que sólo vivieron y resplandecieron
en las edades del oro y en los andantes caballeros."[2]

In view of the disparaging remarks directed toward the
courtier on the whole, it is quite clear that Cervantes in
many passages and episodes of *Don Quijote* intended to
offer a satire and a repudiation of the stereotyped *caballero*
of his age. Quite plain are also the author's condemnation
of court life, and also his hostile attitude toward the

---

[1]   II, xxxviii, 816.
[2]   II, i, 548.

courtier's proverbial values and guidelines for successful living within a courtly environment. Obviously, Cervantes does not disapprove of the abilities of the courtier *per se* or the principles of civilized behavior he embodies; rather he rebuffs the manner in which his diversified talent and knowledge are applied to daily living. Moreover, Cervantes' denunciation of the courtier is not aimed at the courtier's endeavor to improve himself both intellectually and socially, but to courtship as a cult and as an art in itself. Such empty and stylish pastime had apparently, during Cervantes' time, become both an activity and a state of mind of a whole class of individuals, which in his view had seriously undermined traditional social values, chivalric honor, and the individual's commitment to a productive life, and as a result had deeply and adversely affected the economic basic of a whole nation.

Cervantes, however, does not completely reject the *Courtier's* doctrinal material. There is, in fact, a considerable body of thought on which both Cervantes and Castiglione seem to be in agreement. For instance, both writers concur on the need for avoiding affectation. Maese Pedro, for one, warns the young gentleman entrusted with explaining and interpreting the mysteries of the performance at the puppet show not to indulge in affected speech: "Llaneza, muchacho: no te encumbres que toda afectación es mala."[1] Don Quijote also censures the young lad's pedantic way of speaking: "Muchacho no te metas en dibujos . . . sigue tu canto llano, y no te metas en contrapuntos, que suelen quebrar de sotiles."[2]

The two authors also share similar views on matters of proper attire and dressing: "El vestido descompuesto

---

[1] II, xxvi, 732.

[2] II, xxvi, 731.

da indicios de ánimo desmazalado,"[1] says Don Quijote to Sancho before taking over the reigns of his government, and with words reminiscent of the *Courtier* he also informs him that "los trajes se han de acomodar con el oficio o dignidad que se profesa."[2] In another passage that captures the essence of one of Castiglione's suggestions to the courtier in his dealings with the prince, don Quijote tells Sancho that the responsibility "de los vasallos leales es decir la verdad a sus señores en su ser y figura propia, sin que la adulación la acreciente o otro vano respeto la disminuya."[3]

One of the courtier's major attributes, which is also one of Don Quijote's most important traits, is exemplified in the quality of discretion. Cervantes calls Don Quijote "único y sin igual en la discreción."[4] For Castiglione as for the author of *Don Quijote*, *discreción* consists of choosing the middle way as the basis for man's actions. This belief in a golden mean of behavior is clearly expressed in the words of Don Quijote to governor-to-be Sancho: "No seas siempre riguroso, ni siempre blando, y escoge el medio entre dos estremos; que en esto está el punto de la discreción."[5]

---

[1] II, xliii, 843.

[2] II, xliii, 839.

[3] II, ii, 555.

[4] II, viii, 591.

[5] II, li, 911. On the concept of "discretion" in Cervantes, see W. C. Atkinson, "Cervantes, El Pinciano, and the 'Novelas Ejemplares,'" *Hispanic Review*, XVI (1948), pp. 189-208.

Cervantes and Human Perfection

Other parallels and points of contact between Cervantes and Castiglione, particularly in the area of literary criticism—the proper use of language, the idea of the perfect prince, the concept of honor, the idea of fame, the fostering of good habits, and the use of practical jokes—have been already established in the studies by Leonard Mades, Ernesto Krebs, Américo Castro, and Joseph Fucilla. For some ideas on these points, the interested reader can refer to the respective works by these authors mentioned earlier in this chapter.[1]

Evidently, the study of Cervantes' attitude toward the courtier thus far has been based for the most part on the observation of the author's reaction as the main characters of the novel, at different intervals, assume courtly postures or display behavioral patterns descriptive of the stereotyped *caballero cortesano*. There are, however, in *Don Quijote* other figures to whom Cervantes assigns traits resembling the modes of conduct and ideals of the courtly gentleman, and at times, of a whole social class.

One such figure is Don Diego de Miranda, "El Caballero del Verde Gabán," a character portrayed by Cervantes with the physical and mental characteristics reminiscent of Castiglione's courtier. He is described as "hombre de chapa," "la edad mostraba ser de cincuenta años; las canas, pocas, y el rostro aguileño; la vista entre alegre y grave; finalmente en el traje y apostura daba a

---

[1]   For some thoughts on the concepts of honor, man's dignity and glory in Cervantes, as they relate to Castiglione, see: Américo Castro, *El Pensamiento de Cervantes*, pp. 362-69, 370-71, 373-77.

entender ser hombre de buenas prendas."[1] Don Diego introduces himself to Don Quijote as a gentleman of the village and as a family man, moderately rich, whose main occupations are hunting and fishing. He also portrays himself as a man of culture who enjoys the company of friends, wholesome meals, comfortable living, and avoids gossip and prying into other people's lives or doings. No less remarkable is Don Diego's piety and devotion. He tells Don Quijote: "Oigo misa cada día; reparto de mis bienes con los pobres, sin hacer alarde de las buenas obras, por no dar entrada en mi corazón a la hipocrisía y vanagloria . . . procuro poner en paz los que sé que están desavenidos; soy devoto de nuestra Señora, y confío siempre en la misericordia infinita de Dios, nuestro Señor.[2] In addition, Don Diego characterizes himself as honest and careful in reading books that provide only innocent amusement. On the whole, "El Caballero del Verde Gabán" seeks to give the impression of being a model of good behavior, moral excellence, gallantry, intellectual and social sophistication, as well as a picture of Christian dedication and virtue.

But Don Diego's self-characterization, overwhelmingly on the side of righteous smugness, soon becomes the target of the author's satire. Cervantes' mocking of "The Gentleman of the Green Coat" is evident in the description of Sancho's farcical attitude and remarks to Don Diego:

> Atentísimo estuvo Sancho a la relación de la vida
> y entretenimientos del hidalgo; y paraciéndole
> buena y santa y que quien la hacía debía hacer
> milagros, se arrojó del rucio, y con gran priesa

---

[1] II, xvi, 645.
[2] II, xvi, 647-8.

le fue, a asir del estribo derecho, y con devoto corazón y casi lágrimas le besó los pies una y muchas veces.[1]

When Don Diego asked Sancho why he was acting in such a way, he answered: "Porque me parace vuesa merced el primer santo a la jineta que he visto en todos los días de mi vida."[2]

Carlos Varo in his *Génesis y evolución del "Quijote"* summarizes some of the views held by the critics on the figure of Don Diego with these words:

> Este personaje es muy contravertido. Lo cierto es que tanto en la pintura física como en la moral y social la primera impresión que produce es agradable y simpática. Pero, según Vallejo Najera, 'don Diego de Miranda no es otra cosa que lo que hoy llamamos un pacífico burgués acomodaticio e hipócrita, atento a sus intereses, despreocupado del bien común, no obstante sus bien administradas caridades.' Para Ricardo del Arco y Garay es el modelo de 'burguesía medrosa.' Jean Babelón, por el contrario ve en este caballero todas las cualidades del cortesano de Baltasar de Castiglione.[3]

Alberto Sánchez, on the other hand, sees in Don Diego the delineation of Cervantes' own portrayal and all the other things that the author wanted to be and do but

---

[1]   II, xvi, 648.

[2]   *Ibid.*

[3]   Carlos Varo, *Génesis y evolución del "Quijote"* (Madrid: Ediciones Alacalá, 1968), p. 372.

was not able to accomplish.[1] William Byron calls "The Gentleman of the Green Coat" "a good Tridentine boy concerned with his dogs and his table and his handful of devotional books and nervous about his son's being an intellectual."[2]

By and large, it is doubtful that Cervantes wanted to represent in Don Diego the true ideal life of the human being. By closely examining the context and the field of action in which he appears in the novel, Don Diego, far from being an ideal of human perfection, exhibits all the characteristics of a decadent modern knight who is interested in the amenities and comforts of life rather than becoming involved in real knightly pursuits and activities.

Another figure to whom the author attributes courtly qualities and abilities is the shepherd Crisóstomo. Besides being able to sing, play an instrument, and compose verses, Crisóstomo is depicted as a gentle and graceful lad: "Fué único en el ingenio, solo en la cortesía, estremo en la gentileza, fénix en la amistad, magnífico sin tasa, grave sin presunción, alegre sin bajeza y finalmente primero en todo lo que es ser bueno."[3]

The manual dexterity and physical agility of the courtier is well represented in the figure of Basilio:

> Él es el más ágil mancebo . . . gran tirador de
> barra luchador estremado y gran jugador de
> pelota; corre como un gamo, salta más que una

---

[1] Alberto Sánchez, "El caballero del Verde Gabán," *Anales Cervantinos*, IX (1960-1), pp. 169-201. On the symbolism of the color green, refer to Vernon A. chamberlain, "Symbolic Green," *Hispania*, 51 (1968), pp. 29-37.

[2] Byron, p. 431.

[3] I, xiii, 123.

cabra y birla a los bolos como por encantamento;
canta como una calandria, y toca una guitarra,
que la hace hablar, y, sobre todo, juega una
espada con el más pintado.[1]

But here again the author's sardonic attitude toward
Basilio's courtly virtuosity is quite evident not only in
the keen-witted tone and language of the description but
also in the remarks of Don Quijote to Sancho: "Por esa
sola gracia . . . merecía ese mancebo no sólo casarse con
la hermosa Quiteria, sino con la mesma reina Ginebra, si
fuera hoy viva, a pesar de Lanzarote y de todos aquellos
que estorbarlo quisieron."[2]

No less refined and gentlemanly is the figure of Don
Fernando, who is repeatedly described as "mozo gallardo,
gentil hombre, liberal y enamorado,"[3] "astuto y discreto,"[4]
but the author soon brings him down a few rungs by
quickly pointing out his deceitful character and lack of
moral responsibility.[5] Similarly, Don Clavijo after being
depicted by La Dolorida as endowed with the qualities
and virtues of the courtier, is soon labeled as greedy and
dishonest.[6]

This same method and technique by Cervantes of first
praising or presenting under a favorable light and then
mocking many of the principal characters of his novel, in
particular those who embody courtly abilities and talents,
is especially notable in the delineation of the members

[1] II, xix, 672.
[2] *Ibid.*
[3] I, xxiv, 228.
[4] I, xxiv, 229.
[5] I, xxiv, 229-30.
[6] II, xxxviii, 816-20.

of the Spanish nobility. The *duque*, who at first appears under the guise of great courtesy and generosity, is later presented as responsible for the cruel clawing by cats of Don Quijote's face.[1] Furthermore, by Doña Rodríguez' account, he engages and protects an accomplice, in exchange for certain money deals and favors, the very man who had dishonored his daughter.[2] Even the duchess, who is initially portrayed by the author as a picture of beauty, grace, and health, we later discover, through the remarks of doña Rodríguez, that she is plagued by "dos fuentes que tiene en las dos piernas, por donde se desagua todo el mal humor de quien dicen los médicos que está llena."[3] Don Antonio, another member of the Spanish nobility, who at first displays the distinguishing marks of the gentleman, is later presented as a most foolish and insipid host in the description of the showing of the "miraculous head."[4]

Obviously none of the various characters outlined by Cervantes in *Don Quijote* encompasses the perfections of a model or a true hero. In fact, they all differ from each other in some aspect or ability. In some cases the talents and graces that these figures exhibit are described in such manner that it becomes difficult to determine whether the author is truly serious in his praise or appreciation of their respective qualities or he is merely mocking their virtuosity. Besides, even after giving definite signs of willingness to shower someone with praise, Cervantes

---

[1]   II, xlvi, 868.

[2]   II, xlviii, 884.

[3]   II, xlviii, 885. On the episode of Doña Rodríguez and her place in the novel, see the study of Marianela Conchita Herdman, *"Dueñas" and "Doncellas": a study of the "Doña Rodrígues" episode in "Don Quijote"* (Chapel Hill: North Carolina Studies in the Romance Languages and Literatures, 1979), pp. 112-40.

[4]   *Ibid.*

almost invariably manages to find some weakness in the family line or some other flaw in the conduct of the individual as to constantly remind him of his imperfections and humble his humanity.

Perhaps the only conclusion that one can draw from an analysis of the characters in *Don Quijote* is that in Cervantes' perception of the world inhabited by men there are no "quasi-divine" creatures; there exists no one single hero or even one single social or cultural prototype, but there are myriads of mortal beings with limited capacity for self-development. In this many-sided universe, each individual is measured only by his actions and not by controlled and deliberate artifice or by deceptive masking and opportunism. Noble men are defined by noble deeds. The application of any other criteria in judging a man's character and virtue—by noble birth, social and intellectual refinement, military skills, expertise at love—is venturing in the realm of fiction and the world of appearances. As to "perfection," it is a quality and a state of being endemic to the nature of God, not to the world of reality in which men live.

As it appears, the search in *Don Quijote* for an ideal of human conduct or a code of behavior designed to fashion the perfect gentleman results in almost complete disappointment and frustration. As Leland H. Chambers states, "Cervantes' treatment of human existence in *Don Quijote* stresses the relativity of man's worldly experience, the fluidity of all that seems most solid before him,"[1] and therefore "the very basis for moral action and

---

[1] Leland H. Chambers, "Structure and the Search for Truth in *Don Quijote*," *Hispanic Review*, XXXV (Oct. 1967), No. 4, p. 311.

integrity of the soul are constantly at stake; all actions are problematical."[1]

There are, however, in the novel a few references that could guide the student in arriving at some form of tentative appraisal of Cervantes' conception of *el caballero perfecto*. Perhaps a set of rules for the shaping of the true gentleman can be drawn from the admonishments given by Don Quijote to Sancho at the time of his initiation as governor of *ínsula Barataria*. Among the virtues and qualities recommended by Don Quijote to his squire are those which, in his words, contribute to the ennoblement of the soul such as the love of God and the love of the family, the active pursuit of justice, honesty, the practice of humility and compassion, the acquisition of prudence and self-knowledge, and the acceptance of one's own ancestral condition. There are also traits that must adorn the body, namely good manners, cleanliness, the wearing of proper attire, composure in walking, good speaking habits, avoidance of excessive eating, drinking, and sleeping, as well as being unduly lazy.[2]

In another passage directed at the *caballero* of humble origin who aspires to be a distinguished gentleman, the author, through the remarks of Don Quijote to his niece, offers some additional hints as to what he considers the qualities of the true gentleman to be: "al caballero pobre no le queda otro camino para mostrar que es caballero sino el de la virtud, siendo afable, bien criado, cortés, y comedido y oficioso, no soberbio, no arrogante, no murmurador y sobre todo caritativo."[3]

---

[1] *Ibid.*

[2] II, xlii, 840-2; II, xliii, 840-5.

[3] II, vi, 581.

Moreover, the versatility, virtue, and multiple talents of the Renaissance gentleman are perhaps exemplified in the answer Don Quijote gives to Don Lorenzo, the son of Don Diego, when the young man and poet asks him to define the educational basis and background of knight-errantry:

> Es una ciencia . . . que encierra en sí todas las más ciencias del mundo, a causa que el que la profesa ha de ser jurisperto, y saber las leyes de la justicia distributiva y comutativa, para dar a cada uno lo que es suyo y lo que le conviene; ha de ser teólogo para saber dar razón de la cristiana ley que profesa . . . ha de ser médico, y principalmente herbolario, . . . ha de ser astrólogo . . . ha de saber las matemáticas, porque a cada paso se le ofrecerá tener necesitad dellas . . . digo que debe saber nadar como dicen que nadaba el peje Nicolás . . . ha de saber herrar un caballo y aderezar la silla y el freno . . . ha de guardar la fe a Dios y a su dama, he de ser vasto en los pensamientos, honesto en las palabras, liberal en las obras, valiente en los hechos, sufrido en los trabajos, caritativo con los menesterosos, y, finalmente, mantenedor de la verdad, aunque le cueste la vida en defenderla. De todas estas grandes y mínimas partes se compone un buen caballero andante.[1]

There are, of course, other passages in *Don Quijote* from which one can derive a composite of rules for man's moral, spiritual, and social life, but in general the norms for virtuous living suggested in *Don Quijote* are more

---

[1]   II, xviii, 664-5.

consistent with the way of life and heroic ideals of the early knights of chivalry, which Cervantes would have liked to revive,[1] than the lifestyle and code of conduct prescribed by Castiglione for his courtier. As it has been often pointed out in this chapter, it is with a great degree of disappointment and also scorn that Cervantes looks at the courtly pursuits and the drive for self-assertion at all cost by the courtier.

[1]   I, xx, 188.

CHAPTER IV

Courtliness In Calderón's Dramas And Gracián's Treatises On Human Values

The Courtly Gentleman in Calderón's Theater

The theater has always prevailed among art forms as a most useful vehicle for the representation and transmission of man's values and ideals. Fully aware of its suggestiveness and influence over the audiences, playwrights of all ages have often capitalized on their dramatic production to foster attitudes, beliefs, and class idiosyncrasies that mirrored their own group identity and preferences, and at times, also those of their Maecenas under whose patronage they worked and lived.

The connection between the stage and the specific aspirations, manners, and feelings of a whole class of people is particularly highlighted in the dramatic works of Pedro Calderón de la Barca, whose vast literary production aims for the most part at underscoring the inclinations, tastes, and ideals of the Spanish court. "Calderón," says Angel Valbuena-Prat, "es la gran figura sintética que encierra, en apoteosis de brillante escenografía y sabio movimiento de figuras teatrales, la cultura imperial española, en el mundo del pensamiento y de las letras."[1]

Calderón's dramas almost invariably emphasize social decorum, polite usage, virtuous deeds, moral fortitude, personal integrity, and the acquisition of skills and qualities deemed worthy of an aristocrat. In his works, considerable importance is also attached to lengthy and detailed descriptions of specific court functions in all their brilliance and lavishness, and to the elimination from the stage of every plebeian expression, the hiding of all vulgar feelings and the suppression of all base characters. According to Menéndez y Pelayo,

> Calderón . . . instintivamente tiende a presentar sólo lo más ideal de la vida y del sentimiento. De ahí que todas clases de acciones aparezcan como rodeadas de una aureola ideal y heroica, que, por decirlo así, las saca de los límites de la realidad y las sublima sobre las miserias y escorias de la vida presente.[2]

The tendency of Calderón to filter his artistic production of everything coarse and uncouth undoubtedly has helped to make him, even more than previous court dramatists, a true interpreter of the court elitist attitudes and a writer of plays depicting how courtly people would like to be or ought to be, or how the sovereign would like to see them. In view of Calderón's apparent disposition to

---

[1] Angel Valbuena-Prat, *Calderón: su personalidad, su arte dramático, su estilo y sus obras* (Barcelona: Editorial Juventud, 1941), p. 6.

[2] Marcelino Menéndez Pelayo, "Estudio Preliminar" in Pedro Calderón de la Barca, *Comedias de capa y espada* (Madrid: Collección "Cisneros," 1943), I, p. viii.

represent on stage aristocratic tastes and values, it is not unusual that the portrayal of the perfect gentleman should occupy a special place in his works.

It is useful to point out that in the drama of the Golden Age, the figure of the Spanish *caballero perfecto* appears in a number of plays by Lope de Vega, Calderón's predecessor as a dramatist and court playwright For instance, in Lope's *La moza de cántaro*, "the figure of Don Juan is the very embodiment of chivalry and honor."[1] His distinguishing marks are noble origin, good looks, ability to improvise poetry, power of discrimination, and self-restraint. He is also "a loyal and faithful friend" and an emotional and romantic lover who refuses "wealth and position which Doña Ana offers him" in order to be true to Isabel, the servant girl in disguise.[2] In *La cortesía de Espana*, another play by Lope, Don Juan represents the gallant, unselfish, self-controlled, noble-hearted Spanish gentleman who generously forsakes his own love so that he may keep a promise he made to the estranged Lucrezia during their long journey to Toledo.[3] Don Juan of Portugal, the hero in Lope's *El príncipe perfecto*, is another character endowed with qualities that readily identify him with the courtly and chivalric tradition. He is a man of noble birth, great wisdom, and fine manners. He possesses a kind, humble, jovial, and compassionate disposition, as well as a deep sense of justice. He is also well-spoken, courageous in battle, and profoundly religious. In addition, he is a graceful dancer, a lover of music, and an expert

[1] Pauline Marshall, Edition with Introduction and Notes to *"El calallero perfecto" by Alonso Gerónimo de Salas Barbadillo*, p. xxii.

[2] *Ibid.*, p. xxiii.

[3] *Ibid.*, p. xxiv.

in the art of horsemanship, hunting, and the use of arms.[1] Other figures in the drama of the Golden Age that bear the distinctive marks of the courtly and chivalric prototypes can be found in the character of the Count in *El molino* of Lope and in that of don Juan de Mendoza, the *caballero* of *Las paredes oyen* by Ruiz de Alarcón.[2]

In the drama of Calderón, the figure of the gentleman is almost without exception an integral part of the composition.[3] In nearly all of his works one finds a hero or a prototype that personifies ideal human qualities and traits. The stylization of the hero is, in fact, one of the dominant characteristics of Calderón's artistic craftsmanship. Unlike Lope who always managed in his dramas to display two or three characters who equally shared the public limelight, Calderón tends to distinguish and exalt one protagonist or model at the expense of all others. As Valbuena-Prat points out, "el arte dramático de Calderón tiene las características del siglo del barroco. Una . . . es la ley de subordinación de las figuras segundarias al protagonista."[4] In addition, whether the heroes in his dramas are figures representative of the middle-class nobility or princes and great lords, their relative importance in the plays is determined, more often

---

[1] *Ibid.*, p. xxv.

[2] *Ibid.*, p. xxviii.

[3] In Calderón even "the devil" assumes, at times, human characteristics reminiscent of a courtier, with the purpose of influencing the outcome of the action and insuring success. For some thoughts on Calderón's portrayal of "the devil" in human terms, see A. A. Parker, *The Theology of the Devil in the Drama of Calderón* (Blackfriars, 1958), p. 2 et passim. See also Angel L. Cilveti, *El Demonio en el Teatro de Calderón* (Valencia: Albatros Ediciones, 1977).

[4] Angel Valbuena-Prat, *Calderón: su personalidad, su arte dramático, su estilo y su obras* (Barcelona: Editorial Juventud, 1941), pp. 18, 22.

than not, by the degree of influence, nobility, title, and position in the hierarchy of the court. The qualities of the perfect gentleman in Calderón are first and above all combined in the person of the king, his patron and friend.[1] For instance, in *La banda y la flor,* Enrique at first refers to King Philip IV as "El Sol," the Ptolmeic Planet King,[2] and later supercedes this allegory with a typical description of attitudes and marks of the Renaissance gentleman. Among the king's outstanding attributes are those of being expert horseman and warrior:

> Y (aparte la alegoría)
> permite que me detenga
> en pintarte de Filipo
> la gala, el brío y destreza
> con que iba puesto a caballo; . .
> . , que no hay
> agilidad ni destreza
> de buen caballero, que él
> con admiración no tenga.
> A caballo, en las dos sillas

---

[1]   The presence of the royal family in many of Calderón's plays is studied by Everett W. Hesse in "Courtly Allusions in the Plays of Calderón," *PMLA,* Vol. LXV (1950), pp. 531-49. Prof. Hesse points out that Calderón "was a courtier poet . . . who fawned on royalty to curry its favor, perhaps because he knew on which side his bread was buttered." At the end of his analysis, Prof. Hessse asks, "On the basis of the evidence presented in this study, is it not reasonable to conclude that Calderón was chosen court dramatist because he knew how to win the King's favor by his flattery, and having once become aware of the monarch's weakness for it, the dramatist continued in this vein because he knew his future would be secure?", pp. 548-9. See also M. A. Buchanan, "Culteranismo, in Calderón's *La Vida es sueño*" in *Homenaje ofrecido a Menéndez Pidal* (Madrid, 1925), I, 545.

[2]   Everett W. Hesse, "Courtly Allusions in the Plays of Calderón," *PMLA,* Vol. LXV (1950), p. 535.

es, en su rústica escuela,
el mejor que se conoce.
Si las armas, señor, jueja,
proporciona con la blanca
las lecciones de la negra.[1]

In a language reminiscent of *Amadís*, *The Courtier*, and *Don Quijote*, Calderón depicts the king as especially fond of the chase:

Es tan ágil en la caza,
viva imagen de la guerra,
que registra su arcabuz
cuanto corre y cuanto vuela.[2]

Embodying the artistic and intellectual qualities of the Renaissance gentleman, Philip IV is also a painter, a musician, and a lover of the arts:

Con un pincel, es segundo
autor de naturaleza.
Las cláusulas más suaves
de la música penetra.
En efecto, de las artes
no hay alguna que no sepa,
y todas, sin profesión,
halladas por excelencia.[3]

---

[1] Pedro Calderón de la Barca, *La banda y la flor* in *Obras Completas*, ed. Angel Valbuena-Briones (3 vols.; Madrid: Aguilar, 1960), II, p. 429. All quotations from Calderón's works are from this edition.

[2] II, Jornada I, p. 429.

[3] *Ibid.*

The reign itself and the empire of the Spanish ruler are hailed as the symbol and the cradle of "arms and letters";

¡ Oh felice tú, oh felice
Otra vez y otras mil seas
imperio, en quien el primero
triunfo son armas y letras![1]

The courtly milieu in which the king and his courtiers move is the city of Madrid, splendid for its lavishness and pageantry:

Madrid, iris ya divino,
todas las calles cubiertas,
de una bella confusión,
de una confusa belleza,
haciendo campos y mares
las plumas y las libreas.[2]

Obviously, the qualities assigned by Calderón to the king, especially those depicting him as the foremost *caballero* of the court, reflected contemporary ideals and patterns of social and intellectual sophistication. The playwright who was primarily writing for an aristocratic audience that considered codes of behavior and culture as a source of class identification could not have offered the Spanish gentry and nobility a better model to emulate and a more refined setting for the fostering of courtly values and chivalric conduct.

In Calderón's plays, the figure of the perfect gentleman at the lower end of the scale of the Spanish courtly

---

[1]   II, Jornada I, p. 428.

[2]   *Ibid.*

hierarchy is well delineated in the dramas of "cloak and sword." These plays, says Menéndez y Pelayo, always present "al galán como prototipo de la virtud bélica, del pundonor y de la discreción."[1] He also adds: "Más que de comedia realista tienen de representación idealizada de costumbres del tiempo, y esto lo prueba no sólo la repetición constante de los mismos tipos y de unos mismos recursos, sino también ese verdadero desbordamiento de galantería, de honor y de caballerosidad que en todas estas obras se observa."[2]

Eminently representing the traditional chivalric qualities and ideals, honor, courage, discretion, self-assurance, typical of the *caballeros* of the "cloak and sword" dramas, is the figure of Don Carlos, the protagonist of *No siempre lo peor es cierto*, a play which in the words of Menéndez y Pelayo, "no es más la idealización admirable de todos los elementos que entran en la comedia de capa y espada."[3] Don Carlos is described by Doña Leonora as a gentleman first and then a lover:

> Atento te considero
> a la ley de caballero
> primero que a la de amante.[4]

---

1   "Estudio Preliminar" in *Pedro Calderón de la Barca, Comedias de capa y espada*, p. xx.

2   *Ibid.*

3   *Ibid.*, p. xxii.

4   II, Jornada I, p. 1453.

The defense of his lady's honor comes more from a sense of personal responsibility than outside pressure:

> A asegurar me atrevo
> su vida y su honor aquí
> por lo que debo a mí
> no por lo que a ella la debo.[1]

In the words of Doña Leonora, Don Carlos combines gallantry, knowledge, and discretion:

> De galan y de entendido
> juntaste los dos extremos,
> haciendo la cortesía
> capa del atrevimiento.[2]

We gain additional insight into the protagonist's character when later Doña Leonora tells Don Carlos to have fallen in love with him for

> lo ilustsre de tu sangre
> lo honrado de tus respetos,
> lo galán de tu persona
> y lo sutil de tu ingenio.[3]

---

[1] *Ibid.*
[2] II, Jornada I, p. 1454.
[3] *Ibid.*

Don Carlos is also depicted as a strong supporter and protector of the lady he loves. He tells Don Juan:

> Traigo conmigo
> aquesta dama, a quien tengo
> de salvar la vida a costa
> de todos mis sentimientos.[1]

In addition, he is a faithful and sincere lover, whose chivalry is only matched by his self-control and power of restraint:

> De amante y de caballero
> enamorado la adoro,
> y celoso la aborrezco:
> cuyas dos obligaciones
> tan cabal la acción han hecho,
> que desde Madrid aquí,
> si no es hoy, juraros puedo
> que no la hablé dos palabras,
> porque no quise que en tiempo
> alguno de mí dijese
> la fama, que pudo menos
> mi valor que mi apetito;
> que es hombre bajo, que es necio,
> es vil, es ruin, es infame
> el que solamente atento
> a lo irracional del gusto
> y a lo bruto del deseso,
> viendo perdido lo más,
> se contenta con lo menos.[2]

---

[1]   II, Jornada I, p. 1456.
[2]   II, Jordada I, p. 1457.

The courtly setting of this action is Madrid, which in the words of Ines,

> es el centro y la esfera
> de toda la lintura,
> el aseo, la gala y la hermosura.[1]

Another figure typical of Calderón's plays of *capa y espada* is Don Manuel, the central character in *La dama duende*. He is of noble birth, skillful at arms, humble, and refined in manners. He is also a fierce defender of women in need. To the call for help by Doña Angela he responds:

> ¿ Como puede mi nobleza
> excusarse de estorbar
> una desdicha, una afrenta?[2]

Don Manuel is described by Doña Angela as a gentleman whose courage is equaled only by his sense of honor and discretion. He is bold and chivalrous, gallant, and prudent. He will resort to force only after all other attempts and the call to reason have failed. When he is asked by Cosme how he plans to deal with his opponent he states:

> Detenerle con alguna
> industsria; mas si con ella
> no puedo, será forzoso
> el valerme de la fuerza,
> sin que él entienda la causa.[3]

---

[1] II, Jornada II, p. 1467.

[2] II, Jornada I, p. 239.

[3] *Ibid.*

He is both a warrior and a man of learning, as well as a loyal friend. Speaking of his comrade, Don Juan de Toledo, Don Manuel tells Cosme, his squire:

> Don Juan de Toledo es . . .
> el hombre que más profesa
> mi amistad, . . .
> Los dos estudiamos juntos,
> y pasando de las letras
> a las armas, los dos fuimos
> camaradas en la guerra.[1]

Don Manuel is also endowed with a fine diction. He expresses his thoughts well, and in the words of Doña Angela to Doña Beatriz, he writes in the high-flown style of knights of chivalry:

> Digo, pues,
> que tan cortés y galante
> estilo no vi jamás,
> mexclando entre lo admirable
> del suceso, lo gracioso
> imitando los andantes
> caballeros, a quien pasan
> aventuras semejantes.[2]

The portrayal of the chivalric-courtly gentleman delineated by Calderón in the plays of *capa y espada* is somewhat elaborated and enlarged in the so-called

---

[1]   II, Jornada I, p. 238.
[2]   II, Jornada, II, p. 250.

comedias palaciegas.[1] Here the characters are not merely figures of the middle class but representatives of the highest nobility. It is particularly in these plays that the stylization of the Spanish *caballero* becomes even more striking and the socioliterary ideal of the gentleman is presented more emphatically. The heroes of Calderón's court plays are not only generally endowed with the essential qualities and traits that distinguish the protagonists of the "cloak and sword" dramas but as an added quality they also display unusual literary ability and interest in the pursuit of aesthetic pleasure. Indeed, they seem to reflect in many ways the refinement of culture and the aesthetic vision of life that prevailed in the rarefied atmosphere of the academies and salons of the period.

Two representative plays of this genre are *Las manos blancas no ofenden*, a play that Valbuena-Prat calls "una poética danza de salón,"[2] and *Dicha y desdicha de nombre* in which Calderón, according to the Spanish critic, "ha sabido fundir los escondites de los galanes y las carreras iguales de las damas en un fundo de jardín ideal, en líneas elegantes de un salón barroco arquitetónico del siglo XVII."[3] The heroes in these plays show cultural and intellectual sophistication. This is particularly evident in their social mannerisms, their love of fun and games, and also in their unrestrained obsession for elegant diction and virtuosity in conceptual acuity. The artifice in the choice of words and imagery that is pervasive specially in the

---

[1] Angel Valbuena-Briones, "Prólogo General" in Calderón de la Barca, *Obras Completas*, II, pp. 45-7.

[2] *Calderón: su personalidad, su arte dramático, su estillo, y su obra*, p. 165.

[3] *Ibid.*

court plays are well exemplied in the remarks of Cesar to Serafina in *Las manos blancas no ofenden:*

Aunque he visto de tu rostro
el encendido matiz,
dejando mustio el clavel
y ensangrentado el jazmín,
no por eso me acobardo,
viendo que no soy yo aquí
quien ama a lograr amando
porque es su interés su fin.[1]

In like manner, the ideal world and the exquisite setting in which these privileged human beings move are distinctly depicted in *Dicha y desdicha de nombre* in the description that Tristan gives of the room in which he and his master are being hosted:

¡ Qué cuarto, qué galerías,
qué colgaduras, qué telas,
qué escaparates, qué espejos,
qué escritorios, qué alacenas,
qué ropa blanca, qué cama,
qué aparadores, qué mesas,
qué viandas, qué vajillas,
qué cantimploras, qué cenas,
y sobre todo, qué vino![2]

Similarly, Don Felix Colona, the protagonist in the play, in the final verses and summary of the action, accurately reflects by his mode of expression the witticism

---

[1]   II, Jornada II, p. 1109.
[2]   II, Jornada, II, p. 1814.

and intricate rhetoric that had become conventional artistic devices in literary circles and in the academies of the age:

Y si la dicha y desdicha
del nombre dió este suceso,
la dicha de quien le ha escrito
supla en el sagrado vuestsro,
señor, que le perdonéis,
la desdicha del ingenio.[1]

It is worth noticing that in many of Calderón's plays the success and reputation of the main characters, especially in the area of sociability, mental attainments, and winning the praise of the ladies, are frequently decided in situations and in a setting simulating the pedantic worldliness of the academies. Particularly, during Calderón's time, the academies were the center of aristocratic life and the school for intellectual and social refinement of the elite. Admission to a fashionable academy was in part a privilege extended only to a select few and was one of the constant concerns and goals of any gentleman who possessed an exquisite taste and a fine mind. One could not legitimately claim to belong to high society or to be intellectually prominent unless he was known in the academic circles of famous "salons."[2]

From Calderón's dramas we are able to determine that only the more distinguished and cultivated men and women of the Spanish nobility dominated the scene of

---

[1]   II, Jornada III, p. 1846.

[2]   For a study of the "academies" during the Golden Age and the eighteenth century, see Leon H. Vincent, *The French Academy* (London: Houghton-Mifflin & Company, 1901). On the life in the "salon" during the sixteenth and seventeenth centuries, see Clark L. Keating, *Studies on the Literary "Salon" in France: 1550-1615* (Cambridge: Harvard University Press, 1941).

the academies. We know that prominent women generally decided the topics for debate and discussion, most of which centered on the theme of love and literature.[1] Men, on the other hand, gallantly competed with each other in providing those responses and solutions that most enthusiastically met with the approval of the ladies and the admiration of their peers. These parlor games and discussion, at times, became nothing short of a game of wits raised to the level of art. The depiction of the cultural milieu of the academies in a fashion that recalls the framework and the courtly pastimes of Castiglione's *Courtier* is delineated by Calderón in *El secreto a voces*. In this play we find Flérida, the beautiful duchess of Parma, instructing a selected group of *damas y galanes* to take their respective seats and amuse themselves in some form of conversation. She then delegates Arnesto to suggest the argument for debate:

> Flérida - Sentaos todos, ya que el sol
> de pardas nubes cubierto,
> hoy parece que acechando
> sale más que amaneciendo.
> Vosotras tomad lugares
> a esta parte; y vos, Arnesto,
> proponed una pregunat.

[1] Carlos Soler y Arqués in *Los Españoles según Calderón: Discurso acerca de las costumbres públicas y privadas de los españolas en el siglo XVII* (Madrid: Tipografía Guttenberg, 1881), pp. 66-7, deals briefly with the participation of women in the academies and states: "Las mujeres del siglo XVII tienen instrucción y tratan de desarrollar su talento, como lo prueban esos frecuentes certámenes, esas famosas academias de damas y caballeros, verdaderas justas del ingenio, donde se proponen y ventilan cuestiones y problemas psicológicos, á veces de la mayor importancia. El uso de estos certámenes mantuvo vivo por mucho tiempo el afán de instrucción, sin la que de poco hubieran servido las disposiciones naturales, la travesura y el ingenio."

Arnesto - Aunque mis canas pudieran
excusarme, no lo harán
por ver que así te divierto
¿ Cuál es mayor pena amando?[1]

In commenting upon this play, Angel Valbuena-Briones states:

Era costumbre en las cortes ociosas de los
países italianos aguzar el ingenio en juegos de
motivación amorosa. Se planteaba un tema y se
defendían posiciones dispares. No se trataba de
alcanzar cuál fuera la auténtica interpretación,
sino cuál había sido expuesta con mayor
brillantez. En la comedia *El secreto a voces*, la
corte de Flérida es una academia de amor.[2]

In another play, *Hombre pobre todo es trazas*, we find a witty Doña Beatriz offering a reward to the gentleman who most cleverly and tastefully responds to her challenge:

Beatriz – Si es fuerza
que amor de cualquier discurso
principal asunto sea
al que a una pregunta mía
me diere mejor respuesta,
daré esta flor.

Diego - Ya envidiosos
todos la pregunta esperan.

---

[1]   II, Jornada I, 1209-10. See also Carlos Soler y Arqués, p. 67.
[2]   II, p. 1204.

Beatriz - ¿ Cuál es mayor pena amando?[1]

Like witty discourse and gallantry, the pursuit of scholarship and the love of knowledge promoted by the academies are also sublimated in many of Calderón's characters and prototypes. We often find the highest exponents of the aristocracy engrossed in the study of the classics and the humanities. For instance, in the play, *De una causa dos efectos*, Don Carlos is not only the embodiment of great intelligence, courtesy, and discretion but also the personification of serious study and learning. No less aware of the value of culture is his father Federico:

Federico -¿ Qué hace Carlos?

Enrique - Todo el día
encerrado con Platón
y Aristóteles (que son
luz de la filosofía)
se ha estado, sin permitir
que entre a verle, sino solo
su maestro, nuevo Apolo
de nuestsra edad.

Federico -Divertir
no quiero el noble ejercicio
de sus estudios; que aunque
es mi hijo, y en él fué
más curiosidad que oficio
el saber, tanto he estimado
el deseo, la afición,

---

[1] II, Jornada I, p. 211.

el gusto y la inclinación
con que a las letras se ha dado
que no lo quiero estorbar
un punto, por conocer
que tiene más que saber
quien tiene más que mandar.[1]

Carlos' brother, Federico, recognizes as well that not by virtue of birth but by way of learning man becomes knowledgeable:

El mejor, el más supremo
aplauso no es de la sangre,
sino del entendimiento.[2]

Calderón's Aesthetic Perception of Man

The heroes that Calderón presents in the *comedias de capa y espada* and *comedias palaciegas* are only one manifestation of the ideal-type figures that he brings to the stage. If we keep in mind that a great deal of Calderón's artistic production comes to us in the form of allegorical and mythological dramas, it is in these works as well that we must direct our attention to arrive at a better understanding of Calderón's aesthetic perception of man, and consequently of the ideal human being envisioned by him. In these dramas, dominated by the presence of legendary figures, behavior is often expressed in terms of significant acts that express important social values. The human models often embodying cosmic principles

---

[1]   II, Jornada I, pp. 460-1.

[2]   II, Jornada I, p. 477.

and ideals are represented symbolically through allusions to mythology and ancient history. Although the action and the scene of these plays are set in ancient cities and the themes are derived from Greek myths and Roman history, the character drawing, save the anachronism, are men and women of Calderón's days, and are in reality, as Normal Maccoll points out, "Spaniards of the reigns of the Philips."[1]

These plays are characterized by great emphasis on stage decoration and theatrical effects aimed at satisfying the tastes of an aristocratic audience accustomed to lavish spectacle and entertainment, and to the pursuit of aesthetic pleasure for its own sake. It is not without reason that Max Kommerell calls Calderón's drama "a heightening of the ceremony of showing."[2] Heinz Gerstinger states:

> Conscious theatricality in its own right was an aspect of baroque drama. Despite the presence of the most subtle technical devices, such theater was never designed to be an imitation of nature. Rather it represented at once both an expression of the dramatist's inner point of view and an aesthetic principle.[3]

---

[1] Norman Maccoll, *Select Plays of Calderón* (London: Macmillan & Company, 1888), p. 308. Edwin Honiog in his foreword to *Calderón de la Barca; Four Plays* (New York: Hill and Wang, 1970), p. xvi, observes that "Calderón's mythological plays and autos are condensations and fulfillment of a dominant symbology at work in his earlier honor plays and well known cape and sword plays."

[2] Quoted in Heinz Gerstinger, *Pedro Calderón de la Barca*, trans. Diana Stone Peters (New York: Frederick Ungar Publishing Co., 1973), p. 38.

[3] *Ibid.*

"The performances of Calderón's works in Buen Retiro," adds Gerstinger, "may be counted among the rare blissful hours in theatrical history. Spectacle, acting, and poetry were combined in such perfection as has rarely ever been achieved."[1] For instance, during the performance of *El Mayor Encanto Amor*,

> the effects of storms at sea were produced in the park's ponds by means of invisible paddle wheels; whole islands sank in the water; tritons and nixes swam in the waves. To top it all off, the audience was offered the spectacle of fish spurting streams of perfumed water.[2]

In this artificial world of theatrical art, the main characters and ideal figures are not *personajes de carney hueso*; rather, as Valbuena-Prat points out, "son mas bien símbolos y tipos."[3] Although this technique of representation is quite evident in the allegorical dramas, it is even more pronounced in the autos where ideas, virtues, and vices often take human semblance and shape. Obviously, the introduction of symbolism and the use of allegory provided the author with a new and wider range of possibilities and a variety of plots to present to the audiences often presided by the king and his most distinguished courtiers. It also allowed him to escape from the sameness of characters and material prevalent in his earlier dramas.[4] But even more importantly it permitted him to depict prototypes of a more transcendental

---

[1] *Ibid*, pp. 17-8.

[2] *Ibid.*, p. 17.

[3] *Calderón: su personalidad, su arte dramático, su estilo y sus obras*, p. 24.

[4] Edwin Honig, Foreword to *Calderón de la Barca: Four Plays*, p. xvi.

nature and to allude to the process by which these figures and models become functional in their particular environment.

One of the central aspects of Calderón's allegorical dramas is that the hero does not appear in a leisurely mood or in a frame of still-life and ecstatic peace typical of the Renaissance man, but in a state of inner tension and in a continuous process of becoming that involves a period of self-adjustment, discovery, and transformation through self-knowledge and exposure to the world in which he lives. Valbuena-Briones in his *nota preliminar* to Calderón's play, *Primero soy yo*, states:

> Se ha defindo que una de las características del barroco es el dinamismo. La quietud estática clasicista se abandonó por no expresar bien el conflicto conceptual de la nueva época. Las represetaciones necesitaban manifestar la tensión barroca. La columna se retuerce sobre su propio eje generador, las figuras se contosionan, los planos se subdividen. La serenidad huye ante el éxtasis. Dijérase que el hombre barroco tiene una sed inextinguible de espacio, imagen que manifiesta su anhelo de libertad. Este movimiento, esta manifestación dinámica, es la proyección del problema interno, subjetivo, personal del individuo.[1]

---

[1]   II, p. 1167.

Segismundo

Nowhere, perhaps, in Calderón's works is the tension and the struggle of the baroque man to assert himself represented in more graphic terms than in the figure of Segismundo in *La vida es sueño*. Here the civilizing process of the hero takes place through a combination of factors, namely, direct instruction, exposure to civilized behavior, the hero's gradual awakening to the power of love and womanly charm, and his growing awareness, as he confronts reality, of the unpleasantness resulting from the failure to control instinctive and cumpulsive acts.

Dressed in animal skins, a recurrent symbol in the dramas of Calderón of a state of nature and unpolishedness, Segismundo at first appears "como naturaleza sin arte."[1] As Ciriaco Morón explains, "es una naturaleza sin la educadión adecuada[2] . . . no es educado entre hombres y cortesanos." Segismundo himself describes his human condition as "un compuesto de hombre y fiera."[3] Rosaura calls him

un hombre
que de humano no tiene más que el nombre,
atrevido inhumano,
crüel, soberbio, bárbaro y tirano,
nacido entre las fieras.[4]

---

[1]   Pedro Calderón de la Barca, *La vida es sueño*, ed. Ciriaco Morón (Madrid: Ediciones Cátedra, S. A., 1977), p. 27.

[2]   *Ibid.*, p. 26.

[3]   I, Jornada II, p. 516.

[4]   I, Jornada II, p. 517.

Imprisoned in a tower in his early years, he displays violent emotions. He is defiant and unruly. He responds only slightly to Clotaldo's teachings, attempts to murder Rosaura, and he is enraged at the heavens.

In the palace, Segismundo is stubborn. Basilio, his father, calls him "bárbaro . . . y atrevido."[1] In his brief spell of power he insults the whole court from the king down, makes love outrageously to two women, throws a servant out of the window, and tries to murder his former tutor."[2] He also attempts to rape Rosaura, shows a lack of respect to his father, and speaks unkindly to Astolfo. In short, he is the anticourtier at court.

As the play progresses, however, it becomes increasingly evident that Segismundo, although prey to uncontrolled passions, displays certain potentials for self-improvement and adaptation to new forms of behavior. Rosaura, for example, recognizes that "en el traje de fiera yace un hombre,"[3] and Clotaldo says, "La sangre / le incita, mueve y alienta / a cosas grandes."[4] Since the start of the play we gather, in fact, certain clues that point at his princely nature and augur his ascent to high position and status. For one, his speech is polished. He expresses his thoughts well. He shows signs of intellectual curiosity and willingness to learn. We know that he receives instruction in the area of humane letters, the sciences, and religion. Clotaldo tells us that

---

[1]   Jornada II, p. 515.

[2]   E. M. Wilson, "On *La vida es sueño* in Bruce W. Wardropper, ed. *Critical Essays on the Theater of Calderón* (New York: New York University Press, 1965), p. 70.

[3]   I, Jornada I, p. 502.

[4]   I, Jornada II, p. 511.

con él
hablé un rato de las letras
humanas, que le ha enseñado
la muda naturaleza
de los montes y de los cielos.[1]

And Basilio adds that Clotaldo

le ha enseñado ciencias;
éste en la ley le ha instruído
católica, . . .[2]

In his frequent soliloquies and dialogues, Segismundo also demonstrates considerable wit and intelligence. Even more importantly he seems to be very much aroused by womanly beauty and the feeling of love. Upon seeing Estrella, Segismundo exclaims:

¿ Quién es
esta beltad soberana?
¿ Quién es esta diosa humana
a cuyos divinos pies
postra el cielo su arrebol?[3]

When Clarín asks Segismundo what had mostly aroused his interest and admiration while at the royal palace, he responds:

Nada me ha suspendido;
que todo lo tenía prevenido;

---

[1]   *Ibid.*

[2]   Jornada II, p. 508.

[3]   I, Jornada II, p. 514.

mas si admirarme hubiera
algo en el mundo, la hermosura fuera
de la mujer.[1]

He tells Resaura:

Tu voz pudo enternecerme,
. . . tú sólo, tú has suspendido
la pasión a mis enojos,
la admiración al oído.
Con cada vez que te veo
nueva admiración me das,
y cuando te miro más,
aun más mirarte deseo.[2]

For Segismundo the process of acculturation and transformation into a civilized man is gradual and painful. While at the king's palace he is constantly reminded to be considerate and courteous. When he makes a pass at his cousin Estrella in front of Astolfo, she derides him, "Sed más galán cortesano."[3] After throwing a servant off the balcony, Astolfo also warns Segismundo:

Pues medid con más espacio
vuestras acciones severas.
que lo que hay de hombres a fieras,
hay desde un monte a palacio.[4]

---

[1]   I, Jornada II, p. 516.
[2]   I, Jornada I, p. 503.
[3]   I, Jornada II, p. 515.
[4]   I, Jornada I, p. 509.

Basilio states that he is willing to accept Segismundo at court as the legitimate heir to his throne provided that he be "prudente, cuerdo y benigno,"[1] but if he turns out to be "soberbio, osado, atrevido, y cruel,"[2] he will then be returned to his state of captivity. Thus, prudence, good judgment, and graciousness, according to Basilio, are the standard virtues for human interaction and civility, while arrogance, indiscretion, ungentlemanliness, and cruelty are negative qualities inconsistent with the furtherance of harmonious social relationship.

The warnings and instructions that Segismundo receives at court, however, are not sufficient to effect a change in his actions and restrain his natural impulses. In the first place, he finds it very difficult to adjust to the splendid surroundings and to the norms of controlled behavior prevalent at court. His appeals for self-gratification are direct and immediate; he cannot be frustrated without resorting to violence. When Rosaura insists on leaving without his consent, he threatens to retaliate:

> Harás que de cortés pase a grosero
> porque la resistencia
> es veneno crüel de mi paciencia. . . .
> harás que pierda a tu hermosura el miedo;
> que soy muy inclinado
> a vencer lo imposible.[3]

---

[1] *Ibid.*

[2] *Ibid.*

[3] I, Jornada II, p. 517.

Segismundo is also dominated by an incessant passion to seek his interests and pleasures. He tells one of his servants:

> Nada me parece justo
> en siendo contra mi gusto.[1]

Finally when Clotaldo warns him that he might be dreaming with regard to his staying at court, he threatens him with death:

> A rabia me provocas
> cuando la luz del desengaño tocas.
> Veré, dándote muerte
> si es sueño o si es verdad.[2]

Back at the tower, Segismundo, bitterly disappointed that what he had perceived as life had dissipated itself into a dream, gradually begins to realize that he must curb his passions and instincts if he is to avoid further disillusionment. Thus, his *desengaño* becomes the initial step for what will soon be a newly acquired prudence and suspicion of an ever-changing world where nothing is certain. By a process of trial and error, he realizes that instinctive outbursts can only lead to similar disappointments and *desengaños* and that the control of one's impulses is essential for survival in a deceptive world. To Clotaldo's comment that "aun en sueños / no se pierde el hacer bien,"[3] Segismundo responds:

---

[1] I, Jornada II, p. 515.
[2] I, Jornada II, p. 517.
[3] I, Jornada II, p. 522.

Es verdad; pues reprimamos
esta fiera condición,
esta furia, esta ambición,
por si alguna vez soñamos:
y sí haremos, pues estamos
en mundo tan singular,
que el vivir sólo es soñar,
y la experiencia me enseña
que el hombre que vive, sueña
lo que es, hasta despertar.[1]

Interestingly, in this world of appearances, and amidst his confused recollection of his experience at court, there remains only one truth that is pervasive and constant in Segismundo's mind, namely the love he felt for Rosaura:

De todos era señor
y de todos me vengaba;
Sólo a una mujer amaba . . .
Qlue fue verdad, creo yo,
en que todo se acabó,
y esto sólo no se acabá.[2]

It is generally agreed among critics that the factor that has contributed the most to Segismundo's progress toward becoming a virtuous and civilized man is Rosaura's womanly beauty and the refining influence of love. William M. Whitby says: "It was the 'image' incarnated in Rosaura and impelled by his love for her that had become so indelibly stamped in his memory that remained when the rest of the dream ended," and

---

[1] *Ibid.*

[2] I, Jornada II, p. 522.

that later "awakens Segismundo's consciousness of his true nature and brings about his conversion."[1] Michele Sciacca points out that it was the beauty of Rosaura and Estrella, representative of the eternal feminine charm that lead to Segismundo's transformation.[2] A. E. Sloman also believes that Segismundo's recollection of his love sentiments for Rosaura sparked "his later converstion."[3] Menéndez y Pelayo and Arturo Farinelli similarly recognize the overbearing role that Rosaura occupies in the drama and refer to it as a serious flaw in the play.[4] All in all, in the context of modern criticism, it appears that womanly charm and the power of love are at the basis of Segismundo's spiritual and social growth.

According to Everett W. Hesse, however, Segismundo's love for Rosaura "is only one of the elements which impels the prince to change his conduct."[5] According to him the virtues of prudence and temperance that the young prince later displays are acquired through "a process of re-education" based mainly on the ethical and philosophical teachings of Seneca and Saint Thomas."[6] "In the Calderonian concept of the ideal Christian prince,"

---

[1] William M. Whitby, "Rosaura's role in the structure of *La vida es sueño*" in *Critical Essays on the Theater of Calderón*, ed. Bruce W. Wardropper, pp. 104, 102.

[2] Michele Federico Sciacca, "Verdad y sueño de *La vida es sueño* de Calderón de la Barca," *Clavileño*, Año I, núm. 2 (marzo-abril, 1950), pp. 4-5.

[3] A. E. Sloman, "The structure of Calderón's *La Vida es sueño* in *Critical Essays on the Theater of Calderón*," ed. Bruce W. Wardropper, p. 94.

[4] Marcelino Menéndez y Pelayo, *Calderón y su teatro* (Madris, 1910), pp. 278, 265, 275-77. See also Arturo Farinelli, *La Vita é un sogno* (Torinio, 1916), II, pp. 260, 285-6, 276-8.

[5] Everett W. Hesse, "Calderón's concept of the Perfect Prince in *La vida es sueño* in *Critical Essays on the Theater of Calderón*," ed. Bruce W. Warfropper, p. 114.

[6] *Ibid.*, p. 114-5.

says Prof. Hesse, "prudence is composed of two main elements: moderation and knowledge of self." "Prudent moderation," he adds, "corresponds to the Aristotelian conception of the 'golden mean,' which implies the execution of an act 'in accordance with reason.'"[1] Interestingly, prudent moderation and the rule of reason, as noted earlier in this study, were also essential ingredients in the education of Castiglione's "courtier."

We first notice that Segismundo has learned the rule of reason and that he is capable of dominating his passions and acting as a civilized man when he recognizes and credits Clotaldo with his upbringing. Then in a solemn moment of self-restraint, he spares his life. He realizes that regardless of one's awareness and perception of reality, what is important is *obrar bien*:

> Mas, sea verdad o sueño,
> obrar bien es lo que importa. . . .
> obrar bien, pues no se pierde
> obrar bien, aun entre sueños.[2]

A further example of Segismundo's newly acquired self-control and sense of responsibility is that the young prince does not allow his lust for the beautiful Rosaura to interfere with the just restitution of her honor. He tells her:

> ¡ Vive Dios! que de su honra
> he de ser conquistador,
> antes que de mi corona.
> Huyamos de la ocasión,
> que es muy fuerte. . . .

---

[1] *Ibid.*, p. 117.
[2] I, Jornada III, pp. 524-5.

No te responde mi voz,
porque mi honor te responda;
no te hablo, porque quiero
que te hablen por mí mis obras,
ni te miro, porque es fuerza,
en pena tan rigurosa,
que no mire tu hermosura
quien ha de mirar tu honra.[1]

Later in a chivalrous and magnanimous gesture, he restores Rosaura's honor by giving her in marriage to Astolfo:

Pues que ya vencer aguarda
mi valor grandes victorias,
hoy ha de ser la más alta,
vencerme a mí. Astolfo dé
la mano luego a Rosaura
pues sabe que de su honor
es deuda, y yo he de cobrarla.[2]

Thus by temperance and reason, Segismundo has triumphed over himself and his noble deeds are proof of his conversion. Finally he also realizes that man is master of his own destiny and that even ill fate can be overcome by wisdom and prudence:

La fortuna no se vence
con injusticia y venganza,
porque antes se incita más;
y así, quien vencer aguarda
a su fortuna, ha de ser
con prudencia y con templanza.[3]

---

[1] I, Jornada III, p. 530.
[2] I, Jornada III, p. 533.
[3] I, Jornada III, p. 532.

His pride and arrogance have now become humility and compassion. He forgives his father and humbly kneels in front of him. His impulses are now temperate and his actions are controlled by the thought and realization that all earthly goods, pleasures, and honors only last momentarily:

> toda la dicha humana
> en fin, pasa como un sueño,
> y quiero hoy aprovecharla
> el tiempo que me durare.[1]

At the end, Segismundo is acclaimed for his achievement in self-improvement and for his clever mind, wisdom, and discretion:

> Basilio - Tu ingenio a todos admira.
> Astolfo - ¡ Qué condición tan mudada!
> Rosaura - ¡ Qué discreto y qué prudente![2]

Although *La vida es sueño*, as many critics have pointed out, is undoubtedly one of the more complex and transcendental dramas of Calderón, one of the more obvious features of the play is that it depicts the struggle of man for self-realization and traces man's ascendance from a state of instinctive savagery, wild behavior, and incivility to a

---

[1] I, Jornada III, p. 533.

[2] I, Jornada III, p. 533. On the concept of *discreción* in Calderón, see Alexander Augustine Parker, "The Meaning of 'Discreción' in "No h ay más fortuna que Dios" in Hans Flasche, *Calderón de la Barca* (Darmstadt, 1961), pp. 212-29. Angel Valbuena-Briones in *Calderón y la comedia nueva* (Madrid: Espasa-Calpe, S. A., 1977), p. 200, states "Segismundo logra la victoria de sí mismo mediante la prudencia." For an extensive bibliography on Calderón's *La vida es sueño*, see Angel Cilveti, *El significado de "La vida es sueño"* (Albatros Ediciones, 1971), pp. 229-33.

condition of personal refinement and amelioration both in a worldly and spiritual sense. In the process it also reveals the moral and social qualities that in the author's view man must possess to succeed in a world where truth and reality are not easily distinguishable from dreams and appearances. In this universe of unlimited possibilities, where the *desengaño* is the rule rather than the exception, every man, symbolized here in Segismundo, must be guided by self-restraint, prudence, wisdom, and graciousness, from which all other and gentlemanly traits are derived. On the whole, it appears, that the catalyst for the acquisition of these virtues are the influence of womanly beauty and the power of love, both of which, in the play, act as the principal civilizing forces in man's material and moral progress within society.

Coriolano

The portrait of the gentleman who, like Ssegismundo, is incited to noble deeds by his sentiment towards women, and whose violent nature is taimed by the influence of love, is also depicted by Calderón in the figure of Coriolano, one of old Rome's legendary heroes and the protagonist in *Las armas de la hermosura*. In the words of Valbuena-Briones, in this play, Calderón "adoptó la leyenda a sucesos que interesan a sus contemporaneos. . . . Presenta una fábula de acuerdo con los gustos de su generación y proclama en la adaptación del tema, una lección de cortesía y una victoria de sí mismo."[1] Menéndez y Pelayo also states that Calderón transforms Coriolano "en un galante caballero de la Corte de los Felipes."[2]

---

[1]   Pedro Calderón de la Barca, *Obras completas*, I, p. 940.

[2]   Marcelino Menéndez y Pelayo, *Calderón y su teatro*, p. 376.

The play opens in a refined courtly setting where music, poetry, and spectacle are masterfully interwoven and artistically echoed in the expression of mutual love between Coriolano and Veturia and in the chant of two choruses:

> Coro 1.° DE MUSICA. – No puede amor
> hacer mi dicha mayor.
> Coro 2.° - Ni mi deseo
> pasar del bien que poseo.[1]

A patrician by birth and a distinguished gentleman of the city, Coriolano embodies the virtues of a strong magnanimous leader who combines a deep sense of personal honor with an immeasurable tenderness of heart. Veturia, his beloved, repeatedly calls him "noble," "galán," "entendido," "cortesano."[2] Astrea, the queen of the Sabines, greets him as "cortés caballero"[3] and praises his unmatched gallantry. His chivalry with women is well expressed in these kind words of assurance that Coriolano directs to Queen Astrea, who has fallen prisoner of the Roman army:

> has llegado a puerto
> donde las mujeres tienen,
> con franca escala el respeto,
> cortesanos pasaportes
> de inviolables privilegios.[4]

---

[1]   I, Jornada I, p. 941.

[2]   I, Jornada I, p. 954.

[3]   I, Jornada I, p. 951.

[4]   I, Jornada I, p. 949.

Later, after reiterating to Astrea that true soldiers never cease to show courtesy to women even if they are from the enemy side, he gives her freedom:

> Astrea -   ¿ Qué es lo que oigo? Cielos!
> ¿ A mi patria me envías?
> Coriolano -   Sí;
> que los generosos pechos
> lidiamos porque lidiamos;
> mas no nos aborrecemos
> para las cortesanías.[1]

Coriolano is also a faithful friend. He will not compromise his comrade's integrity at any cost. When Enio generously offers to risk dishonor in order to facilitate his escape from captivity, he rejects his friend's help:[2]

> Coriolano - . . . Basta
> que a mí, como delicuente,
> por forajido la patria
> me dé, sin que por traidor,
> yendo contra lo que manda,
> te dé a ti: mira el desdoro
> que hay de una fuga a una infamia.

---

[1]   I, Jornada I, p. 950.

[2]   On Coriolano's perception of the idea of honor and dishonor, see John V. Bryans, *Calderón de la Barca: Imagery, Rhetoric and Drama*. (London: Tamesis Book Limited, 1977), pp. 156-9.

Enio -   Eso salva el dar la vida
            a un amigo.

Coriolano -   Mas no salva
            al amigo que le pone
            en que pierda honor y fama.[1]

We gain additional insight into Coriolano's noble character and ideals when later Enio insists that he accept his aid:

Coriolano - . . . y porque
            tan desconfiado vayas
            que no esperes mi salida
            daré al aire tu esperanza.

Enio -   ¿ Qué has hecho?

Coriolano -   Arrojar la lima
            que si ella es la llave falsa
            de mis prisiones, sin ella
            verás que en vano me aguardas.

Enio -   Eso es desesperación.

Coriolano - Esto es honra.

Enio -   Es temeraria
            resolución.

Coriolano -   Es piadosa.

---

[1]   I, Jornada II, p. 959.

Enio -   Es cruel despecho.

Coriolano -   Es constancia.

Enio -   Es furor.

Coriolano -   Es honor.

Enio -   Es
          ira.

Coriolano - Es valor.

Enio -   Es ingrata
          fe con Veturia.

Coriolano -   Veturia
          me querrá (que es noble dama)
          más con alabanza muerto,
          que vivo sin alabanza.[1]

A further sign of Coriolano's refinement and courtliness is that he feels a strong inclination toward "love," a passion that dominates his thoughts and actions. It was for love's sake, he tells the king of the Sabines, that he had lost the favor of his peers and even that of his own family. His downfall came when upon his return to Rome after a successful military campaign against the Sabines, Coriolano, incited by Veturia, protested the edict passed by the Roman senate during his absence, which stripped Roman women of their traditional rights and privileges. Fully convinced of pursuing a just cause, he appealed to

---

[1]   I, Jornada II, p. 959.

the Romans to support his crusade for women's freedom, thus becoming the champion and protector of their rights:

> Quien fuere de mi sentir
> en que no se vea ofendido
> el honor de las mujeres,
> me siga.[1]

When during a conversation, Aurelio, his father, suggests that love makes men effeminate and lethargic, Coriolano promptly rejects Aurelio's contention, and declaring himself ready to serve Rome, argues that indeed love inspires men to great deeds and enhances rather than discourages valor:

> Y para que mejor veas
> que ser galán en la paz
> no es ser cobarde en la guerra
> el primero seré yo
> que de la patria en defensa
> al oposito le salga.[2]

Although Coriolano suggests that love and patriotism are not mutually exclusive, when forced by his father to choose between the two, he opts for "love." He tells Aurelio, who reminds him of his duty to Rome:

---

[1]   I, Jornada I, p. 954.

[2]   I, Jornada I, p. 944.

Perdida
Veturia, ¿ qué más perdido?[1]

His choice and decision in favor of Veturia is based on
the belief that there can be no honorable men in a society
where women are abused and dishonored.[2] Honor, as
Veturia explains, is a collective quality that reflects itself
equally on both men and women:

> siendo las mujeres
> el espejo cristalino
> del honor del hombre, ¿ cómo
> puede, estando a un tiempo mismo
> en nosotras empañado,
> estar en vosotros limpio?[3]

Coriolano, however, must pay for his act of public
disobedience. Found guilty of treason, he is stripped of
his honor and sentenced to a humiliating life in exile.
Embittered by the cruel treatment, he is overtaken by
anger and dominated by an uncontrollable passion for
revenge unmitigated by reason. For a while he even
forgets his commitment to Veturia, who never wavers
in her loyalty and love for him. In terms reminiscent of
Segismundo's violent outbursts, Coriolano laments his
condition and avows to strike back:

---

[1] *Ibid.*

[2] I, Jornada I, p. 954. On the theme of honor in *Las armas de la hermosura*, see
Albert E. Sloman, *The dramatic craftsmanship of Calderon* (Oxford: Dolphin
Book Co., Ltd., 1963), pp. 68-9.

[3] I, Jornada I, p. 953.

¿ En fin, hijo aborrecido,
Patria, me arroja tu centro,
como bruto a las montañas
como fiera a los desiertos?
Pues teme que, como fiera
rabiosa, que como fiero
bruto irritado, algún día
me vuelva contra mi dueño.[1]

Dismayed by the severe punishment inflicted upon him, he attributes his misfortune to Fortuna, and like Segismundo, raises the question and speculates whether life is nothing but a dream:

Fortuna, si por asunto
de tus variados sucesos
me ha elegido lo inconstante
de tu condición a efecto
de que acrisole en mí
ser verdad aquel proverbio
de que es sueño la vida,
pasándome sus extremos
a preso de victorioso
y a victorioso de preso.[2]

Away from culture and civilization, Coriolano rejects his roots and refuses to reveal his identity:

Sabino -   ¿ Quién eres hombre, me di,
           sin retóricos rodeos?

---

[1]   I, Jornada II, p. 965.
[2]   I, Jornada II, p. 963.

Coriolano - ¿ Cómo he de decir quien soy
si aun de quién fui no me acuerdo?[1]

Later, after winning their confidence and swearing allegiance to the king and queen of the Sabines, Coriolano returns to Rome as commander-in-chief of their army, ready to destroy the city. He rejects all efforts of conciliation and even his father's plea for mercy will not spare the city from destruction. He tells Aurelio:

Di a Roma que yo he venido
a destruirla, y que así
no espere piedad de mí,
porque no la ha de tener
hasta verla perecer.[2]

Coriolano's inherent nobility, however, comes to surface when near the end of the play he yields to Veturia's argument for leniency, fully aware that his act of mercy toward Rome would alienate Sabino, to whom he now offers his life as a price:

Viva, pues, triumfante Roma,
ya que han podido postrarme
a sus siempre victoriosas
municiones de cristales
"Las armas de la hermosura."[3]

---

[1] I, Jornada II, p. 967.
[2] I, Jornada III, p. 973
[3] I, Jornada III, p. 979.

In the words of Coriolano, the noble and kind heart cannot help surrendering to womanly charm and beauty:

el más noble
puede negar justa mente
lo que le pide, a su patria,
a su padre, a sus parientes,
a su amigo y su enemigo;
pero a su dama no puede
a más cuando su hermosura
con armas del llanto vence.[1]

He will not accept Rome's submission until the government of that city gives back to both Roman and Sabine women all their former rights and privileges, and women are left free to pursue interests and activities of their own choice:

las mujeres que hoy
tiranizadas conviene
se pongan en libertad;
y a las que volver quisieran
a Sabinia, no se impidan
ni sus personas ni bienes.
Que las que quieran quedarse,
restituidas se queden
en sus primeros adornos
de galas, joyal y afeites.
Que a la que se aplique a estudios
o armas, ninguno la niegue
ni el manejo de los libros,
ni el uso de los arneses;

---

[1]   I, Jornada III, p. 980.

sino que sean capaces,
o ya lidien o ya aleguen
en los estrados de togas,
y en las lides de laureles.[1]

At the conclusion of the play, the Roman leader imparts a lesson of courtesy to all the gentlemen of his time and of all times:

el hombre que a una mujer,
dondequiera que la viere,
no la hiciere cortesía,
por no bien nacido quede.
. . . se entregue
todo el honor de los hombres
a arbitrio de las mujeres.[2]

Like Segismundo, Coriolano at the end becomes a symbol of prudence, forgiveness, and compassion. A chanting chorus sings his praises:

¡ Viva quien vence!
Que es vencer perdonando
vencer dos veces.[3]

In *Las armas de la hermosura*, like in *La vida es sueño*, the hero's lust for vengeance is tamed by the refining influence of women and love. Both Segismundo and Coriolano in their desire for revenge are immensely human, but even more significant is that they both

---

[1]   I, Jornada III, p. 973.
[2]   I, Jornada III, p. 979.
[3]   I, Jornada III, p. 980.

succumb to the touch of persuasion and tenderness. They are men whose love is perfected and made noble. They both emerge as the champions of women's rights, which in both plays become the gentleman's social code. Both heroes come to realize that honor and glory is to be found in the rule of reason, gallantry, and love.

Ulysses

Another symbolic character and model from classical antiquity that Calderón translates to contemporary stage and presents as an example for imitation by aristocratic society is the figure of Ulysses. Calderón's artistic adaptation of the Homeric hero is not just a dramatic portrayal of a man engaged in a struggle to conquer his sensuality as he "had long been a stock type in Spanish literature,"[1] but an idealization of a prototype that eminently reflected the aesthetical vision and practical necessities of the distinguished human being during the baroque era. Calderón's representation of Ulysses, besides appealing immensely to eighteenth-century sensibilities, also fulfilled, to a greater extent than other characters of his literary production, the specifications of the superior man most able to survive in a world increasingly troubled and uncertain. Ulysses, in fact, is repeatedly presented by Calderón as the embodiment of prudence, sagacity, astuteness, wisdom, and dissemblance—qualities that in baroque thought constituted a useful ideal for man. In addition to these qualities, he also embodies courage, self-confidence, valor in battle, gallantry with women, romantic temperament, and intellectual and

---

[1] Heinz Gerstinger, *Pedro Calderón de la Barca*, p. 98.

social refinement—attributes which have traditionally distinguished the Spanish *caballero*.

In the "auto sacremental" *Los encantos de la culpa*, Ulysses, symbolizing everyman, presents himself as a skillful leader whose principal resources are caution, courage, and cunning. He tells Circe:

> El Hombre soy, a astucias inclinado,
> y por serlo hoy Ulises me he nombrado,
> que en griego decir quiere
> cauteloso.[1]

Later, Circe, in the semblance of Culpa, recognizes him as the mirror of courage, intelligence, and subtlety:

> erais el valiente Ulises
> - que quiere decir en griego
> "hombre ingenioso" (que al fin
> no hay sin cautelas ingenio)-.[2]

It is, however, in the play *El mayor encanto, amor* that Calderón transforms the palace of Circe into a modern court and the Greek hero into a modern prototype of courtly and gentlemanly conduct. Apart from its spiritual and philosophical content and its obvious cosmic implications, the action in the play takes place in a worldly setting dominated by baroque artistic effects and by aristocratic tastes, attitudes, and activities cultivated in contemporary Spanish courtly circles. For its theatrical technique and modernity, *Love, the Greatest Enchantment*, says Heinz Gerstinger, can be considered "the most perfect

[1] III, p. 407.
[2] III, p. 413.

baroque work of that period; for it is a veritable feast of music, technical effects, visual delights, and, above all, poetry."[1]

The background of the play is the court of Circe, a contemporary female wizard, a combination of erudition and voluptuous beauty, with all the magical powers, finesse, and cunning of a contemporary courtly woman. She is described as "muger con belleza y con ingenio," "un ángel en belleza y condición," "una muger hermosa . . . que era la envidia de Diana," "bellísima cazadora."[2] She is also well versed in the study of the humanities, sciences, and mathematics. Her palace is an exotic magical land, *deleitoso paraíso*, where Ulysses, in Circe's words, will be able to experience "todo gusto, / todo aplauso, todo alivio, / todo paz, todo descanso."[3]

In this artificial world of almost ideal perfection appears Ulysses, the hero and the gentleman. At first, he is presented as a man of great valor and discretion. The *Músicos* at his arrival greet him as

el siempre invencible griego,
el nunca vencido Ulises. . . .
el discreto y fuerte Ulises.[4]

Circe also welcomes him as

el griego más generoso
que vio el sol.[5]

[1] Gerstinger, *Pedro Calderón de la Barca*, p. 96.
[2] I, pp. 1513, 1521, 1512, 1514.
[3] I, p. 518.
[4] I, pp. 1514, 1519.
[5] I, p. 1414.

Since the very start of the play, Ulysses shows great courage and gallantry when he risks his life to rescue his crew from the bewitchment of Circe despite the warnings of his lieutenants:

>Antistes - ... vengo a avisarte de esto,
>porque de esta esfinge huyamos. ...
>
>Ulises - ¿ Cómo habemos de dejar
>así a nuestros compañeros?
>
>Clar'in - Perdernos señor, nostros,
>no es alivio para ellos. ...
>
>Ulises - A sus palacios me guía,
>verásme vencer en ellos
>sus hechizos, y librar
>a todos mis compañeros.[1]

Ulysses, reflecting the talents and attributes of the Spanish *caballero* of the eighteenth century, is skilled in both arms and letters. He tells Circe:

>Aunque inclinado a las letras,
>militare escuadrones
>seguí: que en mí se admiraron
>espada y plumas conformes.[2]

As a gentleman well-bred with courtesy, he also displays traditional Spanish chivalry and kindness to women. Although he is fully aware that Circe's trickery

---

[1]   I, Jornada, I, pp. 1513-4.

[2]   I, Jornada I, p. 1515.

and magical powers may cost him dearly, he gallantly accepts the invitation to visit her palace:

Digo
que no pudiera ser noble
quien no fuese agradecido,
y que conmigo he de ser
crüel, por ser cortés contigo.[1]

Ulysses is also depicted as a fierce defender and protector of the woman he loves. When Circe, through a simulated enemy attack, cunningly sought to appraise which of her two suitors—Arsidas or Ulysses—displayed greater courage and loved her more, Ulysses responded by branding his sword and conducting an active search for the enemy in the nearby areas. Arsidas, on the other hand, while pledging to protect Circe from harm, remained unhurried by her side. Later, when Circe informed the two rivals that the enemy alert was nothing but a test designed to assess their relative strength and amorous attachment to her, Arsidas challenged the appropriateness of Ulysses' action, accused him of poor judgment, and proclaimed himself as the more creditable and exemplary lover. Ulysses, in turn, defended his conduct against the insinuations of his competitor and declared himself as the supreme model of courtliness. Here is part of the witty debate between the two:

Arsidas - Yo soy el que me corono
Vencedor, y el que merezco,
Circe, tu favor hermoso,
pues Ulises, acudiendo

<hr>

[1] I, Jornada I, p. 1518.

a sus armas tan heroico,
dejó de mostsrarse amante,
pues en riesgo tan forzoso
no acudió luego a su dama;
que en un amante es impropio.

Ulises - Que acudí a las armas mías
no niego; pero tampoco
niego que de amante ha sido
el efecto más forzoso;
porque si tomo mis armas,
para defensa las tomo
suya. . . .

Arsidas - Si las nobles leyes noto
de caballería, acudir
a las damas es forzoso;
y así como caballero,
no como amante, socorro
a Circe.

Ulises - En las de milicia
es ley, siempre que armas oigo,
acudir a tomar armas;
y así con valor heroico,
yo soldado, caballero
y amante, he acudido a todo.[1]

Reflecting individual preferences and type qualities commonly associated with baroque temperament and personality, Ulysses is also depicted as a man of many resources, of nimble wits, crafty, and skilled at the most

[1]   I, Jornada II, p. 1532.

subtle games. Besides being successful in outplaying his opponents, Ulysses is also able to outsmart Circe, the mistress of all art, in a most critical area of their relationship, namely love. Not only was the Greek hero capable of dissimulating his amorous passion and admiration for her beauty, but even when he is finally ready to confess his love feelings to her, exerting his proverbial self-restraint and always wary of the possibility of *desengaño*, he reveals them in a coded form and by means of a tale. In a confused, almost magical game of wits, at last it was Circe, not Ulysses, who most openly and most passionately admits surrender to love. She tells him:

> Llegaste tú, y queriendo tú homicida
> ser, burlaste mis ciencias: con espanto,
> queriéndote vencer, quedé vencida.
> Sí, mi encanto al mirar asombro tanto
> al incanto de amor, rindió mi vida;
> luego el amor es el mayor encanto.[1]

Ulysses, however, is not immune to love. Like Coriolano he shows loving kindness and delicacy of feeling toward women, and he is particularly touched by their tearful eyes. Responding to Circe's cry for affection, he says:

> Tus encantos vencí, mas no tu llanto;
> pudo el amor lo que ellos no han podido;
> luego el amor es el mayor encanto.[2]

---

[1] I, Jornada III, p. 1536.

[2] *Ibid.*

Finally, as it occurs almost invariably among Calderón's heroes, Ulysses cannot help but yield to womanly beauty and seductiveness:

Circe -   ¿ Quién ha vencido?

Ulises -   El amor,
que, ¿ cómo pudiera ser
que otro afecto me vinciera,
donde tu hermosura viera?
Esclavo tuyo he de ser.
No hay más fama para mí
que adorarte, no hay más gloria
que vivir en tu memoria.[1]

Even Antistes, observing in disbelief his master's sudden change of attitude toward Circe, cannot help concluding that love and beauty conquer all:

¿Quién creerá, que no bastando
tantos encantos, ni tantas
ciencias a vencer sus hados,
una hermosura bastara?
Mas todos lo creerán, todos,
pues todos a ver alcanzan
que un amor y una hermosura
son el encanto del alma.[2]

Strong as it may be, the power of love is not greater than the call of duty or man's thirst for fame. Incited by Achilles, who appears to him in a dream, and reminded

[1]   I, Jornada III, p. 1537.
[2]   I, Jornada III, p. 1534.

of his heroic destiny by his companions, Ulysses finally manages to free himself from Circe's amorous entanglement.

He tells his friends:

¡ Ay amigos! tiempo es ya
que a los engaños me usurpe
del mayor encanto, y hoy
el valor, del amor trunfe.[1]

During Circe's absence, Ulysses sails away with his crew into the open sea:

Huyamos de aquí; que hoy
es huir acción ilustre,
pues los encantos de amor
los vence aquel que los huye.[2]

The sorcerer begs for his return, but in vain. In despair, she destroy herself and her whole island sinks into the sea.

Thus, by the end of the play, Ulysses emerges as a victorious man, who by virtue of his will and courage shapes his life and destiny. Even more importantly, however, he comes forth as an ideal of worldly perfection embodying both the military and social qualities of the knight of chivalry and the intellectual refinement of the Renaissance gentleman. On one hand, in fact, Ulysses combines the main attributes of the medieval knight at arms, namely the knight's independence of character,

[1]   I, Jornada III, p. 1542.
[2]   I, Jornada, III, p. 1543.

his bravery, valor, physical strength, piety, susceptibility to love, gallantry with women, and to some degree, his heroic passion and folly. On the other hand, Ulysses also mirrors the exceptional qualities of the Renaissance courtier, especially the courtier's love of knowledge and spirit of inquiry, his versatility and composure, his sophisticated taste and pursuit of aesthetic enjoyment, as well as his ability for disguise and adopting to shifting roles and changing situations.

What distinguishes, however, Calderón's portrayal of Ulysses, "the extraordinary human being," from previous prototypes is the Greek hero's vigilant and cautious attitude toward the world as it appears, his resourcefulness and faculty to control conflicting passions, his introspective nature, and his self-possession and alertness to the possibility of *desengaño*. These archetypal qualities, as it was pointed out earlier, are also an integral part of Calderón's characterization of Segismundo and Coriolano, but they acquire special relevance in the playwright's dramatic adaptation of the Ulysses theme.

Although dressed in symbolism, the figure of Ulysses—refined and elaborated by Calderón in *El mayor encanto, amor*—may well be the portrait of what the dramatist considered an ideal of gentlemanly perfection and worldly conduct. And the particular traits and attitudes that distinguish the hero may well represent Calderón's aesthetic and practical guidelines for the aristocratic life of the baroque age. Without drastically altering the Greek warrior's traditional nature, Calderón almost effortlessly assimilated the Ulysses-type figure into current fashion and conditions, and transformed it into a model for imitation by the exceptional man of that period.

Nevertheless, the atmosphere of disillusionment,[1] the country's political turmoil and series of military defeats, the sense of failure, and the insecurity that permeated the economic and social life of Spain during this time, together with the rapid growth and concentration of population in large cities—the spirit of competition, displacement, and alienation that the individual often experienced in these densely populated areas, not to mention the widespread skepticism and the nation's general awareness that reality much too easily breaks into illusion, all called for a more pragmatic and systematic approach to the question of human perfectability and to man's knowledge of how to function successfully in an uncertain world.

Gracián and "Worldly Perfection"

During the first half of the seventeenth century it was Baltasar Gracián who zealously devoted his energies to design a more detailed and exacting prescription of worldly wisdom for the aspirant to greatness and heroism in a world where, according to the remarks of "el Veedor de todo" in the *Criticón*, "de una hora para otra están las cosas de diferente data y muy de otro color,"[2] and were in the words of Andrenio "toda inmundicia de costumbres, todo lo bueno por tierra, la virtud dio en el suelo con su

---

[1] On the social and political climate of Spain during the first half of the seventeenth century, see J. H. Helliot, *Imperial Spain: 1469-1716*, pp. 281-351.

[2] Baltasar Gracián, *El Criticón* in *Obras Completas*, ed. Arturo del Hoyo (Madrid: Aguilar, 1967), p. 906. All quotations from Gracián's works will be from this edition.

letrero: '¡ Aquí yace!' la basura a caballo, los muladores dorados, y al cabo al cabo, todo hombre es barro."[1]

Obviously, what in Cervantes had been only a resounding warning of the possibility of *desengaño*, a reserved, watchful attitude, and a somewhat optimistic appraisal of his time and human nature in general, in Gracián had become a total disappointment and an unqualified mistrust of man and the world that surrounds him. "El Siglo de Oro" that Cervantes in *Don Quijote* had characterized as "el siglo de hierro,"[2] in Gracián had now become "el de lodo." Discernibly speaking for the author, Andrenio asks Critilo: "¿ En cual [siglo] pensáis vivir, en el del oro o en el del lodo? – Yo diría- respondió Critilo – que en el de hierro. Con tantos, [yerros] todo anda errado en el mundo y todo al revés, si ya no es de bronce, que es peor." To these remarks Andrenio responded: "No faltará quien diga . . . que es el siglo de cobre, y no de pague, mas yo digo que el de lodo cuando todo lo veo puesto dél."[3]

Even further removed from Gracián's topsy turvy world and assessment of reality is Castiglione's aristocratic and aesthetic view of life and the portrait he draws of the ideal man of his age. The same prototype of worldly perfection that in *Il Cortegiano* appears as a self-confident, outgoing, art-oriented, and pleasure-seeking individual devoid of true practical interests, in Gracián becomes a pragmatic, introspective, self-possessed, crafty schemer. Even the courtier's mastery of *sprezzatura* and his adaptability to changing situations are not matched by the calculating intelligence, self-discipline, and practical competence of Gracián's "héroe" and "discreto." Unlike the courtier who

[1]   *Ibid.*, p. 703.
[2]   Miguel de Cervantes Saavedra, *Don Quijote de la Mancha*, p. 555.
[3]   Gracián, *El Criticón*, p. 703.

seeks perfection and refinement through art, Gracián's models show considerable interests in perfecting their ability to read beyond the realm of outwardly appearances, and thus experimentally discover the world's inner truth. They seem, in fact, constantly engaged in sharpening those aptitudes that more easily will equip them to penetrate "la corteza" or "disfraz"[1] of the empirical world and permit them to successfully deal with the dreamlike qualities and often chaotic conditions of the human experience. As Gracián points out in *El Criticón*, man's greatest ability is:

> Aquello de llegar a escudriñar los senos de los pechos humanos, a descoser las entretelas del corazón, a dar fondo a la mayor capacidad, a medir un cerebro por capaz que sea, a sondar el más profundo interior: eso sí que es algo, esa sí que es fullería, y que merece la tal habilidad ser estimada y codiciada.[2]

For Gracián's heroes, courtliness is not a technique or a method of appearing gracious and refined at court, but the successful application of prudence and craftiness to all interpersonal relationships within the context of a more intricate and more evasive world: that of modern urban society. The new art, as we find it written in *El Criticón*, corresponds "al ver con cien ojos, al oír con cien orejas, al obrar con cien manos, proceder con dos rostros, doblando la atención al adevinar cuanto ha de ser y al descifrar un

---

[1]   *Ibid.*, p. 898. The "truth hidden" vs. "external appearance" in Gracián is discussed by Theodore L. Kassier in *The Truth Disguised: Allegorical Structure and Technique in Gracián's "Criticón"* (London: Tamesis Books Ltd., 1976), pp. 95-113.

[2]   *Ibid.*

mundo entero."[1] Thus, in his pursuit for self-assertion, man must be able to play a variety of roles and take on a mask, as well as adopt an attitude of reserve and caution when dealing with the changing face of reality.

It is useful to point out that, as in Gracián, the question of the relativity of man's experience on earth is also one of Cervantes' main concerns in *Don Quijote*, and it is particularly evident in Cervantes' portrayal of characters engaged in deliberately disguising their identity and playing many roles. Examples calling attention to a deceitful world and a deliberate falsification of reality are: the masquerade of the barber as a damsel in distress and that of the priest as her squire, both with the purpose of enticing Don Quijote's return home; Sansón Carrasco's repeated attempts to pose as a knight-errant with a similar noble intent; the depiction of Don Quijote as a hero showing both periods of mental acuity and intervals of sheer madness; Sancho's aforethought distortion of Dulcinea and the added deception of his master in Sierra Morena; the succession of practical jokes effected on Don Quijote and Sancho by the *duques* under pretense and disguise of courtesy; and Don Quijote's belief in a magic world populated by talking heads, flying horses, and enchanters.

In this world of shifting roles and appearances where everything is subject to change and open to doubt, and where the boundaries between reality and falsehood are blurred, nothing—Cervantes seems to suggest—is ascertainable or exact. Despite human pretensions and claims to knowledge, there can be no absolute sureness of the nature of reality and truth. Confronted with the prospect for change of people and circumstances and

[1] *Ibid.*

man's limited ability to decipher the substance of things, the author of *Don Quijote* is less dogmatic than Calderón or Gracián as to what man's ideal of moral and worldly conduct is or ought to be. Rather, he subtly states the problem and points to reason, discretion, and the love of fellow man—all of which fall within the boundaries of the human potential as guiding principles for virtuous living.[1]

Undoubtedly Cervantes' vision of truth and reality as something undefinable and transcendental not only reflected current concerns and preoccupations, but because of his influence over the reading public, it also heightened even more the moral dilemma and the existential quandary of his age. The theme and queries that Cervantes submits for consideration to his contemporaries are those of *engaño* and *desengaño*, *realidad* and *apariencia*—subject matter that to a large extent constitutes the background of the literature of the baroque period, and particularly of the works of Calderón and Gracián.

As it was pointed out earlier in this chapter, the theme of *engaño* and *desengaño* and the misty nature of man's worldly experience is a recurrent theme in the dramas of Calderón. His consistent escape into the world of allegory and symbolism;[2] his elaborate metaphors and allusions to

---

[1] Marcia L. Wells in *Style and Structure in Gracián's "El Criticón"* (North Carolina Studies in Romance Languages and Literatures, Chapel Hill: University of North Carolina Press, 1976), p. 94, points out that in comparison to Cervantes, Gracián gives less freedom to his characters. Particularly in part 1 and 2 of *El Criticón* "the action takes precedence over the character, whose reaction is inevitable and predetermined by his allegorical significance." For an appraisal of Cervantes' view of man's ideal conduct, see this study, chapter 3, 179-80.

[2] Comparing Gracián's statements on allegory and those of Calderón on the same topic in the "auto sacramental," Marcia L. Wells, p. 92, states: "Unlike Gracián, Calderón does not explore the possibilities that allegory

life as a dream; the repeated references to human passions as powerful forces capable of plunging man into a state of confusion and *desengaño*; the presence of supernatural forces, mythological figures, and ancient heroes in many of his dramas; as well as the exotic scenery and theatrics prevalent in some of his more renowned plays are constant reminders of Calderón's perception of life as a kaleidoscopic plane of shifting transparency, as a semblance of truths beyond our grasp.

It was Gracián, however, who not only called attention to man's critical need to perceive what lies beyond the world of appearances, but at the same time he also mapped a survival strategy for man to follow. As our author often states in his works, it was no longer sufficient for the aspirant to greatness to cultivate, like the courtier, his aesthetic impulses, to possess a fine mind and body, to be versed in literary and artistic pursuits, and to be accomplished in martial skills and worldly charm. Besides these talents and qualities, Gracián, in the chapter "Arte para ser dichoso," through the words of Fortuna, warns his "discerto" to acquire additional know-how and worldly wisdom:

> Andad y procurad ser . . . despierto como el León, prudente como el Elefante, astuto como la Vulpeja y cauto como el Lobo. Disponed bien los medios, y consequiréis vuestsros intentos: y desengáñense todos los mortales . . . que no hay más dicha ni más desdicha que prudencia o imprudencia.[1]

---

offers for duplicity as a 'capa' or 'disfraz.' He is interested in the duality of allegory, in the double levels of meaning that it is capable of expressing simultaneously."

[1] Gracián, *El Discreto*, p. 141.

Thus, vigilance, prudence, cunning, and cautiousness are the overbearing qualities and marks of distinction of what can be properly called "el hombre gracianesco." In view of this, it is not at all surprising that Gracián's composite of the exceptional human being, like that of Calderón, should resemble a man strongly endowed with the Ulysses-type figure and qualities. Gracián, in fact, in *El Criticón*, brushing aside as an anachronism *El Galateo Cortesano* by Lucas Gracián Dantisco—a most popular adaptation of both Castiglione's *Il Cortegiano* and Della Casa's *Galateo*,[1] unequivocally points to the *"Ulisiada de Homero"* as the most up-to-date manual of worldly wisdom and pragmatic behavior.

In *crisi* 11 of the first part of *El Criticón*, Gracián paints the following scene: Andrenio and Critilo upon their arrival at Toledo enter a bookstore for the purpose of acquiring a handbook that was to serve them as a guide in what they call the "laberinto cortesano"[2] of the city. The owner unhesitantly suggests the *Galateo*, which in his view is nothing less than "la cartilla del arte de ser personas . . . y un brinquiño de oro, tan plausible como importante; y aunque pequeño, hace grandes hombres, pues enseña a serlo."[3] But a consummate courtier who overheard the conversation soon takes exception with his comment and remarks that the *Galateo* "aún valdría algo se si platicase todo al revés de lo que enseña."[4] He then adds:

---

[1] Gracián, *El Criticón*, p. 629. See also chapter 2 of this study, p. 122.

[2] *Ibid.*, p. 629.

[3] *Ibid.*

[4] *Ibid.*, p. 630.

En aquel buen tiempo cuando los hombres lo eran, digo buenos hombres, fueran admirables estas reglas; pero ahora, en los tiempos que alcanzamos, no valen cosa. Todas las liciones que aquí encarga eran del tiempo de las ballestas, mas ahora, que es el de las gafas, creedme que no aprovechan.[1]

In his final words of advice to Andrenio and Critilo, the courtier states:

Digo que el libro que habéis de buscar y leerlo de cabo a cabo, ese la célebre *Ulisíada* de Homero. . . . ¿ Que, pensáis que el peligroso golfo que él describe es aquel de Sicilia, y que las sirenas están acullá en aquellas sirtes con sus caras de mujeres y sus colas de pescados, la Circe encantadora en su isla y el soberano Cíclope en su cueva? Sabed que el peligroso mar es la Corte con la Scila de sus engaños y la Caribdis de sus mentiras. . . . Hay encantadoras Circes, que a muchos que entraron hombres los han convertido en brutos. ¿ Qué diré de tantos cíclopes, tan necios como arrogantes, con solo un ojo, puesta la mira en su gusto y presunción? Este libro os digo que repaséis, que él os ha de encaminar para que como Ulises escapéis de tanto escollo como os espera y tanto monstruo como os amenaza.[2]

---

[1]   -

[2]   *Ibid.*, p. 634.

Gracián, at the end, informs us that Andrenio and Critilo "tomaron su consejo y fueron entrando en la corte, experimentando al pie de la letra lo que el Cortesano les había prevenido y Ulises enseñado."[1]

An examination of Gracián's works clearly reveals the author's preference to highlight those special traits and virtues and to delineate those characters and prototypes that distinguish themselves for their affinity and association with the Ulysses-type figure.

For example, in Primor I of *El Héroe*, Gracián warns his candidate that he must be first and above all vigilant, evasive, and crafty:

> Sea esta la primera destreza en el arte de entendidos; medir el lugar con su artificio. Gran treta es ostentarse al conocimiento, pero no a la comprehensión; cebar la expectación, pero nunca desengañarla del todo. . . . Excuse a todos el varón culto sondarle el fondo a su caudal, si quiere que le veneren todos. . . .¡ Oh, varón, candidato de la fama! Tú, que aspiras a la grandeza, alerta al primor: Todos te conozcan, ninguno te abarque, que, con esta regla, lo moderado parecerá mucho, y lo mucho, infinito, y lo infinito, más.[2]

Although Gracián in the succeeding nineteen "primores" plans to train the "héroe" in a multiplicity of talents and skills, and suggests that he acquire, among other virtues and qualities, great knowledge, prudence, discretion, courage, ease of manners, good taste, and

---

[1]   *Ibid.*

[2]   Gracián, *El Heroe*, pp. 6-8.

a fine diction, it appears that the final success of the "héroe" depends for the most part on his mastery of "disímulo"—on the degree of control that he is capable of exerting over his passions and emotions, and on his ability to create an impression of power, leadership, and influence. But nowhere in the works of Gracián are the subtleties of deception, prudence, dissemblance, and cunning raised to the level of art as in *El Discreto*. The twenty-five "realces"[1] that comprise the text aim at providing the seventeenth-century *caballero* with a pragmatic approach to worldly success and self-fulfillment. "El discreto" is a man who seeks self-knowledge: "comience por sí mismo el Discreto a saber sabiéndose."[2] "El primer paso del saber es saberse."[3] Outwardly he displays "una audacia discreta," "una cuerda intrepidez," "señorio en el decir y

---

[1] Evaristo Correa Calderón in *Baltasar Garcián: su vida y su obra* (Madrid: Editorial Gredos, 1961), p. 170, defines the word "realce" as "el retrato moral de una prenda de perfección, y su conjunto la suma de méritos y virtudes deseables en el hombre de mundo, algo así como la culminación en un modelo de las excelencias de muchos." See also "Estudio Preliminar" of Arturo del Hoyo in Baltasar Gracián, *Obras Completas,* p. cxlvii. The similarities between *El Criticón* and *El Discreto* are discussed by Adolphe Coster in *Baltasar Gracián,* trans. Ricardo del Arco y Garay (Zaragoza: Institución "Fernando el Católico," 1947), pp. 113-24.

[2] *El Discreto,* pp. 81-2. Monroe Hafter in *Gracián and Perfection, Spanish Moralists of the Seventeenth Century* (Cambridge, Mass., 1966), p. 107, states that in comparison to other individuals in Gracián's earlier works, "el discreto" stands out for his definite shift toward greater introspection. Evaristo Correa Calderón in *Baltasar Gracián Agudeza y Arte de Ingenio* (Madrid: Clásicos Castalia, 1969), p. 12, says: *El Discreto* "trata de formar no ya al héroe o al político, ni siquiera al cortesano sino simplemente al hombre de mundo, prudente, mesurado, que sepa desenvolverse en los salones con inteligencia y soltura."

[3] Gracian, *El Discreto,* p. 100.

en el hacer," and a certain equilibrium between "genio" and "ingenio."[1] He is also endowed with "gallardía del espíritu con cuyos galantes actos queda muy airoso un corazón."[2] In addition he possesses "cierta subiduría cortesana, una conversable sabrosa erudición, que le hace bien recibido en todas partes y aun buscado de la atenta curiosidad."[3]

"El discreto" is a man of good taste and good manners: in all his actions he must show "despejo," "decoro," "buen gusto."[4] "Ninguno"—warns the author—"consiguirá jamás crédito de consumado en cualquier empleo sin el realce de un plausible gusto,"[5] "sin un buen modo todo se desluce, así como con él todo se adelanta."[6] "El discreto" is also a man who acts with intelligence and good judgment.[7] He must avoid "la hazañería"[8] and "la

---

[1] *Ibid.*, pp. 83, 81-2.

[2] *Ibid.*, p. 89.

[3] Gracián, *El Discreto*, p. 92. "This idea of gusto," says George Gadamer, "is the starting point for Gracián's ideal of social education. His ideal of the educated man (of the *discreto*) is that, as *hombre en su punto*, he achieves the proper freedom of distance from all things of life and society, so that he is able to make distinctions and choices consciously and from a superior position. This ideal of *Bildung* (cultivation) established by Gracián was supposed to be a completely new departure. It replaced that of the Christian courtier (Castiglione). It is remarkable within the history of Western ideals of *Bildung* for being independent of class. It is the ideal of a society based on *Bildung*. (*Truth and Method*, p. 14.)

[4] *Ibid.*, 127.

[5] *Ibid.*, 104.

[6] *Ibid.*, p. 138.

[7] *Ibid.*, 136.

[8] *Ibid.*, p. 122. In *realce* 20 of *"El Discerto"* in "Sátira contra la hazañería," Gracián, while condemning those who engage in what he calls "ridículas proezas," in an obvious satire of Don Quijote, he states: "No todos los ridículos andantes salieron de la Mancha" (p. 137). Although Gracián never

afectación,"[1] and cultivate with enthusiasm his inner qualities since "los varones cuerdos aspiran antes a ser grandes que a parecerlo."[2] Chivalric in spirit, his mind and heart are occupied with noble thoughts and feelings as "en la alteza del espíritu y en los altos pensamientos consiste la grandeza. No hay hidalgía como la del corazón que nunca se abate a la vileza."[3] In summary, "las más sublimes prendas de un varón consumadamente perfecto," according to Gracián, are:

la Alteza de ánimo, la Majestad de espíritu, la Autoridad, la Reputación, la Universalidad, la Ostentación, la Galantería, el Despejo, la Plausibilidad, el Buen Gusto, la Cultura, la Gracia de las gentes, la Retentiva, lo Noticioso, lo Juicioso, lo Inapasionable, lo Desafectado, la Seriedad, el señorio, la Espera, lo Agudo, el Buen Modo, lo Plático, lo Ejecutivo, lo Atento, la Simpatía sublime, la Incomprehensibilidad, la Indefinibilidad, con otras muchas deste porte y grandeza.[4]

---

mentions Cervantes by name, he leaves no doubt of his disliking for the author of *Don Quijote*. For example in "Reforma de libros" in the second part of *El Criticón*, Gracián, after belittling chivalry books in general, he adds: "Replicaron algunos que para pasar el tiempo se le diese facultad de leer las obras de algunos otros autores que habían escrito contra estos primeros burlándose de su quimérico trabajo, y respondioles la Cordura que de ningún modo, porque era dar del lodo en el cieno, y había sido querer sacar del mundo una necedad con otra mayor" (pp. 676-7).

[1] *El Discreto*, p. 110.
[2] *Ibid.*, p. 133.
[3] *Ibid.*, p. 120.
[4] *Ibid.*, p. 142.

Without further adding to the outline and description of "el discreto," it is quite obvious that Gracián's model of perfection displays a number of distinguishing marks and virtues that bear him close resemblance to the knight of chivalry and to the Renaissance courtier. There are, however, important differences that separate "el discreto" from the prototypes of the chivalric and courtly tradition. One of them is undoubtedly his cynical view and almost despairing attitude toward the world and reality.[1] In chapter 7, for example, Gracián, through a letter supposedly written by Juan de Lastanosa, makes the following observation and offers this reminder to "el discreto":

> La vida de cada uno no es otro que una representación trágica y cómica . . . viniéndose a igualar las dichas con las desdichas, lo cómico con lo trágico. Ha de ser uno solo todos los personajes a sus tiempos y ocasiones, ya el de la risa, ya el del llanto, ya el del cuerdo y tal vez el del necio, con que se viene acabar con alivio y aplauso la apariencia.[2]

Even to a greater degree than the courtier, "el discreto" places great emphasis on the art of dissemblance, disguise, and nonchalance. He is constantly reminded of the following:

---

[1]   On the subject of pessimism in Gracián's writings, see Jose Manuel Blecua, "El estilo de 'El criticón' de Gracián," *Archivo de Filología Aragonesa*, I (1945), pp. 7-32.

[2]   *El Discreto*, p. 98.

> La major sabiduría . . . consiste en hacer parecer.[1]
> Las cosas comunmente no pasan por lo que son, sino por lo que parecen.[2]
> Un prudente disímulo es plausible alarde del valor, que aquel esconder los méritos es un verdadero pregonarlos, porque aquella misma privación pica más en lo vivo a la curiosidad.[3]
> Tanto se requiere en las cosas la circumstancia como la substancia; antes bien, lo primero con que topamos no son las esencias de las cosas, sino las apariencias; por lo exterior se viene en conocimiento de lo interior, y por la corteza del trato sacamos el fruto del caudal; que aun a la persona que no conocemos por el porte la juzgamos.[4]

Compared to the courtier, "el discreto" is also far more despondent and critical of his culture and time:

> Estamos ya a los fines de los siglos. Alla en la Edad de Oro se iventaba . . . ya todo es repetir.[5]

He is also far less confident and trustful of the world that surrounds him:

> No hay estado, sino contina mutabilidad en todo.[6]
> Engaña de ordinario la aparente hermosura.[7]

---

[1] *Ibid.*, p. 113.
[2] *Ibid.*, p. 111.
[3] *Ibid.*, p. 114.
[4] *Ibid.*, p. 137.
[5]
[6]
[7]

Finally, in all his dealings and actions, "el discreto" must practice what Gracián often refers to as "astuto arbitrio," "prudente disímulo," "discreto recato," "grave retiro," "prudente encogimiento," "vivir a lo plático," "acomodarse a la corriente," "casar lo grave con lo humano,"[1] and other similar qualities that make him a master of cunning, timeliness, and pragmatic action, as well as a model of worldly wisdom and perfection.

In comparison with the knight-gentleman of chivalric novels who perceived life essentially as a mission and an unselfish dedication to the cause of justice, to his lady, his king, and to God, and in comparison with the Renaissance courtier whose main interest centered on the cultivation of the idea of beauty within himself simply as a matter of art, "el discreto" appears as an art-conscious, self-serving, pragmatic individual who employs all his skills in a multiplicity of roles and disguises as means of survival and also achieving success in a world abound with deception and rivalry.

If Don Quijote—by way of his journey through the fields and villages of La Mancha, and perhaps by artfully playing the part of a madman—was merely trying to probe what seemed a propitious world, and if Segismundo remained perplexed before the shifting fortune of the human condition and could not ascertain whether life is indeed reality or dream, "el discreto" faces no such quandary. He has both intuitively and empirically arrived at a conclusion about the ambivalence of man and the world in general. Observation and experience, the repetitive nature of human behavior, the lesson of history, the admonishments of philosophers, and the example of great men are the basis and the inspiration for the course

---

[1]

of action he must take in his strife for self-assertion. Thus, for "el discreto," attainment is not a matter of personal invention or virtue but a question of appropriate choice and deliberate application of knowledge intellectually and experimentally acquired:

> Todo el saber humano (si en opinión de Sócrates hay quien sepa) se reduce hoy al acierto de una sabia elección. Poco o nada se inventa, y en lo que más importa se ha de tener por sospechosa cualquiera novedad. . . . Vense adelantadas las cosas, de modo que ya no queda que hacer, sino elegir. . . . vemos cada día hombres de ingenio sutil, de juicio acre, estudiosos y noticiosos también, que, en llegando, a la elección, se pierden. Escogen siempre lo peor, páganse de lo menos acertado, gustan de lo menos plausible. . . . Todo les sale infelizmente, y no solo no consiguen aplauso, pero ni aun agrado. Jamás hicieron cosa insigne, y todo por faltarles el grande dono de saber elegir; de suerte que no bastan ni el estudio ni el ingenio donde falta la elección.[1]

Seen in this context, virtue, even to a higher degree than in the courtier, has more to do with appearance than reality. Inner worth is not measured by the possession of great qualities but by skillfully simulating a condition of virtue, even if none exists, when time and circumstances require it. Gracián, however, recognizes in more than one

---

[1]   *Ibid.*, p. 103.

place in his works that the man who possesses true virtue is genuinely superior to those who feign it.[1]

All in all, an analysis of *El Discreto*, with an eye on other treatises of the same genre from the early Renaissance onward, leaves the student with one clear impression: that what is at hand is not as much a new period of history or that new historical realities have emerged, but that the very structure, the internal core of the individual has changed. Although the shift of the individual toward greater introspection, self-control, and internalization of feelings—as it was pointed out earlier in this study—is readily visible in the personality structure of the Renaissance courtier vis-a-vis the more compulsive nature and emotional character of the knight of chivalry, it is quite obvious that by comparison with "el discreto" the overall image of the Renaissance man as an overconfident, enthusiastic, art-loving, and pleasure-seeking individual has been replaced in Gracián's treatise by the profile of a predominantly reflective, wary, astute, calculating, enterprising human being for whom knowledge is essentially a means to an end and success is measured almost exclusively in terms of specific practical results.

It is not an exaggeration to state that in a general sense the philosophy of life outlined by Gracián in *El Discreto* is a sort of Machiavellian doctrine,[2] aimed this time not at the prince but at the common man who aspires to self-distinction and prominence. What the author brings before us in *El Discreto* is in a way the democratization of an ideal whose realization in the past was thought possible only among the noble and the privileged. We have, indeed,

---

[1] *Ibid.*, p. 120.

[2] On the influence of Machiavelli on Gracián, see Werner Krauss, *La doctrina de la vida según Baltasar Gracián* (Madrid, 1963), pp. 70-73, 118-20.

one could argue, the emergence of a new type-figure, that of the "everydayman," who ascends to greatness by a combination of pragmatic virtues. It is useful to point out that the figure of "el discreto," apart from other obvious differences, distinguishes itself from the more fashionable literary prototypes widely romanticized in Europe during the seventeenth and nineteenth centuries, namely the "honnête homme" and the "dandy,"[1] in that both of these examples were mainly representatives of codes and values, of attitudes and feelings considered potentially beyond reach of the common man, yet realizable in the more refined aristocracy and intelligentsia. Moreover, in terms of self-perception, moral conscience, and outlook, "el discreto" displays an air of modernity that appears lacking in the more tradition-oriented figures of the *honnête homme* and the *dandy*, and brings him close, in many ways, to a skillful, self-made entrepreneur of our time.

It would be a subject of considerable interest to explore to what extent the values and ideals of "el discreto" are a part of the training and of the personality structure of the *honnête homme* and the *dandy*[2] and of subsequent generations of exceptional lives, as well as of the successful man of our age.

---

[1] See the study of Donna C. Stanton, *The Aristocrat as art. A Study of the Honnêtte Homme and the Dandy in Seventeenth- and Nineteenth-Century French Literature* (New York: Columbia University Press, 1980).

[2] The relationship between "el discreto" and "l'honnête homme" has been studied to some extent by Carmen Biondo in her thesis, "Gracián et l'Honneste Homme de Faret." For a summary, see *Bulletin Hispanique*, LX, num. 3 (July-September 1958), pp. 394-7. See also Camille Pitollet, "R. Bouvier. La Courtisan, L'honnête homme, L'Heros." *Bulletin Hispanique*, XL (1938), pp. 321-9.

The principles that guide the life of "el discreto" are even further elaborated by Gracián in *Oráculo Manual y Arte de Prudencia*,[1] a most ambitious work that in the tradition of aphoristic literature aims at mapping out a whole science of wisdom and success. It is fundamentally a book of practical rules and advice, whose major themes and intent are consistent with those of *El Discreto*. Restating for the most part in the form of philosophic maxims the concepts and the excellences that characterize the "persona" in *El Discreto*, Gracián here again stresses the value of knowledge and the civilizing influence of culture on man:

> Nace bárbaro el hombre; redímese de bestia cultivándose. Hace personas la cultura, y más cuanto mayor. . . . No hay cosa que más cultive que el saber.[2]

It is the alliance of nature and art that makes the man:

> Pues le hizo la naturaleza al hombre un compendio de toto lo natural por su eminencia, hágale el arte un universo por ejercicio y cultura del gusto y del entendimiento.[3]

---

[1]   See the study of Helmut Hatzfeld, "The Baroquism of Gracián's *El Oráculo Manual*" in *Homenaje a Gracián* (Zaragoza: "Institución Fernando el Católico," 1958, pp. 103-17.

[2]   *Oráculo Manual y Arte de Prudencia*, p. 177.

[3]   *Ibid.*, p. 179.

The interaction of the natural with the artistic in man is the basis of all human perfection:

No hay belleza sin ayuda, ni perfección que no dé en bárbara sin el realce del artificio: a lo malo socorre y lo bueno lo perficiona. Déjanos comúnmente a lo mejor la naturaleza; acojámonos al arte. El mejor natural es inculto sin ella, y les falta la metad a las perfecciones si les falta la cultura. Todo hombre sabe a tosco sin el artificio y ha menester pulirse en todo orden de perfección.[1]

The wise man, however, will acquire knowledge that is applicable to everyday living:

No todo sea especulación, haya también acción. Los muy sabios son fáciles de engañar, porque, aunque saben lo extraordinario, ignoran lo ordinario del vivir, que es más preciço . . . ¿ De qué sirve el saber si no es platico? Y el saber vivir es hoy el verdadero saber.[2]

High on the list of practical virtues is courtesy:

Es la cortesía la principal parte de la cultura, especie de hechizo, y así concilia la gracia de todos; así como la descortesía, el desprecio y enfado universal. . . . Cuesta poco y vale mucho todo honrador es honrado. La galantería y la

---

[1]   *Ibid.*, p. 156.
[2]   *Ibid.*, p. 214.

honra tienen esta ventaja, que se quedan, aquella
en quien la usa, esta en quien la hace.[1]

Other noteworthy virtues of the gentleman are
self-knowledge and self-restraint:

> No puede uno ser señor de sí, sí primero no se
> comprende.[2]
> No hay mayor señorío que el de sí mismo.[3]

One must avoid excessive emotionalism:

> Prevenga la prudente reflexión la vulgaridad del
> ímpetu. . . . Todo exceso de pasión degenera de lo
> racional. . . . Para saber hacer mal a una pasión es
> menester ir siempre con la rienda en la atención, y
> será el primer cuerdo a caballo, si no el último.[4]

"Alteza de animo" is another principal attribute
of the gentleman "porque inflama a todo género de
grandeza: realza el gusto, engrandece el corazón, remonta
el pensamiento, ennoblece la condición y dispone la
majestad."[5] Just as important is *el despejo*, generally
translated into English as "grace":

> Es vida de las prendas, aliento del decir, alma del
> hacer, realce de los mismos realces. Las demás
> perfecciones son ornato de la naturaleza, pero

---

[1]   *Ibid.*, p. 185.

[2]   *Ibid.*, p. 178.

[3]   *Ibid.*, p. 155.

[4]   *Ibid.*, p. 195.

[5]   *Ibid.*, pp. 187-88.

el despejo lo es de las mismas perfecciones. . . .
Sin él, toda belleza es muerta, y toda gracia,
desgracia. Es trascendental al valor, a la
discreción, a la prudencia, a la misma majestad.[1]

Among other things, Gracián also recommends that
the ideal man possess a fertile mind, good judgment,
and a fine taste, as well as great courage and valor.[2] He
must be interested in learning and cultivate those who
can teach him.[3] He must build a good reputation and
avoid those who can discredit him. He should show a
jovial disposition, shun all affectation, master the art of
conversation, and be acquainted with the life story of great
men whom he should learn to emulate rather than imitate.
He must not engage in quixotic pursuits or recklessness.
He should be discreet in the use of criticism and condemn
that which pleases all.

Other indispensable qualities of the successful man are
changeableness and flexibility:

> Múdanse a tiempos el discurrir y el gustar: no se
> ha de discurrir a lo viejo, y se ha de gustar a lo
> moderno . . . acomódose el cuerpo a lo presente,
> aunque le parezca mejor lo pasado, así en los
> arreos del alma como del cuerpo.[4]

---

[1] *Ibid.*, p. 187. On the concept of *despejo* as it relates to that of *grazia* in
Castiglione, see M. Morreale, "Castiglione y *El Héroe*: Gracián y despejo,"
in *Homenaje a Gracián* (Zaragosa, 1958).

[2] *Oráculo Manual y Arte de Prudencia*, p. 298.

[3] *Ibid.*, p. 93.

[4] *Ibid.*, p. 185.

What a man thinks and does must be determined by circumstances; therefore, the following are necessary:

> Vivir a la ocasión. El gobernar, el discurrir, todo ha de ser al caso . . . el sabio sabe que el norte de la prudencia consiste en portarse a la ocasión.[1]

> Dependen las cosas de muchas circumstancias, y la que triunfa en un puesto y en tal ocasión, en otras se malogra.[2]

> Saber hacerse a todos. Discreto Proteo: con el docto, docto, y con el santo, santo. Gran arte de ganar a todos, porque la semejanza concilia benevolencia.[3]

The wise man will proceed with caution, that is "llevar sus cosas con suspención. . . . El jugar a juego descubierto ni es de utilidad, ni de gusto."[4] Moreover, adds the author:

> Conviene ir detenido donde se teme mucho fondo: vaya intentando la Sagacidad y ganando tierra la Prudencia. Hay grandes bajíos hoy en el trato humano: conviene ir siempre calando la sonda.[5]

---

[1] *Ibid.*, p. 227.

[2] *Ibid.*, p. 182.

[3] *Ibid.*, p. 175.

[4] *Ibid.*, p. 153.

[5] *Ibid.*, p. 175.

Deception is not to be shunned:

Las cosas no pasan por lo que son, sino por lo que parecen . . . La buena exterioridad es la mejor recomendación de la perfección interior.[1]

Los sinceros son amados, pero engañados.[2]

Las cosas que se han de hacer no se han de decir, y las que se han de decir no se han de hacer.[3]

Dissemblance is also essential to success:

Cuando no puede uno vestirse la piel del león, vístase la de la vulpeja.[4]

Altérnense la calidez de la serpiente con la candidez de la poloma.[5]

In addition, considering the times, warns Gracián:

Más se requiere hoy para un sabio que antiguamente para siete, y más es menester para tratar con un solo hombre en estos tiempos que con todo un pueblo en los pasados.[6]

---

[1]   *Ibid.*, p. 188.
[2]   *Ibid.*, p. 211.
[3]   *Ibid.*, p. 201.
[4]   *Ibid.*, p. 211.
[5]   *Ibid.*, p. 217.
[6]   *Ibid.*, p. 153.

Without adding further to the list of virtues or to the drawing of the ideal man envisioned by Gracián, it should be noticed that despite the number of extensive studies devoted to the works of Gracián,[1] most of which deal with the author's aesthetic and literary theory as well as his style and system of ideas, the final study on Gracián's idea of the complete man is till to be written.

---

[1] For an extensive bibliography on the works of Gracián, see Baltasar Gracián, *Obras Completas*, ed. Arturo del Hoyo, pp. ccxli-cclxxix. For a concise summary of the works of Gracián, see Virginia Ramos Foster, *Baltasar Gracián* (Boston: Twayne Publishers, 1975), pp. 118-41.

CONCLUSION

This study, as stated in the prologue, limits itself to an analysis of the life ideals of the Spanish *cabellero perfecto* of the sixteenth century as they appear first in Montalvo's *Amadís de Gaula* and later in Castiglione's *Il Cortegiano* after its publication and arrival in Spain. It also appraises how these ideals are viewed and reflected in some major and minor works of sixteenth- and seventeenth-century Spanish authors.

On the basis of the facts presented in the preceding pages, certain observations and conclusions can now be drawn.

For one, the question raised by a number of critics as to whether Montalvo's text can be properly considered a "courtesy book" side by side with Castiglione's *Courtier*, Della Casa's *Galateo*, and other major courtesy books of the period, has been analyzed here at some length and hopefully partially answered. Although *Amadís de Gaula* is in a strict sense a chivalric novel and does not teach by direct instruction but through a series of actions and examples, this study has outlined the essential elements that warrant its classification among the great courtesy books of the epoch and of all times. As a courtesy book, Montalvo's text had considerable impact and held important moral and social implications for the court aristocracy and bourgeois society.

Central to the *Amadís* text are the enormous importance attached to the hero's prowess and reputation and the author's constant emphasis on virtue, honor, and loyalty to a Higher Order. This highlights the general tendency of the author to idealize and elevate the figure of the hero above all other characters in the novel and the effort to present a superior model of chivalric conduct for imitation by the court nobility. The striving toward idealization is quite apparent not only as the author, through the various chapters, underscores the hero's knightly behavior and exquisite sensibility, but also in the description of Amadís' feats of arms and the frequent agonistic contests, consciously placed in strategic parts of the narration with the object of fostering an image of superiority and high achievement not easily obtainable within the normal ambition of the individual.

This process of differentiation and separation had a twofold purpose. On one hand, it served to set the standards of an exclusive profession that reflected the point of view and the self-consciousness of the members of the Spanish nobility. On the other hand, it served to curb the aspirations of the gentry and the middle class that sought to infiltrate the ranks of the courtly aristocracy.

A basic change in the perception of the hero and in the notion of what constituted chivalric conduct and pursuits soon became evident in the *Amadís* sequel. In the continuation of the *Amadís* theme, we readily observe that the field of action of the hero becomes more divorced from the realm of warfare and increasingly associated with the more secular and diversified activities of a growing leisure class whose primary interests centered on staging elaborate games and tournaments and acquiring the refinement of culture.

This spirit of conscious play and the reduction of courtly art to a fashionable pastime reached its highest form of expression in Castiglione's courtier, which became the new universal ideal of human perfection, not only in Italy, but also throughout Europe. Although the courtier, in theory, combined within his own person most of the qualities and sentiments of the chivalric hero, in practice, his truly distinguishing marks were the possession of skills and a personality defined by culture and education rather than by feats of arms on the battlefield. Castiglione believed that the pursuit of scholarship and aesthetic education would give the courtly man an exclusive and more contemporary character, as well as a new class orientation and identity. Interestingly, it was precisely the adoption of this new identity and ideas by the court aristocracy that contributed considerably to the bourgeoisification and secularization of the concept of the courtly gentleman and to the transformation of what was once considered a rigid and exclusive aristocratic code into a more flexible and less class-oriented doctrine.

It is not difficult to see how Castiglione's set of rules and precepts for the courtier, by their very nature, fostered the democratization of the traditional code of the gentleman and made it more accessible to a broader strata of society.

First the endeavor of the courtier to live a life of beauty and his seeking of aesthetic pleasure and self-fulfillment represented an opportunity available to all those who wanted to cultivate within themselves a system of values and acquire certain practical skills. The ideals of the courtier, in fact, fall within the confines of humanism and the culture of the period, which envisioned the development of a civilized world through universal education. Reflecting the point of view of the humanistic movement, the doctrine of the *Courtier*, save the principle of hereditary nobility, is not an exclusionary ideology. Indeed, the pursuit of education and the ability to learn transcend class identity. During the Renaissance in particular, education had become a tool for the intellectual bourgeoisie to readily identify itself with the attitudes and activities of the courtly nobility. The sharing of common educational goals and life ideals on the part of the middle-class intelligentsia and the aristocracy contributed much to establish a network of interdependencies and a new social mix that to a great extent accounted for the gradual assimilation and movement of bourgeois people into the circles of the court. Thus, for the middle class, education represented a means of acquiring power and a pursuit with political and social consequences.

Another element in the *Courtier* that undoubtedly added impetus to the popularization of the code of the gentleman was the adoption of a pluralistic and constantly changing value system that contrasts with the less flexible and more homogeneous code of conduct outlined in *Amadís*. Castiglione's doctrine of contingencies and the courtier's tendency to accommodate his moral standards and personality to circumstances and to practical and aesthetical requirements establish the basis for a code of behavior in which virtue and morality are relative values and in which personal distinction is more readily associated with an outward display of good qualities than the possession of inner goodness. Accordingly, grace, charm, and tact—considered essential elements in the courtier's value system—have no real ethical content. On the whole, they are reduced to plain secularized qualities within the reach of any individual willing to work hard and feign in their pursuit.

The reduction of virtue to role behavior and the condoning of dissemblance as a tool for achieving goals, without a doubt, did much to loosen the social hierarchy, open for many courtiers the road to success, and facilitate the penetration of bourgeois elements and people into the class structure and the range of activities cultivated by the court elite. Transformed almost to a prescription for artful disguise and governed by highly provisional rules, Castiglione's code of conduct, as evidenced by its popularity, not only had an immediate universal appeal among the courtier class, but was also embraced by the rising middle class as a convenient means of climbing the social ladder. Sparked by these new ideas and bourgeois interests, the art of being courtly had thus become less formal and more universalized. Interestingly, even "love," which under the chivalric code was a social obligation and a condition indispensable to the very existence and profession of the knight, is reduced in Castiglione's final analysis and treatment of the theme to a form of fashionable behavior, to an aesthetic experience that assumes a universalized character in the courtier's pursuit of platonic love.

An additional factor in the *Courtier* that is directly related to the idea of contingency and points even further to the secularization of the notion of human perfection in Castiglione is the general tendency to subject all ethical facts to the principle of utility, a motive that historically coincides with the development of bourgeois interests and aspirations. In fact, in an obvious shift from a somewhat more theoretical and artistic treatment of courtly education, Castiglione, at the end of Book III and later in Book IV, sketches the figure of a courtier overly concerned with the useful and the practical and motivated by personal advantage. These changes of attitude and leaning toward a more functional perception of human development underscore the gradual integration and assimilation of middle-class elements into courtly life and ideals, as well as the double movement and reciprocal influence between different social classes and people.

Contributing further to give the *Courtier's* doctrine a secularized character is the degree of autonomy and liberation enjoyed by women at the court of Urbinio. Here, female personalities constantly dominate the discussion and play an important role in shaping tastes and customs and in setting the cultural trends of the age. The attitude of Castiglione toward women reflects the progressive socialization and the growing influence of the role of women in society.

Apart from embodying the ideal of social and aesthetic education and reflecting a more progressive and democratic conception of man relative to his chivalric predecessor, the courtier distinguishes himself from his chivalric counterpart for the easy adaptability and independence of his personality and character. The courtier's ambivalent attitudes and casual approach to questions of morality call particular attention to the split between the individual's inner self and the image he projects outwardly, and to the contrast between appearance and reality.

The problem of deciphering man's true nature, the relativity of human experience, and the lack of definite criteria for judging the world of appearances become later Cervantes' principal preoccupations in *Don Quijote*. Cervantes daringly challenges the premise of the humanistic argument upholding man's inherent dignity and perfection by pointing to man's deceptive nature and to the limitations of human knowledge. Through the characters of his novel representing all strata of society, the author of *Don Quijote* illustrates that examples of good and bad conduct are more or less spread evenly among men irrespective of birth, position, or wealth. Cervantes also stresses that the courtier's ideal and profession, which by the seventeenth century had been widely popularized and to a large extent had become the field of activity of status seekers and mercenaries, contained no essential moral significance or specific class connotation.

That the code of the perfect gentleman had become operational within a larger group of people and among different social classes is quite evident in the theater of Calderón. Although Calderón's dramas are eminently aristocratic in character and are directed to sophisticated court audiences, the heroes and prototypes portrayed in these plays are more often than not representatives of the lesser nobility and of the middle class. Particularly in the plays of cloak and sword, we find that certain forms of behavior and qualities, which at one time were the distinctive marks of the highest nobility, here become the sphere of action and the attributes of middle-class *caballeros* and their squires, who often equal and sometimes surpass their masters in wisdom and courtliness.

The ideal of social education and worldly perfection become even more independent of class in the works of Gracián and especially in the figure of the *discreto*. Like the courtier, the *discreto* is a true intellectual and an artful schemer who is mostly concerned with the appearance of things rather than with their substance. The *discreto*, however, goes somewhat further than the courtier in pursuing wholly terrestrial goals. He frees himself from all closed world views and class-oriented ideology and prominently reflects the secular man's preoccupation with the useful and the practical. The *discreto*, in fact, sees the world as a series of problems and projects where *homo honinis lupus* is the watchword. His understanding of the truth and his *modus operandi* are mainly functional and pragmatic. His courtship consists for the most part in working out forms of defense against the unreliability of sensory experience. Thus he sets out to achieve the desired success and results by the simple application of his human abilities and intelligence. He also rejects all myths and theories about the influence of the supernatural in determining man's condition or fate.

The *discreto* symbolizes by and large the self-made man who need not accept as his destiny the possibilities defined for him by birth. This view and approach of the *discerto* to the world and reality clearly reflect the skeptical crisis of the seventeenth century. His classless ideology and personal characteristics, when compared to those of the courtier-knight, call attention to the gradual secularization of what was once considered chivalric and courtly and to the conventionalization of a profession formerly open only to a selected few. These changes in thought and outlook not only reveal the accelerated social mobility and the transitional nature of that period of history, but also bring into focus the disintegration of the old order, as well as the new perception man had of himself and the world around him.

All in all, it is quite obvious that the notion of what constituted human perfection and the system of beliefs that traditionally defined the perfect human being have through the centuries acted as a powerful force in shaping man's views and the society in which he lived. Recent studies, notably those of Maurice Magendie, Ruth Kelso, W. W. Wiley, and F. R. Bryson have undoubtedly contributed a great deal to an understanding of the doctrine and the social ideals that from the early Renaissance to the later part of the eighteenth century nourished the well-bred man and the "perfect gentleman" in England, France, and other Western European countries. Nevertheless, the contribution that the doctrine has made to modern literature and social ideals has not been sufficiently investigated to suggest an abatement of the question.

Especially in the area of Spanish literature over the past two hundred years, and the areas already mentioned in the final pages of the last chapter, there is a dire need for scholarly research aimed at interpreting the extent and the manner in which the ideal of the perfect gentleman of the Renaissance and of the Baroque period affected the minds of the nineteenth- and twentieth-century authors and the role it played in forging new and more current literary prototypes.

BIBLIOGRAPHY

Primary Sources

Aretino, Pietro. *The Courtesan.* Translated by Samuel Putnam. New York: Charles Scribner's Sons, 1926.

Calderón de la Barca, Pedro. *Obras Completas.* Critical edition and commentary by Ángel Valbuena-Briones. 3 vols. Madrid: Aguilar, 1960.

———. *Comedias de capa y espada.* Edited with "estudio preliminar" by Marcelino Menéndez Pelayo. Madrid: Colección "Cisneros," 1943.

———. *Four Plays.* Edited with foreword by Edwin Honig. New York: Hill and Wang, 1970.

———. *Selected Plays of Calderón.* Edited by Norman Maccoll. London: Macmillan and Company, 1888.

———. *La vida es sueño.* Edited by Ciriaco Morón. Madrid: Ediciones Cátedra, 1977.

Casa, Giovanni della. *Il Galateo ovvero de' Costumi,* in *Opere,* Vol. III. Venezia: Pasinello, 1728.

Castiglione, Baldesar. *Il Cortegiano con una scelta delle opere minori*. Edited with introduction and notes by Bruno Maier. Torino: Unione Tipografico-Editrice Torinese, 1964.

————. *Il Cortegiano*. Edited with commentary by Vittorio Cian. Firenze: Sansoni, 1929.

————. Lettere. Edited by Pierantonio Serassi. 2 vols. Padova: G. Comino, 1769-1771.

————. *El Cortesano*. Translated by Juan Boscán. "Estudio preliminar" by Marcelino Menéndez Pelayo. Edited by A. González Palencia. (Añejos de la Revista de Filología Española, Añejo XXV.) Madrid: Aguirre, 1942.

————. *El Cortesano*. Translated by Juan Boscán. Edited by Teresa Suero Roca. Barcelona: Editorial Broguera, 1972.

————. *The Book of the Courtier*. Translated from the Italian by Sir Thomas Hoby with an introduction by Walter Raleigh. New York: A.M.S. Press, 1967.

————. *The Book of the Courtier*. Translated with notes by Leonard Eckstein Opdycke. New York: Scribner's, 1901.

————. *The Book of the Courtier*. Translated with introduction and notes by Charles S. Singleton. Garden City, New York: Doubleday and Company, 1959.

Capellanus, Andreas. *The Art of Courtly Love*. Translated by J. J. Perry. New York, 1941.

Caxton, William. *The Book of Ordre of Chyualry.* Edited by A. T. P. Byles. London: E.E.T.X., 1926.

Cervantes, Saavedra, Miguel de. *Don Quijote de la Mancha.* Edited with introduction and notes by Rodolfo Schevill and Adolfo Bonilla. 4 vols. Madrid: Gráficas Reunidas, 1928-1941.

————. *El ingenioso hidalgo Don Quijote de la Mancha.* Edited with commentary by Francisco Rodríguez Marín. 10 vols. Madrid: Ediciones Atlas, 1947-1949.

————. *Don Quijote de la Mancha.* Edited with introduction and notes by Martín de Riquer. 2 vols. Barcelona: Editorial Juventud, 1958.

————. *The Ingenius Gentleman Don Quijote de la Mancha.* Translated with introduction and notes by Samuel Putnam. 2 vols. New York: Viking Press, 1949.

Dantisco, Lucas Gracián. *Galateo Español.* Edited with introduction by Margherita Morreale. ("Consejo Superior de Investigaciones Científicas." Madrid: Clásicos Hispánicos, 1968.

Erasmus, Desiderius. *The Education of the Christian Prince.* Translated by Lester K. Born. New York: Columbia University Press, 1936.

Gracián y Morales, Baltasar. *Obras Completas.* Edited with introduction and notes by Miguel Batlori and Ceferino Peralta. Vol. I. In B.A.E. Vol. CCXXIX. Madrid: Ediciones Atlas, 1969.

————. *Obras Completas.* Edited with introduction and commentary by Arturo del Hoyo. Madrid: Aguilar, 1967.

Guazzo, Stefano. *The Civile Conversation.* Translated by George Pettie. 2 vols. London: Constable, 1925.

Guevara, Antonio de. *Despertador de Cortesanos.* París: Sociedad de Ediciones Luis Machaud, 1929.

————. *Menosprecio de Corte y Alabanza de Aldea.* Madrid: Ediciones de "La Lectura," 1961.

Guicciardini, Francesco. "Relazione di Spagna," in *Opere Inedite.* Vol. VI. Firenze: M. Cellini, 1864.

————. *History of Italy and History of Florence.* Translated by Cecil Grayson. New York: Washington Square Press, 1926.

Leone, Ebreo. *The Philosophy of Love.* Translated from *Dialoghi d'Amore* by J. Friedeberg-Seeley. London: Soncino Press, 1937.

Machiavelli, Niccoló. *The Prince and the Discourses.* New York: The Modern Library, 1950.

Milán, Luis D. *El Cortesano: Libro de Motes de damas y caballeros.* Madrid: Imprenta y Estoreotipia de Aribau, 1874.

Pérez de Oliva, Hernán. *Diálogo de la dignidad del hombre.* Edited by J. L. Abellán. Barcelona: Cultura Popular, 1967.

Possevino, Giovanni Battista. *Dialogo dell'honore*. Vinegia: Gabriel Giolito de Ferrari, 1556.

Pulgar, Hernando del. *Claros varones de Castilla*. Edited with introduction by Domínguez Bordona. Madrid: Ediciones de "La Lectura," 1923.

Rodríguez de Montalvo, Garci. *Amadís de Gaula*. Edited with introduction and notes by Edwin Place, 4 vols. Madrid: Consejo Superior de Investigaciones Científicas, 1959-1969.

———. *Amadís de Gaula*. Edited with "discurso preliminar" by Pascual de Gayangos in *Libros de Caballerías*. "Biblioteca de Autores Españoles," Vol. XLI, Madrid: Ediciones Atlas, 1950.

———. *Amadís de Gaula*. Edited with introduction by Arturo Souto. México City: Porrua. "Sepan Cuantos," 1969, 1975.

———. *Amadís de Gaula*. Edited with introduction by Felicidad Buendía, in *Libros de Caballería Españoles*. Madrid: Aguilar, 1954.

———. *El primer manuscrito del "Amadís de Gaula"* with commentary by A. Rodríguez-Moñino. Madrid: Aguirre Torre, 1957.

———. *Amadís de Gaul*. Translated by E. B. Place and H. C. Behm. Lexington: University of Kentucky Press. Studies in Romance Languages, II, 1974.

Seneca. *Moral Essays*. Translated by John W. Basore. Harvard University Press, 1928.

Vega, Garcilaso de la. *Obras*. Edited by Tomás Navarro. Madrid: Clásicos Castellanos, 1974.

————. *Obras con Anotaciones de Fernando de Herrera*. Seville, 1850.

Vassari, Giorgio. *Lives*. Edited by W. Gaunt. London: 1963.

Villalón, Cristobal de. *El Scholástico*. Madrid: Clásicos Hispánicos, 1967.

Secondary Works

Adams, Hilary. "Il Cortegiano and Il Galateo," *Modern Language Review*, No. 42 (1947), 457-466.

Adler, Mortimer J. and Van Doren, Charles. *The Great Treasures of Western Thought*. New York: R. R. Bowker Company, 1977.

Alvarez-Fernández, Manuel. *La sociedad española del Renacimiento*. Madrid, 1974.

Arbo, Sebastián Juan. *Cervantes: The Man and His Time*. New York: The Vanguard Press, 1955.

Arco y Garay, A. *La sociedad española en las obras de Cervantes*. Madrid, 1951.

Astrana, Luis Marín. *Estudio Crítico.* Madrid: Editorial Castilla, 11947.

Atkinson, W. C. "Cervantes, El Pinciano, and the *Novelas Ejemplares*," *Hispanic Review,* XVI (1948), 189-208.

Babelón, J. "Carlos V y la decadencia de la caballería," *Cuadernos Hispanoamericanos,* XXXVI (Madrid, 1958), 296-302.

Baret, Eugéne. *De l' "Amadís de Gaule" et de son influence sur les moeurs et la littérature au XVIᵉ et au XVIIᵉ siecle.* Genéve: Slatkine Reprints, 1970.

Benton, John. "The Court of Champagne as a Literary Center," *Speculum,* XXXVI (October, 1961), 551-582.

Blanchard, Harold H. *Prose and Poetry of the Renaissance in Translation.* London: Longman, Green and Company, 1958.

Glanco-González, Bernardo. *Del Cortesano al Discreto: Examen de una "decadencia."* Madrid: Editorial Gredos, 1962.

Blecua, Jose Manuel. "El estilo de *El Criticón* de Gracián," *Archivo de Filología Aragonesa,* I (1945), 7-32.

Bleznick, Donald W. "Don Quijote's advice to Governor Sancho Panza," *Hispania* XL (1957), 62-4.

Blunt, Anthony. *Artistic Theory in Italy 1450-1600.* Oxford: Clarendon Press, 1940.

Bonet, Carmelo. "El arte de escribir: la lección del cortesano" in *Despuntes Críticos*. Buenos Aires: Academia Argentina de Letras, 1969, 200-212.

Bourciez, Edward. *Les moeurs polies et al littérature de cour sous Henri II*. Paris, 1886.

Briffault, Robert S. *The Troubadours*. Bloomington: Indiana University Press, 1965.

Bryans, John V. *Calderón de la Barca: Imagery, Rhetoric and Drama*. London: Tamesis Book Limited, 1977.

Bryson, F. R. *The Point of Honor in Sixteenth-Century Italy*. New York, 1935.

Buchanan, M. A. "Culteranismo en Calderón's *La vida es sueño*" in *Homenaje ofrecido a M. Pidal*. Madrid. 1925.

Burckhardt, Jakob C. *The Civilization of the Renaissance in Italy*. New York: Oxford University Press, 1968.

Burke, Edmund. *A Philosophical Inquiry into the Origin of our Ideas of the Sublime and the Beautiful*. Edited by J. J. Bouton. New York: Columbia University Press, 1958.

Burke, Peter. *The Renaissance*. Longmans, 1976.

Byles, A. T. "Medieval Courtesy Books and Prose Romances of Chivalry" in *Chivalry*. Edited by Edgar Prestage. New York: Alfred A. Knoff, 1928.

Byron, William. *Cervantes: A Biography*. Garden City, N. Y.: Doubleday and Company, 1978.

Campbell, Joseph. *The Hero with a Thousand Faces*. Second Edition. Bollingen Series, 17. Princeton: Princeton University Press, 1968.

Castro, Americo. *El Pensamiento de Cervantes*. Madrid: Hernando, 1925.

———. *Hacia Cervantes*. Madrid: Hernando, 1925.

———. "Algunas observaciones acerca del concepto del honor en los siglos XVI y XVII," Revista de *Filología Española*, III (1916), 1-50.

Cartwright, Julia. *Baldassare Castiglione: The Perfect Courtier*. 2 vols. New York: P. Dutton, 1908.

Cassier, Ernst. *The Renaissance Philosophy of Man*. Chicago: University of Chicago Press, 1948.

Chamberlain, Vernon A. "Symbolic Green," *Hispania*, 51 (1968), 29-37.

Chambers, Leland H. "Structure and the Search for Truth in *Don Quijote*," *Hispanic Review*, XXXV October, 1967), 309-326.

Chandler, Richard and Schwartz, Kessel. *A New History of Spanish Literature*. Baton Rouge: Louisiana State University, 1961.

Chaves, Jose M. *Intergroup Relations in Spain of Cervantes*. New York: Editorial Mensaje, 1974.

Chevalier, Maxime. *Lectura y Lectores en la España de los Siglos XVI y XVII*. Madrid: Ediciones Turner, 1968.

Chrétien de Troyes. *Cligés*. Translated by W. W. Comfort. London, 1914.

Cian, Vittorio. *Un ilustre nunzio pontificio del Rinascimento: Baldassar Castiglione*. Città del Vaticano: Biblioteca Apostolica del Vaticano, 1951.

Cienfuegos, Alvaro. *La heroyca vida de S. Francisco de Borja*. Madrid, 1917.

Cilveti, Angel L. *El Demonio en el Teatro de Calderón*. Valencia: Albatros Ediciones, 1977.

———. *El Significado de "La Vida es Sueño."* Albatros Ediciones, 1971.

Cioranescu, Al. *L'Arioste en France des Origenes a la fin du XVIIIᵉ Siecle*. Paris: Les editions de Presses Modernes, 1939.

Cline, Ruth H. "The Influence of Romances on Tournaments of the Middle Ages," *Speculum*, 20 (1945), 204-211.

Correa, Calderón Evaristo. *Baltasar Gracián: Su Vida y Su Obra*. Madrid: Editorial Gredos, 1961.

Corsano, Antonio. "L'ideale Estetico Morale del Castiglione," in *Studi sul Rinascimento*. Bari: Adriatica, 1949.

Coster, Adolphe. *Baltasar Gracián*. Translated by Ricardo del Arco y Garay. Zaragoza: Institución "Fernando el Católico," 1947.

Cosman, Madeleine P. "The Education of the Hero," in *Arthurian Romances*. Chapel Hill: University of North Carolina Press, 1966.

Cotarelo, Emilio y Mori. *Ensayo sobre la vida y obras de Calderón de la Barca*. Madrid, 1924.

Crane, Thomas F. *Italian social customs of the Sixteenth Century and their influence on the Literature of Europe*. New Haven: Yale University Press, 1920.

Croce, Benedetto. *Poeti e scrittori del pieno e del tardo Rinascimento*. Bari: Laterza, 1970.

———. *La Spagna nella vita italiana durante la Rinascenza*. Bari: Laterza, 1949.

———. *Estetica*. Bari: Laterza e Figli, 1958.

Cross, T. P. and Nitze, W. A. *Lancelot, Guenevere: A Study of the Origin of Courtly Love*. Chicago, 1930.

Curtius, Ernst. *European Literature and Latin Middle Ages*. New York: Pantheon Books, 1920.

Da Vinci, Leonardo. *Notebooks*. Edited by I. A. Richter. Oxford: University Press, 1952.

Deleito y Pinuela, José. *Solo Madrid es Corte*. Madrid, 1942.

Denomy, Alexander J. "Courtly Love and Courtliness," *Speculum*, 28 (1953), 44-63.

Díaz-Plaja, Fernando. *Cervantes*. Barcelona, 1974.

Dickens, A. G. *The Courts of Europe, politics, patronage, and royalty, 1400-1800*. New York: McGraw-Hill, 1977.

Dowling, John C. "A Title of Distinction," *Hispania*, 41 (1958), 449-456.

Duchesne, Julien. *Histoire de poémes épiques français du XVIIe siecle*. Paris: Hachette, 1970.

Durán, Manuel, *Cervantes*. New York: Twayne Publishers Inc., 1974.

————. *La ambiguedad en le "Quijote."* Xalapa: Universidad Veracruzana, 1960.

Elias, Norbert. *The Civilizing Process: The History of Manners*. Translated by Edmund Jephcott. New York: Urizen Books, 1978.

Elliot, J. H. *Imperial Spain 1469-1716*. New York: The New America Library, 1966.

Entwistle, W. J. *A lenda arturiana nas literaturas de peninsula iberica*. Lisboa, 1942.

Estelrich, J. H. *Influencia de la lengua y de la literatura italiana en la lengua y literatura castellana*. Madrid, 1913.

Farinelli, Arturo. *La Vita é un Sogno*. Torino, 1916.

Ferguson, Arthur B. *The Indian Summer of English Chivalry*. Durham, North Carolina: Duke University Press, 1960.

Fletcher, Jefferson B. *Literature of the Italian Renaissance*. Port Washington, N. Y.: Kennikat Press Inc., 1934.

Foster, Virginia Ramos. *Baltasar Gracián*. Boston: Twayne Publishers, 1975.

Frappier, Jean, *Amour Courtois et Table Ronde*. Genéve: Librarie Droz, 1973.

Fucilla, Joseph. "The Role of the *Cortegiano* in the Second Part of *Don Quijote*," *Hispania*, XXXIII (1950), 291-6.

Gadamer, Hans-Georg. *Truth and Method*. New York: The Seaburg Press, 1975.

García, J. C. *Selección de Escritos*. Bogotá: Editorial Centro, 1935.

Gerstinger, Heinz. *Pedro Calderón de la Barca*. Translated by Diana Stone Peters. New York: Frederick Ungar Publishing Company, 1973.

Giannini, A. "La carcel de amor y el *Cortegiano* de B. Castiglione," *Revue Hispanique*. XLVI (1919), 547-468.

Girard, René. *Deceit, Desire and the Novel: Self and Other in Literary Structure*. Translated by Yvonne Freccero. London: The John Hopkins Press, 1969.

González, Alberto Navarro. *El Quijote Español del Siglo XVII*. Madrid: Ediciones Rialp, 1964.

Green, Otis H. "Boscán and *Il Cortegiano*: 'The Historia de Leandro y Hero,'" *Literary Mind of Medieval and Renaissance Spain*. Lexington, Ky.: The University Press, 1970.

———. "Realidad, voluntad y gracia en Cervantes," *Iberia: Revista de filología,* 3 (1961), 113-28.

———. "Courtly Love in Spanish Cancioneros," in *Literary Mind of Medieval and Renaissance Spain*. Lexington: University Press, 1970.

Hafter, Monroe. *Gracián and Perfection: Spanish Moralists of the Seventeenth Century*. Cambridge, Mass., 1966.

Hale, John H. *Renaissance*. New York: Times Inc., 1976.

Hatzfeld, Helmut. "The Baroquism of Gracián's *El Oráculo Manual'* in *Homenaje a Gracián*. Zaragoza: Institución "Fernando el Católico," 1958.

Hauser, Arnold. *The Social History of Art*. 2 vols. New York: Vintage Books, 1957.

Haywood, Charles. "Cervantes and Music," *Hispania*, XXXI (1948), 131-151.

Heltzel, Virgil. *Check List of Courtesy Books*. Chicago, 1942.

Herdman, Marianela Conchita. *"Dueñas" and "Doncellas": A Study of the "Doña Rodríguez" Episode in "Don Quijote."* Chapel Hill: North Carolina Studies in the Romance Languages and Literatures, 1979.

Hernshaw, F. J. "Chivalry and its Place in History," *Chivalry*. Edited by E. Prestage. New York 1928.

Hesse, Everett W. "Calderón's Concept of the Perfect Prince" in *Critical Essays on the Theater of Calderón*. Edited by Bruce Wardropper. New York: New York University Press, 1965.

———. "Courtly Allusions in the Plays of Calderón," *PMLA*, 65 (1950), 531-549.

Hexter, J. H. "The education of the aristocracy in the Renaissance," *Journal of Modern History*, XXII (March, 1950), 1-20.

Hofstadter, Albert. *Philosophies of Art and Beauty: Selected Readings from Plato to Heidegger*. New York: The Modern Library, 1964.

Holdane, R. B. *The Philosophy of Humanism*. London, 1972.

Holme, J. W. "Italian Courtesy Books of the Sixteenth Century," *Modern Language Review*. 5 (1910), 145-166.

Hook, Sidney. *The Hero in History: A Study in Limitation and Possibility*. Boston: Beacon Press, 1976.

Huizinga, Johan. "The Political and Military Significance of Chivalric Ideals in the Late Middle Ages" in *Men and Ideas*. London: Meridian Books, 1959.

———. *Homo Ludens: A Study of the Play-Element in Culture*. Boston: The Beacon Press, 1964.

Jaeger, Werner Wilhelm. *Paideia: The Idelas of Greek Culture*. 3 vols. Translated by Gilbert Highet. New York: Oxford University Press, 1965.

Judson, Alexander Corbin. "Spenser's Theory of Courtesy," *PMLA*, XLVII (1923), 122-136.

Karl, Frederick R. "Don Quijote as Archetypal Artist and *Don Quijote* as Archetypal Novel," *Adversary Literature*, pp. 55-67. New York: Farrar, Straus & Giroux, 1974.

Kassier, Theodorre L. *The Truth Disguised: Allegorical Structure and Technique in Gracián's "Criticón."* London: Tamesis Books Limited, 1976.

Keating, Clark L. *Studies in Literary "Salon" in France 1550-1615.* Cambridge: Harvard University Press, 1941.

Kelso, Ruth. *Doctrine of the English Gentleman in the Sixteenth Century.* University of Illinois Studies in Language and Literature. Vol. XVI, Nos. 1-2 (Urbana, 1929).

Kilgour, Raymond Lincoln. *The Decline of Chivalry as Shown in the Decline of Decline of French Literature of the Late Middle Ages.* Cambridge: Harvard University Press, 1937.

Krauss, Werner. *La doctrina de la vida según Baltasar Gracián.* Translated by Ricardo Estarriol. Madrid: Rialp, 1962.

Krebs, Ernesto. *"El Cortesano* de Castiglione en España," *Boletín de la Academia Argentina de Letras*, VIII (1940), 93-146, 423-435; IX (1941), 135-142, 517-543; X (1942), 53-118, 689-748.

Laurencín, Marqués de. Documentos inéditos referentes al poeta *Garcilaso de la Vega.* Madrid, 1915.

Ledesma, Francisco Navarro. *Cervantes: The Man and the Genius.* Translated by Don and Gabriela Bliss. New York: Charterhouse, 1973.

Leturia, Pedro. *Íñigo de Loyola*. Translated by Aloysius J. Owen. Syracuse: Le Moyne College Press, 1963.

Lewis, C. S. *The Allegory of Love*. London: Oxford University Press, 1936.

Lipking, Lawrence. "The dialectic of *Il Cortegiano*," *PMLA*, 81 (1966), 355-362.

Little, Charles E. *Historical Lights*. New York: Funk and Wagnalls Company, 1886.

Mades, Leonard. *The Armor and the Brocade: A Study of "Don Quijote" and the "Courtier."* New York: Las Americas Publishing Company, 1968.

Magendie, Maurice. *La Politesse mondaine et les théories de l'honnêté en France de 1600 a 1660*. 2 vols. Paris, 1925.

Malkiel, María Rosa Lida de. "Árthurian Literature in Spain and Portugal" in *Arthurian Literature in the Middle Ages*. Clarendon Press, 1959.

———. *La idea de la Fama en la Edad Media Castellana*. México: Fondo de Cultura Economica, 1952.

Marasso, Arturo. *Cervantes: La invención del "Quijote."* Buenos Aires: Colección Academus, 1947.

Marichalar, Antonio. "*El Cortesano* en el Centenario de Boscán," *Escorial: Revista de Cultura y Letras*. Diciembre, 1942.

Mariejol, Jean Hippolyte. *The Spain of Ferdinand and Isabella*. Translated by Benjamin Keen. New Brunswick: Rutgers University Press, 1961.

Marshall, Pauline. *Edition with Introduction and Notes to "El Caballero Perfecto" by Alonso Gerónimo de Salas Barbadillo*. University of Colorado Studies: Language and Literature, No. 2. University of Colorado Press, 1959.

Mason, J. E. *Gentlefolk in the Making*. Philadelphia, 1935.

Mazzeo, Joseph. *Renaissance Revolution.* New York, 1965.

McEóin, Gary, *Cervantes*. Milwaukee: The Bruce Publishing Company, 1950.

Menéndez Pelayo, Marcelino. *Historia de las ideas estéticas en España*. 5 vols. Santander. Consejo Superior de Investigaciones Cientificas, 1946-1947.

————. *Orígenes de la Novela*. Santander: Aldus, S. A. de Artes Cientificas, 1943.

————. *Calderón y Su Teatro*. Madrid, 1910.

Menut, A. D. "Castiglione and Nicomachean Ethics," *PMLA*, LVIII (1943), 309-321.

Moorman, Charles. "The First Knights," *Southern Quarterly*, I (1962), 13-26.

Morreale, Margherita. *Castiglione y Boscán: El ideal cortesano en el Renacimiento español.* ("Añejos de Boletín de la Real Academia Española," Añejo I.) Madrid: Aguirre, 1959.

————. "Castiglione y El Héroe: Gracián y despejo" in *Homenaje a Gracián.* Zaragoza, 1958.

Mott, L. F. *The System of Courtly Love as an Inroduction to the "Vita Nuova" of Dante.* Boston, 1896.

Mottola, Anthony. "The *Amadís de Gaula* in Spain and in France." Unpublished PhD dissertation. Fordham University, 1962.

Navarrete, Fernández de. *Vida del celebre poeta Garcilaso de la Vega.* ("Colección de documentos inéditos para la Historia de España," XVI.) Madrid, 1950.

Neilson, W. A. *The Origins and Source of the Courts of Love.* Harvard, 1899.

Nelson, John Charles. *Renaissance Theory of Love.* New York: Columbia University Press, 1958.

Newstead, Helaine. "The Origin and Growth of the Tristan Legend" in *Arthurian Literature in the Middle Ages.* Oxford: Clarendon Press, 1959.

Nicolson, Harold. *Good Behavior.* Garden City: Doubleday & Company Inc., 1956.

O'Connor, John. *Amadís de Gaule and its Influence on Elilzabethan Literature*. New Brunswick: Rutgers University Press, 1970.

Olmeda, Mauro. *El ingenio de Cervantes y la locura de don Quijote*. México: Editorial "Atlante," 1958.

Ortiz-Domínquez, Antonio, *La sociedad española en el siglo XVII*. Madrid, 1963.

Palacín, G. B. "Influencia de Castiglione en las letras Españolas," *Le Lingue del mondo*, XVII (1951), 195-197.

Panofsky, Erwin. *Idea*. Translated by Joseph Peake. Columbia: University of South Carolina Press, 1968.

Parker, Alexander Augustine. "The Meaning of 'Discreción' in *No hay más fortuna que Dios*" in Han Flasche *Calderón de la Barca*. Darmstadt, 1961.

————. *The Theology of the Devil in the Drama of Calderón*. Blackfriars, 1958.

Picatoste, Felipe D. *Estudio sobre la grandeza y decadencia de España*. 2 vols. Madrid: Imprenta de la viuda de Hernando Y Cª, 1887.

Pierce, Frank. *Amadís de Gaula*. Boston: Twayne Publishers, 1976.

Place, Edwin B. "*El Amadís* de Montalvo como manual de cortesanía en Francia," *Revista de Filología Española*, XXXVIII (1954), 151-169.

Ponseti, Helena Percas de. *Cervantes y su concepto del arte; Estudio crítico de algunos aspectos y episodios del "Quijote."* 2 vols. Madrid: Gredos, 1975.

Purcell, Mary. *The First Jesuit, St. Ignatius Loyola.* Westminster, Maryland: The Newman Press, 1957.

Rand, Edward Kennard. *Founders of the Middle Ages.* Harvard University Press, 1967.

Rebhorn, Wayne A. *Courtly Performances.* Detroit: Wayne State University Press, 1978.

Reed, A. W. "Chivalry and the idea of the gentleman," in *Chivalry.* Edited by E. Prestage. New York, 1928.

Reyes, A. "Influencia del ciclo artúrico en la literatura castellanlla" in *Capítulos de Literatura Española.* México: 1945.

Reynier, Gustave. *Le Roman sentimental avant l'Astrée.* Paris, 1908.

Riley, E. C. *Cervantes: Teoría de la Novela.* Madrid: Taurus, 1962.

Riquer, Martín de. *Cavalleria fra realtá e letteratura nel Quattrocento.* Bari: Adriatica Editrice, 1970.

Roeder, Ralph. *The Man of the Renaissance.* New York: Garden City Publishing Company, 1973.

Rosamund, Mitchell. "Italian 'nobiltá' and the English Idea of the Gentleman in the Fifteenth Century," *English Miscellany*, No. 9 (1958), 23-37.

Rougemont, Denis de. *Love in the Western World*. New York: Pantheon, 1956.

Ruiz, de Conde, Justina. *El amor y el matrimonio secreto en los libros de caballerías*. Madrid: Aguilar, 1945.

Salazar, Adolfo. "Música, Instrumentos y Danzas en las obras de Cervantes," *Nueva Revista de Filología Hispánica*, II (1948), 118-173.

Sánchez, Alberto. "El Caballero del Verde Gabán," *Anales Cervantinos*, IX (1960-1), 169-201.

Schenk, Wilhelm. "*The Cortegiano* and the Civilization of the Renaissance," *Scrutiny*, XVI (1949), 93-105.

Schiller, Friedrich. *On the aesthetic education of man*. Translated by Elizabeth M. Wilkinson and L. A. Willoughby. Oxford: The Clarendon Press, 1967.

Sciacca, Michele Federico. "Verdad y sueño de *La Vida es Sueño* de Calderón de la Barca," *Clavileño*, Año I, Num. 2 (marzo-abril 1950), 1-9.

Sedgwick, H. E. *In Praise of Gentlemen*. Boston, 1935.

Sloman, Albert E. *The dramatic craftsmanship of Calderón*. Oxford: Dolphin Book Company, 1963.

―――. "The Structure of Calderón's *La vida es sueño*" in *Critical Essays on the Theater of Calderón*. Edited by Bruce Wardropper. New York: New York University Press, 1965.

Smith, Pauline. *The Anti-Courtier Trend in Sixteenth Century French Literature*. Genéve: Librairie Droz, 1966.

Soler y Arqués, Carolos. *Los Españoles según Calderón: Discurso acerca de las costumbres públicas y privadas de los españoles en el siglo XVII*. Madrid: Tipografía Guttenberg, 1881.

Spitzer, Leo. *Classical and Christian Ideas of World Harmony*. Baltimore, 1963.

―――. "Linguistic Perspectivism in *Don Quijote*" in *Linguistics and Literary History, Essays in Stylistics*. Princeton: Princeton University Press, 1967.

―――. "On the Significance of *Don Quijote*," *Modern Language Notes*, 77 (1962), 113-129.

Stanton, Donna C. *The Aristocrat as Art: A Study of the Honnête Homme and the Dandy in Seventeenth and Nineteenth-Century French Literature*. New York: Columbia University Press, 1980.

Stone, Lawrence. *The Crisis of the Aristocracy 1558-1641*. Oxford: Oxford University Press, 1965.

Strong, Roy C. "Queen Elizabeth and Oriana," *Studies in Renaissance*, Vi (1959), 251-257.

Thomas, Henry. *Spanish and Portuguese Romances of Chivalry*. Cambridge: Cambridge University Press, 1920.

Tiraboschi, G. *Storia della Letteratura Italiana*. Florence, 1905.

Toffanin, Giuseppe. *Il Cinquecento*. Milano: Vallardi, 1950.

Trilling, Lionel. *Sincerity and Authenticity*. Cambridge: Harvard University Press, 1973.

Vaganay, Hugues. *Ámadís en Français: essai de bibliographie*. Florence: Olschki, 1906.

———. "Les Trésors d'Amadís," *Revue Hispanique*, LVII (1978), 115-126.

Valbuena-Briones, Angel. *Calderón y la Comedia Nueva*. Madrid: Espasa-Caple, S. A., 1977.

Valbuena-Prat, Angel. *La Vida Española de la Edad de Oro*. Barcelona, 1943.

———. *Calderón: su personalidad, su arte dramático, su estilo y su obras*. Barcelona: Editorial Juventud, 1941.

Va Doren, Mark. *La Profesión de Don Quijote*. México D. F., 1962.

Vargas, Tamaio de. *Garcilaso de la Vega natural de Toledo, principe de los poetas Castellanos*. Madrid, 1622.

Varo, Carlos. *Génesis y evolución del "Quijote."* Madrid: Ediciones Alcalá, 1968.

Viñas y Mey, Carmelo. "Espíritu Castellano de aventura y empresa y la España de los Reyes Católicos," *Archivo de Derecho Público*, V (1952), 13-83.

Vincent, Leon H. *The French Academy*. London: Houghton-Mifflin & Company, 1901.

Voight, George. *The Revival of Classical Antiquity*. Berlin: Reimer, 1859.

Von Martin, Alfred. "Sociology of Renaissance" in *Renaissance Medieval or Modern*. Edited by Karl H. Dannenfeldt. Boston: Health & Company, 1957.

Wardropper, Bruce W. "Cervantes' Theory of the Drama," *Modern Philology*, 5 (1955), 217-21.

Weber de Kurlat, Frida. "Estructura novelesca del *Amadís de Gaula*," *Revista de Literaturas Modernas*, 5 (1967), 29-54.

Wells, Marcia L. *Style and Structure in Gracián's "El Criticón,"* (North Carolina Studies in Romance Languages and Literatures) Chapel Hill: University of North Carolina Press, 1976.

Werner, Krauss. *La doctrina de la vida según Baltasar Gracián*. Madrid, 1963.

White, John S. *Renaissance Cavalier*. New York: Philosophical Library, 1959.

Wiley, W. W. *The Gentleman of Renaissance France.* Cambridge, 1954.

Williams, Grace S. "The Amadís Question." *Revue Hispanique*, XXI (1909), 1-67.

Williamson, Edward. "The Concept of Grace in the Work of Raphael and Castiglione," *Italica*, XXIV (1947), 316-324.

Wilson, E. M. "On la *Vida es Sueño*" in Bruce Wardropper's edition of *Critical Essays on the Theater of Calderón.* New York: New York University Press, 1965.

Wingfield-Stratford, E. *Making of a Gentleman.* London, 1938.

Withby, William M. "Rosaura's Role in the Structure of *La vida es sueño*" in *Critical Essays on the Theater of Calderón.* Edited by Bruce W. Wardropper. New York: New York University Press, 1965.

Woodhouse, J. R. *Baldesar Castiglione: a reassessment of the "Courtier."* Edinburgh University Press, 1972.

Woodward, W. H. *Studies in education during the age of the Renaissance 1400-1600.* Cambridge, 1906.

Yates, Frances Amelia. *The French Academies of the Sixteenth Century.* London: Warburg Institute, University of London, 1947.

About The Author

George Udeozor is the unlikely author of this literary marvel which takes the reader on a breath-taking journey through the chilling nightmares of the darkness and evil that may lurk at the edges of the American Dream. Like most success-driven immigrants, the author, after a childhood plagued by civil war and economic hardship, worked his way through High School in Nigeria and College in the United States before launching a career in banking with Barclays Bank of California, Los Angeles. Although successful as a banker, the author could not resist the lure of profit and adventure in the International Business arena. His quick success as a Finance/Defense Consultant and marriage to his beautiful wife, a glamorous Medical Doctor gave the appearance of nothing less than the actualized American dream. In this book, the author tells the story of his plight from one nation to another and the struggles of political power intertwined with culture which appears to be at the base of each judicial system and those in its charge.